FARMER'S MARKET
COOKBOOK

FARMER'S MARKET
COOKBOOK

making the most of fresh and seasonal produce with over 140 recipes

YSANNE SPEVACK

HERMES HOUSE

Dedicated to my mum, Coral,
for all her inspiration both in and out of the kitchen,
to Steve, for his support throughout the writing of this book,
and to John at the Organic Delivery Company, for his fantastic fruit and veg.

Hermes House is an imprint of Anness Publishing Ltd
Hermes House, 88–89 Blackfriars Road, London SE1 8HA
tel. 020 7401 2077; fax 020 7633 9499; info@anness.com

© Anness Publishing Ltd 2002, 2003

A CIP catalogue record for this book is available from the British Library.

Publisher: Joanna Lorenz
Managing Editor: Linda Fraser
Senior Editor: Margaret Malone
Editor: Joy Wotton
Copy Editors: Jenni Fleetwood and Jane Bamforth
Editorial Reader: Jan Cutler
Indexer: Hilary Bird
Designer: Nigel Partridge
Photographers: Peter Anderson and Simon Smith
Home Economist: Annabel Ford
Stylist: Helen Trent
Production Controller: Wendy Lawson

Previously published as *Organic Cookbook*

1 3 5 7 9 10 8 6 4 2

NOTES
Bracketed terms are intended for American readers.

For all recipes, quantities are given in both metric and imperial measures and, where appropriate, measures are
also given in standard cups and spoons. Follow one set, but not a mixture, because they are not interchangeable.

Standard spoon and cup measures are level.
1 tsp = 5ml, 1 tbsp = 15ml, 1 cup = 250ml/8fl oz

Australian standard tablespoons are 20ml. Australian readers should use 3 tsp in place of 1 tbsp
for measuring small quantities of gelatine, flour, salt, etc.

Medium (US large) eggs are used unless otherwise stated.

CONTENTS

INTRODUCTION

Organic food is the fastest growing sector of the entire food industry. Step into any supermarket and you will see an impressive array of organic produce, not tucked away at the end of an aisle, but proudly and prominently displayed. This is often the first point of contact for shoppers unfamiliar with organic food, but having experienced the superior flavours and learned of the undeniable health benefits, many people go on to investigate box schemes, farmers' markets featuring organic produce and small, local organic suppliers.

Interest in organic food and farming is at an all-time high. This is partly due to the fact that people are better informed about nutrition, more concerned about the environment and more cautious about the short- and long-term effects of diet on health than at any time in the past, but there are also more fundamental reasons, such as flavour. To put it simply, we appreciate good food. This generation is more widely travelled than any previous one, and is discovering

Below: Organic sheep and lambs graze on unsprayed grass, free from pesticides.

exotic cuisines and exciting new tastes from all over the world. People eat out more, and are more adventurous when cooking at home. As palates become increasingly sophisticated, we demand more from the ingredients that make up our meals, so it is hardly surprising that we increasingly favour organic food.

But What Is Organic Food?

Organic farming is the cultivation of crops and rearing of livestock with natural soil fertility at the heart of the system. Organic farmers believe that by working hard to maintain and encourage good soil structure on their land, the crops and livestock grown and bred there will flourish. They work with nature, rather than trying to bend nature to their purpose, so produce is grown without the routine use of pesticides or artificial fertilizers, and animals are reared without being treated with growth promoters or unnecessarily dosed with antibiotics.

If this sounds like a return to the way things used to be, it is, but only to a point. Modern organic farming is highly scientific and makes considerable use of

Above: Organic pumpkins and squash are grown free from artificial fertilizers.

technology. Research into more efficient organic farming methods is ongoing. For food to be labelled organic, it must have been produced according to strict guidelines, which are rigidly regulated.

Soil fertility is promoted by crop rotation, composting and planting crops that supply specific nutrients. Farmers encourage predator insects such as ladybirds (ladybugs) to visit by planting their favourite flowers. They may also sometimes introduce other predators to control pests biologically. When coupled with preventative methods, such as growing in polytunnels, where insects can be kept out, the need to use agrochemical pesticides is avoided.

Agrochemical Farming

The cultivation of crops and rearing of livestock using agrochemicals was first promoted on a large scale in the 1950s, in response to widespread food shortages during and immediately after World War II. This was a period of modernism, with technologies of all kinds being optimistically embraced. Agrochemicals held the promise of maximizing food production, so they were universally adopted. They achieved

Right: Organic cattle are less susceptible to disease because they are always free-range and have access to the outdoors.

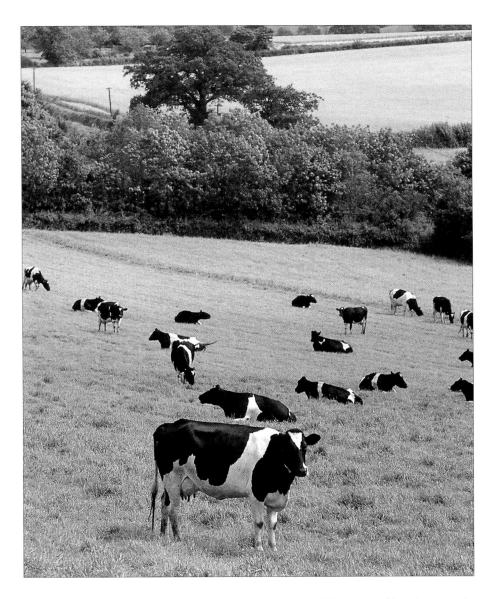

their immediate objectives, but at a cost to the environment that is only now beginning to be fully appreciated.

Yields from organic and agrochemical farms are now almost identical, and organic yields continue to grow as a result of continued research into intensive organic agriculture. Organic farmers also benefit from access to much wider seed banks than those customarily used by agrochemical farmers, so can select the best varieties of crops for their climate and terrain.

Organic farming now utilizes some of the same non-invasive technology as agrochemical farming. Satellites, for example, are used to predict weather patterns or map insect migrations.

The Cost of Going Organic

If yields are improving and organic food production is becoming steadily more efficient, why does organic food tend to cost more than agrochemical food? The answer lies in outdated government subsidy schemes, which are based on the aspirations and knowledge of post-World War II policymakers. Agrochemical farmers receive a much higher amount of taxpayers' money than organic farmers. Historically, this was because farmers were encouraged to experiment with chemicals to increase yields. Thinking has changed radically since those days, but subsidizing policy has not altered for the last fifty years.

Farmers are actively encouraged to spray their fields with chemical pesticides and fertilizers. When these chemicals run off farms and pollute the water table, huge sums of money must be spent internationally in clean-up operations. It is not the chemical companies or the farmers who pay for this pollution management; it is the taxpayer.

Consumers pay for agrochemical products three times. First at the checkout, then – about half the price of the item again – through taxes as a subsidy to agrochemical farmers, and finally through further taxes to clean up the water table. This economic breakdown does not include any costs incurred to industry through the ill health of agrochemical farm workers who have been exposed to toxins.

Organic food will continue to be marginally more expensive than agrochemical food until government policies change. However, the difference in food quality that organic food offers more than justifies this price premium. An organic apple contains more vitamins, minerals and phytonutrients than a non-organic apple. It also contains about 25 per cent less water. It is likely to be a more interesting variety, will almost certainly taste better and will have a more enjoyable texture. Most importantly, it will not be coated in an untested cocktail of up to twenty artificial chemicals and waxes.

Organic Livestock

Animal welfare is a fundamental principle of organic livestock, poultry and dairy farming. Organic animals are always free range. Because they have access to the outdoors and are not intensively reared in enclosed spaces, they are less susceptible to disease and, although farmers will take appropriate action if an animal becomes unwell, there is no need for the routine administration of antibiotics that is standard preventative practice on agrochemical farms.

Above: These dairy cows are being reared organically, free from hormones that increase milk production or encourage growth.

Organic farmers will often use such complementary medicines as homeopathic treatments to cure a sick animal and inject antibiotics only as a last resort when other treatments have failed.

Organic farmers are not allowed to use hormones to encourage animal growth or increase milk production. In countries where growth hormones such as BST (bovine somatotropin) are administered, dairy cows often suffer intense pain from unnaturally swollen udders. Their milk – and dairy products produced from it – contains the same hormones, increasing the consumer's risk of multi-generational cancers and hormone disruption disorders.

Fish
Organic fish, whether wild or farmed, should come from sustainable fisheries and farms, and be caught using fishing practices that protect the environment.
Wild Fish Logic dictates that all wild fish are organic, since they swim and eat where they will. However, pollution, insensitive fishing methods and proximity

to major shipping lanes all have a detrimental effect on wild fish stocks, and there is no standard for organics in wild fish. The Marine Stewardship Council is an international organization offering an accreditation scheme for sustainable wild fisheries.
Farmed Fish The conditions under which fish are farmed vary widely. For farmed fish to be labelled organic, they must be reared responsibly. This means giving them adequate room to move, letting them grow and develop naturally and giving them organic feed. This is not the case on many agrochemical fish farms, where fish populations can be so high and intensive that infestation and disease are commonplace and chemical pesticides must be used liberally to control them. Pesticides, waste fish food and sewage from agrochemical fish farms frequently pollute our rivers and waterways, and it is not just these substances that escape. Fish get under the wire, too, and in many European rivers, four out of every five salmon caught originated on an agrochemical farm.

Farmed fish are bred to mature later and be less aggressive than their wild counterparts in order to produce a greater yield and be easier to manage.

The damage from wild and farmed salmon interbreeding is immense, with natural fish stocks at ever increasing risk. Intensive fish farms are beginning to address these problems in many areas of the world, but to be sure that your farmed fish is produced responsibly, make sure it carries the mark of an organic certification body that you trust.

Hemp
This is a wonder crop that puts more nutrients back into the soil than it needs to grow. It is therefore ideal for farmers who are converting their land to organic methods. The conversion period required for organic certification can be a difficult time financially for farmers. While the land is renewing itself, farmers may not sell their produce as organic even though they are not using agrochemicals. Hemp can usefully bridge the gap by providing a saleable crop while improving soil fertility.

The applications of hemp are extraordinary. The ropes and sails used on the ships that first charted our seas were made of hemp. So was the first pair of Levi's jeans. Hemp also made the paper on which the original American Constitution was written. Hemp is the most versatile organic crop we have. You

Below: Organic fish are farmed with care for the environment.

Above: *Organic fruit contains more vitamins, minerals and phytonutrients than non-organic fruit. It also tastes better.*

can make cosmetics from its oil, power cars with it, and even use it for making plastics. In fact, hemp can do anything that a hydrocarbon can do. In these times of dwindling fossil fuel reserves, hemp is potentially a major part of the solution because it actually reduces greenhouse gases plus it manufactures oxygen when it grows, and can easily be processed into a powerful fuel source to rival oil.

Hemp seed is the only complete vegetable protein known, with a nutritional make-up that is even more balanced than soya. Sixty-five per cent of the protein in hemp is in globular edestin form, which is the most easily digestible form of protein. The oil content of hemp seeds typically consists of 60 per cent Omega-6; 20 per cent Omega-3 and 10 per cent Omega essential fatty acids (EFAs). This is seen as the most suitable ratio of dietary fat for long-term human consumption. Hemp seed oil also contains GLA, which is the active constituent of evening primrose oil. This makes the oil ideal for the treatment of PMS, eczema, joint conditions and even some cancers.

Left: *Hemp products include such beauty products as soaps, moisturizers and loofah-like scrubs.*

NOT EVERYTHING ORGANIC IS FOOD!

Non-organic cotton and tobacco are two pesticide-dependent crops grown widely in the Americas and in developing countries. Dangers to the consumer from agrochemicals used in the cultivation of non-food crops are minimal, but when the soil's natural fertility is undermined by artificial fertilizers, farmers become reliant on agrochemicals. Concerns are high for farm workers in developing countries exposed to pesticides deemed too strong for use on food crops. Where protective clothing is absent, they have a higher than average incidence of cancers and respiratory conditions. There is also a high rate of early mortality among the farmers themselves.

Organic cotton and tobacco are available. The Scandinavian Oeko-Tex mark is an assurance that fabrics are organic or sustainable. The American Spirit tobacco company manufactures organic cigarettes.

Seeds and garden flowers are two more areas of environmental concern. Because it is vital that no weed seeds contaminate the product, agrochemical seed producers spray their crops liberally with herbicides.

Cut flowers are not regulated as stringently as food crops, so farm workers and the environment can lose out. Buying organically grown flowers benefits both the people who grew them and the planet.

Organically grown hyacinths

WHY GO ORGANIC?

There are dozens – many would say hundreds – of excellent reasons for choosing the organic option. Apart from benefits to the individual in terms of health, avoidance of chemicals and the sheer enjoyment of eating food that is full of flavour, there are environmental issues to consider, as well as moral questions such as animal welfare, the health of farm workers and fair trade.

Improved Health

All organic food is good for you. Fresh organic produce contains more vitamins, minerals, enzymes and other micro-nutrients than intensively farmed produce. It also tastes better. Organic fruit and vegetables are full of juice and flavour, and there are many different

Below: *Organic cauliflower, cabbage, broccoli and Brussels sprouts are high in glucosinolates, which help prevent cancer.*

varieties to try. Organic meat, poultry and dairy produce are of excellent quality and usually lower in saturated fat.

Vitamins and Minerals The reason why fresh organic produce contains more vitamins and minerals than the agrochemical equivalent is largely due to the method of cultivation. Unlike agrochemical fruit and vegetables, which are sprayed with artificial fertilizers that force the plants to grow quickly, even in inferior soil, organic fruit and vegetables are allowed to grow and ripen more naturally in richer soil, obtaining the maximum variety of micronutrients.

These micronutrients are also more concentrated in organic fruit and vegetables, because they contain much less water than agrochemical produce.

Phytonutrients Organic produce is rich in naturally occurring chemical compounds known as phytonutrients. These are found in fresh fruit and vegetables and

help to fight disease and promote good health. More research is needed to pinpoint the precise benefits of all these compounds, but much is already known. Glucosinolates in cabbage, broccoli, cauliflower and Brussels sprouts help to prevent cancer. Flavonoids are powerful antioxidants. The strongest flavonoids are found in onions and garlic. Eating onions and garlic regularly significantly reduces the risk of heart disease and the spread of cancer.

While all fresh produce contains phytonutrients, organic produce contains more than its non-organic equivalent. This is because all plants produce phyto-nutrients as part of their natural defence against pests. If a plant is protected from pests by agrochemicals, there is no need for it to produce phytochemicals in the same quantity. Also, studies have found that when plants take up high levels of nitrogen from the soil, they produce

Above: *Just some of the fruits available organically: apples, grapes, pineapple, oranges, kiwi fruit and passion fruit.*

fewer and less diverse phytonutrients. Agrochemical crops are liberally sprayed with nitrogen fertilizers to make them grow quicker, whereas organic crops are grown in more balanced and less nitrogen-rich soil.

Fats Hydrogenated fats are oils that have had hydrogen added to them so that they become solid or semi-solid at room temperature. They are widely used in the food industry despite the fact that nutritionists universally agree that they are a major cofactor in heart disease, cancer, diabetes and obesity. The surest way to remove hydrogenated fats from your diet is to go organic. Organic food regulations throughout the world prohibit the use of hydrogenated fats.

Eating too much saturated fat is a contributing factor in cardiovascular diseases such as heart attacks and stroke. Saturated fat is present in organic beef as well as in intensively reared beef, but the percentage is likely to be lower. Saturated fat is also easier to remove from organic beef. In intensively reared

cattle saturated fat is more evenly distributed, so is harder to cut away when you are preparing the meat for cooking. Since it clogs up your arteries, the more saturated fat you can remove from your food the better.

Meat, poultry, eggs and milk from grass-fed animals also contain more conjugated linoleic acid or CLA. This substance helps those who consume it to maintain a healthy weight, and studies have shown that it reduces the risk of heart disease and may help to prevent cancer. So although organic meat contains saturated fat, it also contains CLA to balance it.

The Balanced Diet

A wholesome, organic diet provides balanced nutrition, including a healthy range of vitamins, minerals and phytonutrients. This is an important consideration in a world where many people opt for convenience foods that are

often high in fat and sugar and offer little in terms of nutrition. The body craves the nutrients it lacks, and this can drive people to overeat, yet remain malnourished. There is a direct correlation between over-consumption malnutrition trends in industrialized nations and eating non-organic food. Obesity epidemics have occurred in countries that rely on agrochemicals to grow and process their foods.

Improved Immunity There is evidence to suggest that people who eat organic food build up a stronger immunity to disease than those who consistently eat food that is laden with chemicals. Eating over-processed, non-organic junk food puts a strain on immune systems already compromised by living in a polluted world, by forcing the liver and kidneys to work harder to remove the toxins they frequently contain.

A New Zealand report into the possible benefits of an organic diet suggested that people who follow an organic diet benefit from a very marked decline in influenza and experienced far fewer colds and catarrhal problems than other members of the population. Further reported benefits included clear, healthy skin, improved dental health and excellent general health.

Below: *Organic eggs are high in linoleic acid, which helps maintain a healthy weight.*

Above: *Eating an organic diet before conception and during pregnancy will help rid the body of toxins.*

Increased Fertility Studies appear to support a link between organic diets and increased fertility in men. The World Health Organization estimates that the average sperm count for male adults is about 66 million/ml. Two recent studies recorded that men who eat organic food have between 99 and 127 million sperm/ml. More research is needed to confirm these findings. However, the fact that a balanced organic diet is more nutritionally sound and contains fewer chemicals or artificial hormones than a non-organic diet, is bound to offer the best option for men – and women – wanting to support their sexual health and improve their chances of conceiving.

Avoiding the Chemical Cocktail

The average adult living in one of the industrialized nations has between 300 and 500 agrochemical pesticides in his or her body at any one time. Each of these toxic chemicals is stored in body fat, and each is toxic enough to kill insects. In combination, they are certainly more

poisonous. Pesticides can remain stored in body fat for many years. No long-term studies have truly evaluated the damage to our health that these chemicals pose, but there is evidence to suggest that they exacerbate chronic conditions and seriously undermine health.

Children are particularly susceptible to agrochemical toxins. They have a higher intake of food than adults in relation to their body weight, and their bodies are less efficient at eliminating toxins. Breast milk from mothers whose diets are not organic generally contains concentrations of pesticides. These have been shown to adversely affect brain development in babies. Ideally, a woman planning to conceive a child should adopt an organic diet at least one year before falling pregnant. This gives her body time to detoxify, helping to create a healthier environment for the foetus to grow in and then purer breast milk for the baby once it has been born.

Artificial Additives Every year, the average American eats more than two kilograms of chemical food additives. Seven thousand artificial additives are permitted to be used in conventional food. Only seven of these – the most innocuous – are allowed to be used in processed organic food. Artificial additives are used by manufacturers to improve the shelf life, flavour, colour, sweetness and saltiness of non-organic

Below: *Organic fruit and vegetables, on sale at a local farmers' market, are fresh and full of goodness.*

processed foods. Flavour enhancers may be added to disguise inferior quality ingredients. Although some artificial additives are absolutely harmless, many undermine our health. Generally they are used in combination, unleashing an unresearched toxic combination upon the consumer, which may well have implications in terms of cancer, asthma, liver disease and osteoporosis.

When food deteriorates naturally, you can see at a glance when it is past its best. Preservatives may artificially prolong a food's shelf life, but they do not prolong the life of all the nutrients within the product. When preservatives are banned, as in processed organic food, you can be sure that as long as the food is fresh, it is full of goodness.

Antibiotics and Hormones Intensively reared livestock are routinely fed and injected with antibiotics to keep them healthy. These substances pass into their meat. People who eat this meat develop reduced immunity through over-exposure to antibiotics. On the other hand, bacteria that become over-exposed to antibiotics become increasingly resistant to them. The British Medical Association has stated that: "The risk to human health of antibiotic resistance…is one of the major health threats that could be faced in the 21st century."

Hormones and endocrine disrupting chemicals (EDCs) also pose a threat to health. Five out of the twelve most commonly used pesticides in the world are known to be EDCs. This means that they are known to affect the delicate balance of human hormones. Some women in Hawaii have extremely high rates of breast cancer. Hawaii also has a high rate of zeno-oestrogens from pesticides in its groundwater. A Danish scientific study, which tracked more than seven hundred Hawaiian women over twenty years, concluded that there is a probable link between the pesticides in the water and breast cancers.

There is also evidence that growth hormones from intensively farmed meat can lead to a wide variety of human endocrine disorders, from obesity to multi-generational cancers.

Food Safety
All organic animals that are naturally

Above: Heirloom and rare varieties of potatoes are appearing at markets as organic farmers seek out new crops.

vegetarian are fed only vegetarian food. This was a huge benefit during the UK's BSE (Bovine Spongiform Encephalopathy) crisis. BSE was caused and spread because cows were fed contaminated food, which was itself animal in origin. All organic farms in the UK are completely BSE-free because organic cows are always fed food that is 100 per cent vegetarian.

Organic meat and dairy produce is free from genetically modified organisms or GMOs because all food for organic animals must be GMO-free by law. The diet of organic animals is also solvent free. This may seem obvious until it is considered that non-organic animals regularly eat food contaminated with solvents. Non-organic cooking oil is usually produced by soaking oil-rich vegetable matter in solvents. The oil is then extracted from the liquid, and the remaining solid matter is used for animal feed. Solvent-extracted animal feed is banned from organic farms.

Natural Flavours
During the year 2000, 43 per cent of consumers who bought organic food in Britain declared that they did so because they thought it tasted better than non-organic food. Tastes vary from person to person, but there are sound

reasons why organic food tastes better.

Most agrochemical crops are grown from seeds bred to produce a high yield. Organic fresh produce, however, comes from seeds bred primarily for flavour. Many organic farmers take pride in growing heirloom crops. These crops were once highly prized but have been overlooked in recent years because they were less commercially profitable than modern varieties. Organic growers in industrialized nations regularly produce about a hundred different kinds of potato. This is considerably fewer than the thousand or more varieties on sale at the farmer's market in the town of Cuzco in Peru, but at least five times more than the twenty or so varieties of agrochemically grown potatoes on sale in the USA or UK.

The slower growth rates of organic crops allow more time for flavour to develop naturally. Phytonutrients often help to flavour the fresh produce in which they occur so, as well as being good for health, high levels of certain phytonutrients boost the taste factor. Sugar levels are often slightly higher in

Above: *Flowers planted among vegetables encourage the predator insects that control pests in an environmentally friendly fashion.*

organic fresh produce than in non-organic varieties; this is particularly obvious in carrots and apples. Organic fruit is more likely to be allowed to ripen naturally on the tree, granting more time for flavours and sweetness to develop.

The lower percentage of water in organic fresh produce concentrates the nutrients and intensifies the flavour. If you were to evaporate all the water from an agrochemical carrot and an organic carrot of equal weight, the remaining dry matter from the organic carrot would be some 26 per cent heavier.

Food animals raised organically also benefit from growing more slowly than their agrochemical equivalents, and their meat becomes more flavoursome during the lengthy process. Another reason why meat from organic farms tastes better is because flavour is an important factor in selecting which type of animal to raise, and farmers are increasingly choosing the traditional heritage breeds that are noted for the tastiness of their meat

Right: *Fresh produce grown in an organic vegetable garden is an excellent option for the health-conscious consumer.*

above yield.

Organic prepared foods are allowed to contain very few of the chemical flavourings and flavour enhancers found in non-organic foods. Monosodium glutamate, for instance, is outlawed in organic food. This substance, commonly known as MSG, has been linked to nausea, dizziness and even asthma attacks. Organic foods taste so good that they do not need flavour enhancers.

Although much organic produce is currently grown a long way from the point of sale, it is best to buy it fresh from local producers. Not only will it have the finest flavour and highest concentration of nutrients, it will not contribute to pollution by having to be transported long distances. The range of fruit and vegetables may not be as great as that on offer in supermarkets, but the pleasure of enjoying seasonal treats such as strawberries in summer is more than adequate compensation.

Animal Welfare

Organic farm animals and poultry are treated with respect, without recourse to artificial hormones, antibiotics or routine drug therapies. Inhumane practices such as battery farming are banned. Dairy cows raised organically have, on average, 50 per cent more room in their barns than non-organic

cows, and unlike the latter, they are always provided with bedding. They also enjoy much more time out of doors. The same holds true for organic poultry.

Wildlife and the Environment

Our environment is under immense threat. Over the last 30 years, intensive farming in many countries has led to dramatic erosion of the soil. Bird populations have declined by up to 70 per cent, and some species of butterflies, frogs, grass snakes and wild mammals have been brought near extinction. Wild flowers and shrubs that once flourished in the fields are now seldom seen. Intensive farmers grub up ancient hedgerows that surround their fields to allow access for their giant machinery.

Organic farmers actively promote biodiversity by cherishing hedges, not just for their natural beauty, but for the practical support they offer. They play a vital role in supplying a habitat for the birds and insects that an organic farm needs in order to function. Wild flowers at the edge of a field attract butterflies and useful predators to the crop, so organic farmers always keep a strip of wild land around a field. Intensive farmers destroy resources such as these, either mechanically or by using pesticides. Many chemical pesticides are directly related to nerve gases. They are

Above: *A willow fence forms a natural field boundary and encourages butterflies.*

designed to kill. Those pests that survive being drenched with pesticides may develop immunity. Stronger pesticides must be developed and this leads to an ever-increasing cycle.

Although agrochemical farmers use pesticides to target specific pests, they are toxic to many creatures. Small mammals and birds are often killed or weakened by agricultural pesticides. Equally damaging are agrochemical seeds that have been treated with organochlorides in an attempt to prevent them being eaten. These highly poisonous chemicals, which last for years in the environment, kill numerous birds and animals every year.

Chemicals sprayed on crops eventually either penetrate the plants or trickle down into the soil, polluting the land and draining into the water table. The poisons then flow into streams and rivers, polluting the ecosystem. Agrochemical fertilizers are just as damaging to the ecosystem as pesticides. Nitrate-based fertilizers also seep out of the fields into the water system. In rivers and lakes, they stimulate the growth of algae. Excessive algae throws the whole ecosystem out of balance, poisoning waterways.

Farm Workers' Health and Fair Trade

On agrochemical farms, especially those in such developing countries as India, workers are often at direct risk from pesticide pollution. Protective clothing and machinery is expensive, whereas pesticide chemicals are relatively cheap. The result is that many farm workers are forced to apply these poisons to crops while unprotected. It is not only the farm workers themselves who are at risk — pesticides also endanger the general population.

Many farm workers in developing nations are exposed to horrifying amounts of poisons every day from childhood onwards. Pesticide exposure can lead to multi-generational diseases and cancers. The children of farm workers are more likely to have genetic defects that continue to successive generations. The workers often receive only subsistence wages for working long and back-breakingly hard days. In some countries, the average age of death for farm workers is around fifty.

Going organic avoids supporting these types of injustices. Using spending power sensitively is a direct way of working towards a fairer trading world. Many organic products are fairly traded, which means that a buyer will offer a reasonable price for crops. The majority of trading between the developed and the developing world does not currently

follow this principle. A cash-poor farmer may be forced to sell his crop for less than its worth because he does not have the bargaining power of a multinational company. For assurance that an organic product is fairly traded, look out for the Fairtrade seal and consult your supplier or shopkeeper.

Packaging

While packaging provides a valuable method of food preservation without the use of additives, unnecessary packaging is wasteful and environmentally insensitive. Many smaller organic companies are beginning to use recycled and recyclable containers for their products, but too many organic foods are still wrapped in the same plastics and bleached non-recycled papers as non-organic products.

Lobbying these organic companies to change their practices can help, but it is equally vital that organic consumers make every effort to recycle their waste. Glass, aluminium and paper are all candidates for recycling. Paper and plastic bags can be reused, and a compost bin is valuable for disposing of waste organic matter.

Below: *Recycling organic waste matter in compost bins is good for the environment and enriches the soil of any garden.*

THE ORGANIC KITCHEN

The organic cook has a vast array of ingredients, from fresh fruit and vegetables to fine quality meat and store-cupboard staples. Take the same care with preparation as you do with selection and storage and you'll be rewarded with delicious dishes. Exploring the range of organic fresh and store-cupboard items is a rewarding experience. If you buy fresh produce direct from the grower, ask the names of varieties so you can seek out your favourites. The selection that follows is not intended to be an exhaustive guide to every organic item, but it does introduce some of the best buys from organic growers and producers around the world.

FRESH PRODUCE

Good fruit and vegetables are at the heart of organic cuisine. The main point of agreement between health experts and nutritionists throughout the world is that we need to eat more fruit and vegetables. The United Nations World Health Organization has stated that if you eat five portions of fresh produce every day, you halve your chances of getting cancer.

If you can't afford to buy organic produce every day, it is better for you to supplement your diet with non-organic alternatives than to cut back on fruit and vegetables. Organic fresh produce is, however, nutritionally richer, tastier and more diverse. As well as the usual varieties on sale, you will find rare heirloom types of fruit and vegetables.

There is a huge global market for both organic and agrochemical produce,

Below: *Stock up on fresh organic vegetables at local farmers' markets.*

and imported fruit and vegetables often travel thousands of miles before they reach our shores. Because demand for organic produce is growing at such a high rate in industrialized countries, many organic fruit and vegetables are likely to have been transported long distances.

Local Produce

If you can get it, it is better to buy locally grown produce. There are two main reasons why this is superior to imported organic fruit and vegetables: nutrition and the need to avoid increasing pollution.

Locally grown food is more nutritious than food that has been flown in from another country. Fruit and vegetables for export are often picked before they are fully ripe and kept chilled to avoid spoilage. This means that they fail to develop the complex flavours and nutritional compounds available in produce that has been allowed to ripen naturally and has been freshly picked

Above: *Growing your own organic herbs will add taste and nutrition to your cooking.*

and transported no further than to the nearest farmers' market. Also, organic standards vary in different countries. Some are not as stringent as others in terms of conversion periods from agrochemical to organic farming, or in nurturing natural soil fertility.

The other major advantage of buying locally grown organic produce is to avoid contributing to pollution. Long-distance transportation of food, whether it be organic or agrochemical, currently uses enormous quantities of petrochemicals, to fuel aeroplanes, ships or road vehicles. Burning fossil fuels is the antithesis of the organic ideal. Major ecological advances, such as fuel cell technology, are in the pipeline for green transportation. However, as long as petrochemicals power organic food imports, it is preferable to buy locally grown organic produce where possible.

That said, buying imported organic fruit is sometimes the only option. Citrus trees do not grow outdoors in cool climates, and date palms prefer arid climates to wet ones. Supplementing locally grown organic produce in season with the occasional imported organic treat is probably a good balance for most organic connoisseurs.

Growing and Buying

The best way to take advantage of the hundreds of different varieties of organic fruit and vegetables is to grow your own. Whether you have a couple of tubs on the patio, a vegetable plot or an impressive garden, preparing the soil,

Above: *Freshly dug organic potatoes have a flavour all of their own.*

nurturing the plants and then reaping the harvest is richly rewarding. The pleasures of gardening aside, the fresher the produce, the tastier and more nutritious it will be.

If you don't have green fingers, the best way to ensure that vegetables and fruit are fresh is to buy them from a local farmers' market or through a box scheme. Such schemes are operated by small individual growers or co-operatives. Customers opt for regular deliveries, either specifying which seasonal vegetables and fruit they would like to receive, or paying a fixed amount each week and leaving the selection of produce to the grower. The arrival of the box is then a delightful surprise, and often there will be extra treats, such as a few fresh herbs, a small box of berries or a head of the new season's garlic.

Buying Direct
One key benefit of buying fruit and vegetables direct from the grower is to maintain a valid connection with our food. Purchasing vegetables from the man who grew them allows information about the produce to be exchanged. Stories about an individual crop can be passed on and cooking tips and recipes shared. A farmer might also welcome feedback on a new variety that he is experimenting with, and customers can let him know which fruit or vegetables they have particularly enjoyed.

Children who have watched carrots being lifted or have sifted through sacks of potatoes with soil still clinging to

them, will soon make the connection between their food and the place it comes from, and will be much more likely to enjoy their organic greens.

Farmers get a much better deal selling their organic food directly. Not only do they obtain about double the price at a farmers' market than they would if they sold to the supermarket, but they enjoy the contact with the townsfolk who tuck into their produce. Never before has the connection between urban and rural societies been so weak. Farmers' markets and box schemes help to bridge the gap.

Supermarkets
It is possible, of course, to shop at the supermarket. While it is heartening that supermarkets are providing greater access to organic fresh produce than before, it is useful to be aware of a couple of negative aspects. Supermarkets generally spray non-organic produce with pesticides after it has left the field to ensure that stores remain free of insects. And, to avoid contamination of organic produce, they have to protect it in plastic packaging. This does not alter the organic status of the produce but the packaging does contribute to the environmental pollution that organic farming techniques aim to minimize. With increased public pressure, larger supermarket chains are likely to address this issue.

Another point to consider is that of food miles. Supermarkets tend to pool their products at central depots. This makes for easier distribution, but can be very wasteful of fuel and energy. An organic potato grown near Town A might well be driven to a central washing plant hundreds of miles away, near Town B. It may then be driven to the central supermarket distribution depot a similar distance away in Town C, only to be transported back to Town A for sale in the supermarket there.

Right: *Some packaging, such as this mug and spoon made out of recycled paper, is not harmful to the environment.*

Enthusiastic organic cooks would doubtless prefer always to buy and cook fresh ingredients, but there are occasions when it is useful to have ready-made meals and frozen foods to hand. The wide range of organic convenience foods extends to pasta sauces, soups, TV dinners and freshly prepared sandwiches.

Organic convenience products are unlikely to be as tasty or nutritionally balanced as organic foods prepared at home, but they are better for you than the non-organic alternative. They contain only a small number of artificial additives and are prohibited from containing hydrogenated fats. Such foods may not be irradiated and are not allowed to contain genetically modified ingredients.

Many non-organic processed foods contain excessive levels of refined white sugar and salt, both of which should be avoided. The quick energy rush provided by white sugar is followed always by energy depletion. Complex natural unrefined sweeteners, such as organic fruit syrups, produce a far more balanced response from the body. Too much salt raises blood pressure, increasing the risk of heart disease and strokes. The majority of organic prepared foods offer a safe level of salt, but it is important to check the salt and sugar content on the label of all convenience products.

The good news is that some convenience foods, such as frozen organic fruit and vegetables, can be more nutritious than the fresh non-organic equivalent. This is because produce is frozen within hours of being picked, whereas fresh non-organic produce may have been picked many days before.

Storing Fresh Fruit and Vegetables

It is very important to store organic produce carefully because it will not keep as long as non-organic examples.

Store ripe fruit in a cool place, away from direct sunlight. Green bananas will ripen within a couple of days if they are stored in a plastic bag with an over-ripe banana. Soft fruits such as tomatoes, kiwi fruits and avocados can be placed on a sunny window sill to help them ripen. This also brings out the flavour and encourages their natural juices to flow.

Most fresh vegetables are best stored in the refrigerator. Salad crops, including lettuces, rocket (arugula) and spinach, should be eaten within a few days of purchase. Root vegetables should be left unwashed, as the soil or mud coating helps to keep them fresh. Moisture is retained within the root or tuber, so unwashed carrots, turnips and potatoes keep for much longer than the shiny, scrubbed vegetables that look so pretty but perish so much quicker.

Right: Making flavourful juices from fresh fruit and vegetables is easy and delicious, as in this power booster mix of apple, carrot and beetroot (at back). Blend cucumber, tomatoes, garlic and lemon juice for an energizing summer drink (at front).

Cooking Organic Fruit and Vegetables

Cooking fruit reduces valuable vitamins and minerals, so, if you can, eat it raw. Over-cooking vegetables depletes their nutritional value, destroys their texture, impairs their flavour and spoils their natural colour. It is always advisable to steam vegetables rather than boil them. Boiling vegetables destroys up to half their nutrients, although this figure can be reduced if the vegetables are cooked whole and sliced afterwards. Better still, serve vegetables raw. They will contain many more enzymes than if cooked. Enzymes help us to digest the micronutrients in fresh produce, so, apart from potatoes, aim to cook for as short a time as possible.

Juicing

If you need to use up a stock of fruit or vegetables quickly, simply juice them. This is the most direct way of accessing the nutrients. Any vegetables can be mixed together satisfactorily, but apples are the only fruit that work well with vegetables. By the same token, any combination of fruit can be juiced, but if you want to add a vegetable, make it a carrot. Following these rules ensures that juices do not curdle and are refreshing, delicious and nutritious.

Preserving

For added variety during the winter months, you can preserve organic fruit. Marmalades and jams are easy to make. Drying slices of fruit, such as apples, by baking them overnight in the oven on a very low heat maintains much of the nutritional value while concentrating the taste. It is important to use organic fruit when preserving, as the peel is included. All kinds of organic dried fruit can be bought, from apricots to bananas and mangoes. Non-organic dried fruits are generally treated with sulphur, fungicides and mineral oils, whereas organic varieties are preserved naturally.

Left: Pickling is a great way to preserve extra stocks of all sorts of vegetables, including garlic, small onions and shallots.

ALLIUMS

This family of plants includes onions, leeks, chives and garlic, all of which owe their characteristic odour and flavour to a compound called allicin. Organic alliums contain more allicin than their non-organic counterparts, so have stronger flavours and more health benefits. Organic onions are sweeter, and organic garlic is more pungent. Unfortunately, allicin is also the constituent in alliums that makes us cry, so organic onions should be chopped at arm's length – or by someone else!

Alliums help to lower cholesterol. They also have antibacterial qualities and can help to relieve asthma, bronchitis and other sinus and chest ailments. The cycloallin they contain is an anticoagulant, which thins the blood and helps to protect the heart. Alliums also have anti-fungal properties; the juice can be rubbed on to the skin to relieve fungal infections. Garlic is the most powerful healer of the alliums and has been praised for its medicinal powers for hundreds of years, but all members of the family contain some allicin, so they all have beneficial qualities.

All alliums should be stored in a cool place. It is important to keep them dry or they will begin to sprout. Organic alliums keep just as well as non-organic ones. The wide variety of onions can be enjoyed raw or cooked and, with garlic, add flavour to many savoury dishes.

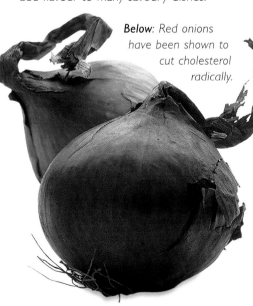
Below: Red onions have been shown to cut cholesterol radically.

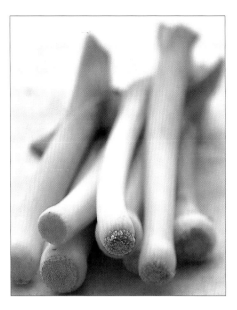
Above: A bunch of baby leeks is a bonus in the autumn organic vegetable box.

Onions
These are indispensable in the organic kitchen and form the basis of innumerable savoury dishes, including salads, stews, soups and gravies. There are many varieties, including big Spanish onions and small, sweet red onions. Add onions on the side when making a classic organic cooked breakfast. Not only do they taste delicious with bacon and sausages, but they have been shown to cut cholesterol radically.

Garlic
Although it is the most powerful healer of the allium family, this is not garlic's only attribute. It also has a superb flavour. Both hard- and soft-neck varieties are on sale in the organic market, and there is a wealth of taste and colour to explore. Hard-neck garlic, like Pink Music, has a central woody stem surrounded by five to ten easy-to-peel cloves. It has a richer, more rounded flavour than soft-neck garlic, which is the type you often find twisted together, French fashion, to form plaits or braids. Soft-neck garlic, such as Mother of Pearl, has a spicy flavour. Each bulb contains a seemingly endless amount of increasingly smaller cloves.

Above: Bulb spring onions (scallions) are at their most nutritious when they are raw.

This type of garlic can be stored for up to a year, unlike hard-neck garlic, which must be used within six months. Fresh organic garlic is available but it is at its best when dried and cured. When the thin skin is papery dry, the cloves are mature and will burst with flavour. Look for a firm head when buying garlic.

Above: Garlic

Leeks
A bunch of sweet, young leeks is a bonus in the autumn organic vegetable box. They are good enough to eat raw, but also taste great when lightly steamed or sautéed with garlic.

Spring Onions/Scallions and Chives
These vegetables taste delicious, especially when raw, when they are at their most nutritious. Organic growers often sell bunches of thin, young spring onions which make delicious snacks.

TUBERS

Whether you are shopping for potatoes, yacons or Jerusalem artichokes, you'll be spoilt for choice, since there are many more varieties of organic tubers available than the few agrochemical types.

Potatoes

A farmers' market or box scheme will provide opportunities to sample unusual types of organic potatoes. There are huge variations in the size and flavour of potatoes, and colours include yellow, red, pink, purple and black. There are two textures: waxy and floury. Common waxy varieties include new potatoes, Pink Fir Apple and Charlotte. Maris Piper and Estima are floury. Yukon Gold and Alaskan Sweetheart are also good.

All potatoes are a good source of vitamin C and the B group vitamins. Organic potatoes are helpful in supporting the body's natural resistance and keeping energy levels steady. Their peel can safely be eaten, boosting fibre levels, nutrition and flavour.

Waxy potatoes are ideal for frying and steaming, while floury potatoes are better for mashing or creaming. Use floury potatoes in leek and potato soup or for chips (French fries) that are soft in the middle, and waxy new potatoes as a springtime accompaniment for lamb chops. Potatoes should be stored in a dark, cool place that is perfectly dry.

Jerusalem Artichokes

Widely available in the autumn months, these delicious vegetables have an unusual, slightly bitter yet buttery flavour, and are excellent served alone or incorporated into dishes. Their bitterness is due to the presence of a compound called *cynarine*. This is a powerful liver stimulant, so eating Jerusalem artichokes will support liver

Above: *Jerusalem artichokes help detoxify the body.*

action, helping to detoxify the body. Organic Jerusalem artichokes also help to alleviate rheumatism and arthritis. Try Jerusalem artichokes lightly steamed with fish, or mashed with potatoes and swedes (rutabagas).

Sweet Potatoes

When cooked, sweet potatoes become sticky and soft with a gorgeous, smooth taste. Organic varieties are particularly sweet and are an excellent source of vitamins, including vitamins C, E and betacarotene, which helps to prevent cancer. They encourage eye and skin health, too. Because organic sweet potatoes are free of fungicides, they can be scrubbed and cooked whole for a wonderfully caramelized alternative to the ubiquitous baked potato. They are also good when steamed and mashed in the same way as regular potatoes.

Yacon Tubers

Almost all yacon tubers are organic. A staple food of the people of the Andes, they can be savoured cooked or raw. They are a good source of complex carbohydrates, with lots of vitamins and minerals. Their crunchy flesh is sweet and juicy like that of a water chestnut or jicama. Try them sliced or grated in leaf or rice salads. When steamed or roasted, the yacon becomes even sweeter. Yacons are not widely available, but can be found through box schemes and at farmers' markets. Store them in the salad drawer of the refrigerator.

Above: *Sweet potatoes are a good source of vitamins, including vitamins C, E and betacarotene.*

Below: *Organic farmers produce many varieties of white and red potatoes.*

ROOTS

The roots are a plant's powerhouse, and root vegetables provide us with a delicious way of tapping into this energy store. Organic root vegetables are often more knobbly and curly than agrochemically grown root vegetables. They deliver more nutrition and flavour than their more uniform counterparts, as well as being more individual in appearance.

All root vegetables should be stored unwashed. As with tubers, a layer of soil helps to seal moisture and nutrients into the roots.

Below: Swedes (rutabaga) contain vitamins A and C.

Carrots
Organically grown carrots are extremely high in betacarotenes, giving them a rich orange colour. Celebrate this with a sweet Middle Eastern salad. Grate four small carrots and mix with the juice of one orange, a few sesame seeds and 5ml/1 tsp honey. Alternatively, simply steam lightly or add to stews and stir-fries.

Below: Turnips are credited with soothing aching joints.

Parsnips
Organic parsnips are fragrant and intense. When roasted, they caramelize more successfully than non-organic ones because they are sweeter. Their flavour concentrates and the texture becomes chewy, with a crunch at the tip.

Swedes/Rutabaga and Turnips
There is nothing more comforting on a cold winter night than mashed swede with a little butter and seasoning. Organic turnips have a subtle flavour, underpinned with a bitter edge that people love or hate. They are delicious lightly steamed and served as a side dish for fish. Turnips deliver calcium and potassium and are credited with soothing aching joints.

Beetroot/Beets
Organic beetroot comes in an amazing variety of types. From yellow mangels to the Italian bull's-eye beet, these are the most colourful root vegetables. Young beetroot tastes very good when it is raw and grated. Alternatively, roast them with a medley of other root vegetables.

Left: Radishes are a good source of anti-cancer phytochemicals.

Radishes
When grown organically, radishes are very hot and spicy. They also have more concentrated amounts of anti-cancer phytochemicals. Traditionally, radishes are eaten to stimulate the gall bladder to manufacture digestive juices. The many varieties range from Japanese daikon to the classic red cherry belle. As with all root vegetables, any sign of springiness indicates that a radish is not fresh. Radishes are delicious sliced raw in salads, especially with watercress or rocket (arugula), and are also good in stir-fries.

MAKING A BASIC VEGETABLE STOCK
Homemade stock is a healthier option than the store-bought version and is easy to make. It can be stored in the refrigerator for up to four days. Alternatively, prepare it in large quantities and freeze.

INGREDIENTS
15ml/1 tbsp olive oil
1 potato, chopped
1 carrot, chopped
1 onion, chopped
1 celery stalk, chopped
2 garlic cloves, peeled
1 sprig thyme
1 bay leaf
a few stalks of parsley
600ml/1 pint/2½ cups water
salt and freshly ground pepper

1 Heat the oil in a large pan. Add the vegetables and cook, covered, for 10 minutes, or until softened, stirring occasionally. Stir in the garlic and herbs.

2 Pour the water into the pan, bring to the boil, and simmer, partially covered, for 40 minutes. Strain, season with salt and pepper, and use as required.

PUMPKINS and SQUASHES

Organic farmers grow many more varieties of pumpkins and squashes than agrochemical farmers. Summer squashes include the thin-skinned courgettes (zucchini), marrows (large zucchini) and patty pans, while winter brings the heavyweights, such as pumpkins and acorn squashes, with their glowing colours, thick skins and superb keeping properties. The natural sweetness of these vegetables makes them a favourite with small children. To cook, simply cut open, scoop out the seeds, slice into cubes and steam or roast until soft.

Courgettes/Zucchini and Marrows/Large Zucchini
Organic courgettes range in colour from pale yellow to deep green. They can easily be grown in a garden or on a balcony, and are readily available in stores and farmers' markets. Slice them into salads, or fry with onions, garlic, coriander and paprika for a quick side dish. Marrows are best baked. Try stuffing them with brown rice, almonds, onions and cheese.

Summer squash are effective diuretics and their potassium content helps to relieve high blood pressure.

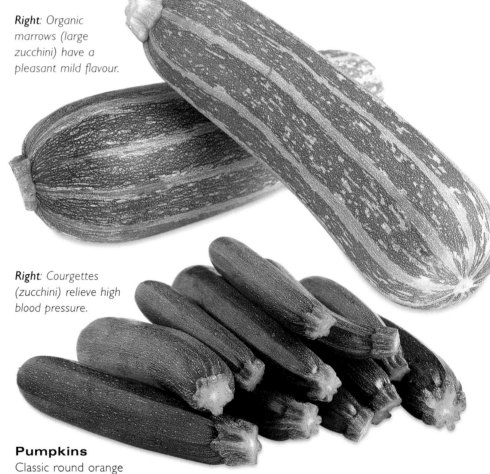

Right: Organic marrows (large zucchini) have a pleasant mild flavour.

Right: Courgettes (zucchini) relieve high blood pressure.

Pumpkins
Classic round orange pumpkins are full of betacarotene. This has been proven scientifically to help prevent cancer, particularly lung cancer. Pumpkin seeds can be washed, seasoned and roasted for a delicious snack that is rich in protein, minerals and B vitamins. Shell them after roasting to enjoy their nutty flavour, and reap the benefits of their protective action on the human reproductive system.

Above: Pumpkins are full of betacarotene, which has been scientifically proven to help prevent cancer.

ROASTING SQUASH
Cooking squash this way brings out its flavour and retains the goodness.

1 Preheat the oven to 200°C/400°F/ Gas 6. Cut the squash in half, scoop out the seeds and place it cut side down on an oiled baking sheet.

2 Bake for 30 minutes, or until the flesh is soft. Serve in the skin, or remove the flesh and mash with butter and seasoning.

GREENS

Green-leaf vegetables, such as cabbages, broccoli, chard, Brussels sprouts and cauliflower, are among the best sources of phytochemicals when organic. They help to defend the body against cancer, and should be eaten every day if possible. Leaf vegetables are a rich source of vitamins and minerals, too, including vitamin C, calcium, iron and betacarotene.

Agrochemical green-leaf vegetables are heavily sprayed with the strongest fungicides, insecticides and herbicides. Some include a compound, lindane, which is banned in the USA but still used in other countries. Organic vegetables are not sprayed in this way. They are nutritionally richer, with a more complex phytochemical profile and a more complex flavour. Lightly steamed or freshly stir-fried they are full of colour, crunch and vitality.

Below: Organic cabbages are among the best sources of phytochemicals.

Cauliflowers

When grown organically, cauliflowers are often quite small, around the size of tennis balls. Try to find vegetables that still have their outer leaves. The leaves should be green rather than yellow to indicate freshness, and they are a usable part of the cauliflower. Remove them from the cauliflower head and steam for a few minutes.

Above: Organic cauliflowers are often quite small, which was how they looked when they were first cultivated.

Below: Spinach is high in folic acid.

Swiss Chard and Spinach

Vegetarians and vegans are advised to eat chard and spinach regularly. Swiss chard is a rich, deep green with bright red or creamy white veins, and is almost exclusively found organically grown. Rich in iron, calcium, vitamins A and C and carotenes, Swiss chard is excellent for menstruating women and also as a treatment for anaemia.

Organic spinach is available as small baby salad leaves or fully-grown. A superb source of chlorophyll and folic acid, it is an excellent food for preconception and pregnancy.

To prepare, cut chard leaves away from their stems. Steam the stems for two to three minutes, adding the leaves at the end for only a few seconds. Likewise, steam spinach for about 20 to 30 seconds as the delicate leaves wilt almost immediately. Alternatively, lightly fry the leaves in organic olive oil or butter for a few moments, or simply eat them raw in a salad.

Cabbages

These versatile vegetables come in a variety of organic types, from wrinkly January kings to smooth purple red cabbages. Some have tight, compact heads; while others are loose-leaved. Thinly sliced cabbage makes a very good salad or slaw. Stir-frying cabbage leaves brings out their natural sweetness.

SALAD VEGETABLES

Fresh vegetables are at the heart of organic cuisine, and the most nutritious way to eat them is in salads. Most vegetables, with the exception of potatoes, can be used raw in salads, but some are particularly well suited to this treatment.

Lettuces

Along with other salad leaves, lettuces are the classic basis of a salad, and organic ones are extremely tasty and nutritious. All lettuces contain tiny quantities of opiates, which give the vegetable relaxing qualities that help to relieve stress and relax the lungs. It is these compounds that contribute the characteristic, slightly bitter taste. Organic lettuces contain more phytochemical compounds than agrochemical examples. Nutritionally, lettuce is best eaten raw, but it can also be braised or steamed.

Salad Leaves

Pak choi (bok choy), Chinese mustard greens, mizuna and tatsoi are just some of the salad leaves grown organically. Try raising your own lettuces and salad leaves from seed. They are easy to grow all year round on a window sill, or outside in spring and autumn. When buying prepared salads, it is absolutely essential to choose organic. Non-organic prepared salads are washed in chlorine to prevent the leaves from going brown. This is why a home-prepared salad composed of similar ingredients will not last as long. Organic prepared salads and ready-cut vegetables are simply preserved by oxygen exclusion and modern refrigeration methods.

Left: Organic pak choi is free from harmful chemical pesticides and fertilizers.

Cucumbers

Organically grown cucumbers are full of flavour and there are lots of different kinds. The tiny lemon cucumber looks rather like its namesake. Yellow in colour, it is so short and plump that it is almost round. These cucumbers have an extraordinary ability to absorb radiation, an attribute that was underlined during experiments with organic lemon cucumbers at the Los Alamos nuclear research centre in the United States. Lemon cucumbers are just one of the many traditional and heirloom varieties of cucumbers that are grown organically alongside the more familiar long, green cucumbers. With their refreshing, mild flavour cucumbers are perfect in salads.

Below: Traditional cucumbers are available in organic varieties.

Below: Lettuces are easy to grow all year round on a window sill or outside in the spring and autumn.

Above: Watercress helps to relieve the symptoms of lung cancer and skin complaints.

Above: Avocados contain essential fatty acids.

Watercress and Celery

Unless they are organic, watercress and celery are generally both treated heavily with pesticides and fertilizers. Because it has a high water content, agrochemical watercress can be particularly toxic and could well be laced with nitrates.

Organic watercress may be smaller but the flavour is sharper and more concentrated. The pungent taste is due to an antibacterial phytonutrient, so watercress works well against bacterial disorders such as food poisoning. It is also believed to protect against – and relieve the symptoms of – lung cancer and skin complaints. It can be used in smaller quantities than agrochemical watercress because of its intensity. Try it in salads, or make it into a peppery soup with onions, cream and nutmeg.

Celery helps to flush out excess fluid from the body and is a useful remedy for constipation. It is great in a mixed vegetable juice or stock. When finely sliced, fresh celery adds crunch to a Waldorf salad. Celery is also delicious braised and will add flavour to a stuffing for roast chicken.

Avocados

These are possibly the most indulgent of vegetables. Many dieters are deterred from eating these delicious vegetables because of their relatively high calorie content, but they are packed with the right sorts of fats, essential fatty acids. Non-organic avocados are often picked while they are still bullet hard and ripened artificially, whereas organic avocados ripen naturally over a longer period. The result is creamy flesh that relieves PMS, is great for the skin and helps prevent cancer. Slice or cube avocado for salads, or mash with lemon juice and chilli for an instant guacamole dip. You can even use the empty avocado skins to moisturize your skin.

PREPARING FENNEL

With a sharp knife, cut the fennel bulb in half lengthwise, then either cut into quarters or slice thinly.

Fennel

The aromatic fennel bulb has a very similar texture to celery and is topped with edible feathery fronds. Organic fennel is smaller and tastier than non-organic fennel, with essential oils that help combat digestive complaints such as flatulence. Its distinctive aniseed flavour is most potent when eaten raw in salads. This tasty vegetable can also be braised, when it acquires a delicious sweetness. Fennel is at its best when it is fresh and should be eaten as soon as possible after purchase.

Below: Fennel contains essential oils that can help combat digestive disorders.

VEGETABLE FRUITS

Tomatoes, aubergines (eggplant), (bell) peppers and chillies are treated as vegetables in cooking but classified botanically as fruit.

Tomatoes

There is simply no comparison between the flavour of a freshly picked organic tomato that has been allowed to ripen naturally and the taste of an artificially ripened tomato. Organic growers select the sweetest, tastiest varieties, and whether you buy tiny cherry tomatoes or big beefsteaks, you won't be disappointed.

In terms of nutrition, tomatoes contain a beneficial carotenoid called lycopene. This important micro-nutrient helps to protect the body from cancer, especially cancers of the gastrointestinal tract, breast, cervix and prostate. Lycopene is present in the fresh fruit and is released from the skin when fresh tomatoes are cooked. This means that levels of lycopene are even higher in canned or processed products, such as tomato purée (paste), canned tomatoes, ketchup and pasteurized tomato juice, than they are in fresh tomatoes. However, fresh tomatoes are

Left: Chadwick tomatoes are sweet and juicy.

higher in vitamin C, which is destroyed in cooking. It is absolutely essential to buy organic tomato products since almost all non-organic prepared tomato products contain GMO tomatoes.

Chillies

Fresh chillies come in a wide variety of shapes, sizes and colours, with flavours ranging from mild and fruity to intensely fiery. Organic growers like to experiment with the rarer varieties, so you may find unusual types at a farmers' market. More than 200 different types of chilli are available and they now form an integral part of very many cuisines, including Indian, Thai, Mexican, South American and African.

Right: Serrano chillies contain capsaicin, a phytochemical that is essential for heart health.

Chillies are the concentrated relations of sweet peppers, and there are wonderful stories concerning their heart-strengthening abilities. They also have antibacterial properties and help respiration and chest complaints.

Like peppers, chillies contain *capsaicin*. In chillies, however, it is concentrated, and accounts for their heat. Handle them with care, as the *capsaicin* can damage sensitive skin, especially around the lips and eyes. The hottest part of a chilli is the white membrane that connects the seeds to the flesh. Removing this membrane and the seeds removes most of the heat. The heat can also be moderated and the sweetness released if chillies are roasted or grilled (broiled) until charred, and then peeled in the same way as peppers. Chillies prepared in this way freeze well.

Above: Naturally ripened organic tomatoes contain a beneficial carotenoid called lycopene, which helps protect the body from cancer.

Left: Organic aubergines are meaty and delicious.

Aubergines

Organic aubergines are both meaty and delicious. They come in a range of beautiful varieties, from the pretty dappled pink Listada de Gandia to the creamy White Sword. The phytochemical that gives aubergines their bitter flavour helps to prevent and cure the common cold. If you prefer a less bitter taste, slice each vegetable and sprinkle it with salt. Leave for about an hour and the salt will leach out the bitterness, then rinse thoroughly and pat dry before cooking. This also prevents the absorption of excessive oil when frying.

A great way to release the sweetness of aubergines is to bake them. Simply put them, on a baking sheet, in an oven preheated to 180°C/350°F/Gas 4. Cook for about 30 minutes or until tender, then peel the skin from the flesh, chop them and serve drizzled with olive oil, tahini and lemon juice. This popular dish is known as baba ganoush. Aubergines are also delicious roasted, griddled and puréed into garlic-laden dips.

Peppers/Bell Peppers

Agrochemical peppers are often grown hydroponically, which is why they tend to taste inferior to organic ones. Organic peppers are full of vitamin C as well as containing the phytochemical capsaicin that is great for heart health. Green peppers are fully developed but less ripe than other examples, which can make them hard to digest. They have refreshing juicy flesh with a crisp texture. In addition to being more mature, orange, red and purple peppers have sweeter flesh and are more digestible than less ripe green peppers. Roasting or chargrilling peppers enhances their sweetness. Peppers are also delicious when they are served stuffed, sliced into salads or steamed.

Below: Sweet (bell) peppers are members of the capsicum family. The very best organic peppers are firm and glossy with unblemished skins.

PEELING (BELL) PEPPERS

1 Roast the peppers under a hot grill (broiler) for 12–15 minutes, turning regularly, until the skin chars.

2 Alternatively, place on a baking sheet and roast in an oven preheated to 200°C/400°F/Gas 6 for 20–30 minutes, until the skin blackens and blisters.

3 Put the peppers in a plastic bag and leave until cool. The steam will encourage the skin to come away from the flesh easily.

4 Peel away the skin, then slice in half. Remove the core and scrape out any remaining seeds. Slice or chop according to your recipe.

MUSHROOMS

Non-organic mushrooms are subjected to vast amounts of chemicals, on the crop itself and to sterilize the straw on which they grow. Fungicides and insecticides are sprayed over them and their growing sheds are regularly bleached. Organic mushrooms have no such hazards. They are also much tastier than most non-organic varieties, whether simply sliced raw in a salad or fried with tamari or soy sauce.

Most organic mushrooms do not contain a wealth of nutrients, but are a useful source of B vitamins, potassium, iron and niacin. Organic shiitake mushrooms, however, are fantastic for the immune system, and have been prized for centuries in Japan for their medicinal properties. They are also a good source of phytochemicals and other nutrients. Dried shiitake mushrooms are readily available in organic stores.

Button (white), cap and flat mushrooms are the most common cultivated variety of mushrooms. They are all one type of mushroom in various stages of maturity, from small button mushrooms, through cap mushrooms to the largest, strongest-flavoured flat mushrooms. Flat mushrooms are good grilled (broiled) or baked on their own or with stuffing.

Left: *Fresh and dried shiitake mushrooms are fantastic for the immune system.*

Chestnut (cremini) mushrooms look similar to button mushrooms but have brown caps and a nutty flavour. Field (portabello) mushrooms are wild and have intense, rich flavour which makes them ideal for grilling and stuffing. Chanterelles are a pretty yellow colour, with a funnel-shape and a fragrant but delicate flavour. Available dried as well as fresh, they are delicious sautéed, baked or added to sauces.

Store fresh organic mushrooms in paper bags in the refrigerator, and use within a few days of purchase. When you are ready to eat them, wipe the mushrooms gently with damp kitchen paper and trim the stems. Wild mushrooms often harbour grit and dirt and may need to be rinsed briefly under cold running water but they must be dried thoroughly. Never soak fresh mushrooms or they will become soggy.

PREPARING DRIED SHIITAKE MUSHROOMS

Dried shiitake mushrooms are a useful store-cupboard stand-by. Before they can be used in cooking, however, they must be rehydrated.

1 Quickly wash off any dirt under cold running water, then soak dried shiitake mushrooms in tepid water for about 2–3 hours, or overnight. If you are short of time, soak for at least 45 minutes before cooking.

2 Remove the shiitake from the soaking water, and gently squeeze out any excess water. With your fingers or a knife, trim off the stem and then slice or chop the caps to use in cooking. Add the stems to soups or stock. Don't discard the soaking liquid; rather drain it through muslin (cheesecloth), then use it in soups or stews or for simmering vegetables.

Left: *This mixed selection of organic mushrooms is a useful source of B vitamins, iron, potassium and niacin.*

PEAS, BEANS and CORN

These popular organic vegetables can be bought frozen as well as fresh so you can enjoy them all year round. They are frozen within hours of being picked and so are still high in nutritional value.

Left: Organic corn cobs have sweet kernels.

Peas and Beans

Organic farmers often rely on legume crops to keep their fields fertile, so there is usually an abundant and varied supply of peas and beans, from sweet mangetouts (snow peas) to meaty broad (fava) beans. Early summer brings the first garden peas, so sweet and tender that you can eat them raw, straight from the pod. This season is short, but other delights lie ahead. Crisp French (green) beans, sugar snaps and runner beans soon appear on organic market stalls.

Shelled peas are best eaten lightly steamed or added to sauces and stews in the last few minutes of cooking. Mangetouts and beans can be sliced raw into salads, stir-fried or lightly steamed as a side dish. Store fresh peas and beans in the salad compartment of the refrigerator and use them within a week to ensure the best taste.

Corn

Organic corn cobs are often smaller and paler than the agrochemical equivalent, but the kernels are beautifully tender and sweet. Corn cobs are best eaten soon after picking, before their natural sugars start to convert into starch, the kernels begin to toughen and their flavour fades. Remove the green outer leaves and cook whole or slice off the kernels with a sharp knife. Baby corn can be eaten raw, and are also good in stir-fries. One delicious way to serve corn on the cob is to fry it whole in hot olive oil for just a few minutes. The heat will be just enough to release the natural sweetness and caramelize the exterior.

Eda-mame

These are fresh soya beans. They are widely available in Japan and in many parts of the USA. Eda-mame deliver a complete balance of protein and phytochemicals that are good for maintaining healthy hormone levels.

PREPARING EDA-MAME

This is a good way to appreciate young soya beans in the pod.

1 Separate the pods from the stalks, if they are still attached, and trim off the stem end. Sprinkle the pods generously with salt and rub the salt into the bean pods with your hands. Leave for 15 minutes.

2 Boil plenty of water in a large pan, then add the beans and boil over a high heat for 7–10 minutes, or until the beans are tender but still crunchy. Drain immediately and refresh briefly under running water.

3 Serve hot or cold in a basket or a bowl with drinks. To eat, squeeze the pods with your teeth to push out the beans into your mouth.

Left: Organic mangetouts and sugar snap peas have a fresh flavour.

SEA VEGETABLES

Also known as seaweeds, these amazing vegetables, with unusual, tangy flavours and exotic colours, provide our strongest natural source of minerals and trace elements. Nori, wakame and hijiki are the richest sources of minerals. Nori is also the best source of protein.

Although Japan and China are the countries best known for their use of sea vegetables, seaweeds have been collected all over the world for centuries.

One interesting property of seaweeds is their ability to detoxify the body thanks to the alginic acid they contain. When we ingest this substance, it binds with heavy metals in our intestines and allows them to be released, cleansing the body. Nori, laver, dulse, kombu, wakame and arame are all types of seaweeds with these detoxifying properties.

Fresh seaweed requires little preparation. Having been gathered in clean and unpolluted water, it needs to be rinsed in fresh water before being dried in the sun or in an oven on a very low heat. It can also be chopped and frozen.

Most seaweeds are only available dried. Once reconstituted they can be used as substitutes for fresh green vegetables, toasted and crumbled over soups, salads or stir-fries, or used in sushi. Unopened packets of dried sea vegetables keep well for several months if stored in a cool place. Canned organic seaweeds often taste stronger than the dried versions.

Nori

The traditional sushi wrap, nori is one sea vegetable that does not require soaking. It comes in purple-black sheets which, when toasted for use as a garnish, turn translucent green.

Above: *Dried and cut wakame can be used in stews and salads.*

Below: *Toasted nori sheets add crunch when used as a garnish.*

TOASTING NORI
This brings out the flavour and makes nori crispy. Take care not to scorch the nori sheets – or your fingers.

1 Hold a sheet of nori with a pair of tongs about 5cm/2in above a gas burner for about 1 minute, moving it around so it toasts evenly and turns bright green and crisp.

2 Leave the nori to cool for a few moments. Crumble between your fingers and sprinkle over soups, salads or stir-fries, or use in sushi.

Wakame

A dark-coloured seaweed with a delicate flavour, wakame adds body to stews and can also be used in salads. A small strip, cooked with beans and pulses, will help to soften them. Prepare it in the same way as arame.

Kombu

A strongly flavoured seaweed with flat fronds, kombu, or kelp as it is also known, is used in slowly cooked dishes. It is an essential ingredient in the Japanese stock, dashi.

Above: Hijiki requires longer cooking than most sea vegetables.

Below: Laver is high in minerals and vitamins.

PREPARING DRIED HIJIKI

Soaking and cooking times vary depending on how the hijiki is to be used.

1 Rinse the hijiki in a strainer under cold, running water, then place in a bowl and cover with tepid water. Leave to soak for 15 minutes – it will expand to several times its dried volume. Drain and place in a pan.

2 Add fresh water to cover the hijiki and bring to the boil. Simmer for about 20 minutes until tender.

Arame

Mild-tasting arame is a good sea vegetable to try if you haven't tasted these vegetables before. It must be soaked in warm water for 20 minutes before using in salads or stir-fries, but can be added straight from the packet to slow-cooked noodle dishes and soups.

Hijiki

This twiggy, black sea vegetable looks similar to arame but is thicker and has a stronger flavour. It requires longer cooking than most sea vegetables.

Laver

Commonly found around the shores of Britain, laver is used in regional dishes such as Welsh laverbread, where it is combined with oatmeal. It can be added to sauces and stuffings.

Dulse

A purple-red sea vegetable, dulse has a chewy texture and spicy flavour when cooked. It can be added to salads. In Wales, Ireland, North America and Canada, dulse is gathered in summer and sold in health food stores and fish markets. It is great in noodle dishes and soups or toasted and crumbled for a nourishing garnish.

Right: Dulse has a spicy flavour.

Agar-agar

A setting agent, derived from a type of seaweed called "rock flower vegetable" in China, agar-agar is an ideal vegetarian alternative to gelatine. Available in strips or as powder, it can be used to make excellent sweet or savoury jellies.

HERBS and EDIBLE FLOWERS

Fresh and dried herbs have been prized by cooks for centuries for their ability to enhance the flavour of any ingredient they accompany and enliven even the simplest meal. It is a bonus that many herbs have remarkable healing qualities.

Typically, organic herbs have stronger flavours than non-organic ones because they have a higher concentration of phytochemicals. These active components are the main source of a herbal plant's flavour and health-promoting properties. Non-organic herbs all have the medicinal and taste benefits of organic herbs, but often contain much smaller amounts of the essential oils vital for these purposes. Since it is rare for cooks to wash fresh herbs thoroughly before use, pesticide residues on non-organic herbs can be inadvertently included in a meal. Dried non-organic herbs carry the same risk.

Another big plus when buying herbs from organic growers is the sheer variety and number of plants on offer, including unusual and heirloom varieties such as apple mint, purple basil and Chinese chives. By shopping from organic growers direct, or sourcing organic seeds, the organic cook has access to a much broader selection of flavours.

Growing Herbs

It is essential to use fresh herbs before they start to wilt, and the best way to guarantee freshness is to grow your own herbs in pots or in a window box. Good herbs that grow all year round are parsley, thyme, chives, marjoram, winter savory, sorrel and tarragon. These perennials are quite difficult to grow from seed, so they are best bought as young plants.

Annual herbs such as mint or basil can be grown from seeds sown from late March onwards. They should be sown in seed compost in shallow trays and transferred to bigger containers after about a month. Herbs should always be grown outside, and stone or terracotta pots are best. Traditional herb pots not only look attractive, with their little pockets on the sides, but also work well. All herbs need to be kept under cover on the very coldest nights of winter, but can otherwise stay outside on a window sill or balcony, or in the garden.

Right: Basil is said to have a calming effect on the stomach, easing constipation, sickness and cramps, and aiding digestion.

MAKING BOUQUET GARNI

Tie herbs in a bundle, or bouquet garni, when you want the flavour but not the herbs themselves in a dish.

1 With a long piece of string, tie together a few parsley stalks, a sprig of thyme and a bay leaf, or your own choice of herbs. Add a piece of celery stick to flavour poultry dishes, a spring of rosemary for lamb, or a piece of fennel or leek for fish dishes.

2 Dried or chopped herbs can be bundled together in a small muslin (cheesecloth) bag. Break or tear the herbs into small pieces and place in the centre of a 10–13cm/4–5in square of clean muslin. Bring the edges of the muslin up over the herbs and tie firmly into a bag with a length of string. Make muslin bundles in batches so that they are readily at hand for cooking.

3 Tie one end of the string to the pan handle or leave it hanging over the edge of the casserole to make it easy to remove and discard the herbs before serving the dish.

Culinary Combinations

The reason why particular herbs are traditionally added to certain dishes has something to do with complementary flavours, but there are other practical considerations, too. The classic combination of fried lamb's liver with sage not only tastes superb, but the sage helps the body to digest the meat. Organic rosemary contains powerful essential oils that stimulate the digestive system to make extra bile. This makes it the perfect partner for lamb and chicken dishes. Bay leaves added to bolognese sauce aid the digestion of a pasta meal, and the mint tea that customarily concludes the meal in many countries helps to counter indigestion. It also sweetens the breath and because it is a mild stimulant, the diner is less likely to fall asleep on a full stomach.

Preparing Leafy Herbs

Organic herbs do not need to be washed, but different herbs should be prepared in different ways. Such woody-stemmed herbs as sage and thyme need their leaves removed from the stems before adding to dishes. Large leaves can be picked off with the fingers. For small leaves, hold a sprig of herb at the tip and strip off the leaves with a fork.

Leafy herbs, including parsley, can simply be chopped once any coarse stalks have been removed. Cutting herbs with a knife or scissors damages the essential oils from the plant, making them taste more bitter. Try tearing the delicate leaves and stems to encourage a sweeter flavour.

Lightly crushing, or bruising, whole leaves or sprigs of herbs with a mortar and pestle helps to release their flavour into dishes that are cooked quickly.

Use herbs as soon as possible after picking. If you must store them briefly, do so in the refrigerator, wrapped in foil or paper, or chop and freeze them.

Herb Oils

Flavoured oils are delicious for cooking chicken and fish or drizzling over roasted vegetables. Strongly flavoured herbs such as thyme, bay, basil, rosemary, marjoram and tarragon are best suited to flavouring oils. Push several sprigs into a clean, empty bottle. Fill with light olive or sunflower oil and store in a cool place for two weeks. Then strain through muslin into clean bottles. Herb oils will keep for three to six months.

Edible Flowers

Whole flowers or individual petals can enhance savoury and sweet dishes with their delicate flavours. The visual appeal of adding whole flowers or individual petals to a recipe is immediate and wonderful. Flowers from plants with other culinary uses usually taste like a milder version of that plant.

Cooking with organic flowers rather than non-organic flowers is hugely preferably because they are more likely to be strongly scented and, therefore, strongly flavoured. They are available in a fantastic range of species.

Cut deep pink carnation petals from the bitter base of each flower and soak in white wine for half an hour.

Left: Chives and bay leaves add flavour to any organic meal.

Above: Rosemary and sage

DRYING HERBS

Woody-stemmed herbs, including rosemary, thyme, oregano and sage, can be dried for use in winter dishes when fresh herbs may not be available.

Pick herbs before they flower, preferably on a sunny morning after the dew has dried. Tie them in bunches and place each bunch inside a roomy paper bag that you have perforated in several places. Tie the bag closed and hang it in a warm place, with the leaves dangling down. The paper cover helps to prevent the leaves from fading and the bag catches any that drop.

The leaves should be dry and crisp after a week. Leave the herbs in bundles or strip the leaves from the stems and store in airtight jars.

Pour the mixture over a fruit salad. Raw sunflower petals add vibrancy to stir-fries. Deep blue cornflowers and bright orange calendula petals transform a green salad, and nasturtiums add peppery bite. Passion flowers, fuchsias, pansies and violas are a dramatic garnish for cakes. Violet and rose petals are traditionally used throughout Europe candied as cake decorations. Lavender and rose waters are made by steeping the flowers in hot water until it cools, then straining the mixture. In Eastern Europe and the Middle East, dried rose petals and rose water are mixed into such dishes as couscous and tagines.

APPLES and PEARS

Few sights are more pleasing than an orchard of mature organic apple and pear trees in summer. Fallen white and pink blossoms litter the grass like confetti, and birds and bees dart between the branches overhead. The fruits are beginning to form. Soon they will start to swell and ripen, the fragrance redolent of times in childhood spent climbing trees and scraping knees. Later, in autumn, the ants and other insects on the ground might be lucky with a windfall. But we will be luckier still. The fruit grown in an organic orchard are delicious, self-packaged parcels of vitamins, minerals and phytochemicals.

Agrochemical pears and apples are grown in startlingly different circumstances from the organic ideal described above. Single species trees grow in regimented rows, over-laden with fruit that is systematically sprayed with toxic

Above: *Selection of organic apples including Granny Smith, Red Spartan, Bramley and Chive.*

fungicides, herbicides, insecticides and growth-regulating hormones. The insecticides are often organophosphate-based products, similar to nerve gases. Before going on sale, the fruit may be treated with preservatives. This process lengthens its shelf life but does nothing to preserve the natural nutrients within the product. Because the fruit is picked before it is ripe, its nutritional value is further undermined. If you buy non-organic apples and pears, peel them to remove the chemical covering. The paradox is that the skin is the most nutritious part of the fruit.

Above: *Spartan, and other, apples can cleanse and purify the blood.*

1 Peel, core and thickly slice the apples. Drop the apple pieces immediately into a bowl of cold water to which a few drops of lemon juice or cider vinegar have been added to prevent discoloration.

2 Barely cover the base of a pan with cold water. Add the apple pieces and cook gently, with the lid on, until soft. Add honey to taste towards the end, if you like.

3 If you are using firm eating apples, which will not disintegrate to a purée, cook until very tender, then rub through a coarse strainer with a spoon for a smooth purée.

DRYING APPLES AT HOME

The drying process boosts levels of vitamin C in apples.

1 Peel the apples, remove the cores and slice the fruit into rings. Soak in salted water for a few minutes to prevent discoloration.

2 Thread the apple rings on to a length of string. Hang them from the ceiling or suspend across the room until they are completely dry.

3 Alternatively, arrange the rings in a single layer on a wire rack on a baking sheet, making sure that they are not touching. Place in an oven set to 70°C/150°F/Gas Low for several hours until dried.

Apples

Rich in pectin and potassium, apples are a good general tonic for the immune system. While an agrochemical apple might look fresh, it could have lost many of its most valuable active vitamins and compounds.

Organic apples can be found in a wealth of varieties, from classic heirloom fruits to modern hybrids. Some varieties, including Bramley's Seedling, are particularly good for cooking and make wonderful pies and crumbles or crisps. The latter are particularly tasty – and even more nutritious – when oats, ground almonds and cinnamon are mixed into the topping. Eating apples, such as Cox's Orange Pippin and Spartan, are often favoured for cooking, too. Their slices stay whole when baked. Classic apples still grown organically include deep red American Salome and the Flower of Kent, an old English variety, which legend has it was the apple that landed on Sir Isaac Newton's head convincing him of the force of gravity. Modern apples range from the sweet and juicy Japanese Shizuka to the multipurpose Australian King Cole. Look out for unusual varieties like these at farmers' markets.

Above: Conference pears are good at lowering cholesterol as well as easing constipation.

Below: Red Williams pears are high in soluble fibre.

Pears

Most pears are all-purpose – they can be eaten fresh or cooked. Popular varieties include Conference, Williams, Comice, Bartlett and Anjou. It is good to buy pears slightly under-ripe, as they will ripen over a few days on a sunny window sill. Conference pears, by contrast, should have a little "give" when you buy them. Like organic apples, pears are a good source of soluble fibre and great at lowering cholesterol as well as easing constipation.

Eating and Storing

When eaten fresh, organic apples and pears should be cut immediately before serving to limit oxidization. Some varieties of apples do not go brown as quickly as others when exposed to air, especially Ginger Gold. Apples and pears can also be eaten cooked or dried. Both fruits juice well, and the juice can be frozen for a few months without losing its nutrient content and flavour. Store apples and pears in a cool, dark place and do not let them touch each other. Check them frequently, especially the pears, as they tend to spoil more quickly than agrochemical fruit.

SUMMER FRUITS

The delicate juicy sweetness of organic summer fruits is one of the greatest joys of the summer months. Like all fruit, these are generally best when home-grown and in season.

Cherries and Plums

From the palest of yellow varieties to the dark-red morellos, cherries are the prettiest of fruits. Plums are just as varied, from tiny greengages to regal Victorias. Agrochemical plums and cherries are treated with differing levels of respect by the farmers who grow them, from widespread use of agrochemicals

Above: Cherries are high in phytochemicals.

in some countries to near abstinence in the UK's cherry industry. Unless you can be certain that no agrochemicals have been used, it is safer to choose organic plums and cherries to eat unpeeled. Both plums and cherries are a good source of phytochemicals and may help to prevent cancer and relieve rheumatism and arthritis. Plums contain malic acid and betacarotene, so they can provide protection against heart disease and circulatory disorders. Plums also relieve fluid retention and are good for digestion. Plums can be sweet and juicy or slightly tart; the latter are best cooked in pies and cakes or made into a jam.

Sweet plums can be eaten as they are but are also good in fruit salads and fruit pies. There are also two types of cherries: sweet and sour. Some, such as the popular Bing, are best eaten raw, while others, such as Morello, are best cooked.

Above:
Elegant Lady
peaches

Above: Organic plums contain malic acid and betacarotene, which protect against heart disease.

Below: Victoria plums may help relieve rheumatism and arthritis.

Peaches, Nectarines and Apricots

Organic peaches, nectarines and apricots tend to be smaller and more intensely coloured than non-organic fruit, and are much sweeter and tastier. They help to regulate the system and ease constipation. Ripe peaches and apricots should be stored in the refrigerator but brought to room temperature before eating.

STONING A PEACH

1 Slice through the seam line all around the peach.

2 Twist the two halves in opposite directions to separate them.

3 Lever out the stone with a knife.

BERRIES and CURRANTS

Among the most popular of all fruits are berries and currants, with their glowing colours and sweet, scented juices. Strawberries, raspberries, currants of all colours, cranberries, blackberries and blueberries are just some of the delights that are sold throughout the summer. These are strictly seasonal crops. Buy them out of season and they will be inferior in terms of taste, texture and nutrition and they will almost certainly have been brought great distances by air.

Berries are delicate fruit. Washing them can spoil their texture and flavour. This is just one of the reasons why it is best to buy organic. It is perfectly safe to pop an organic berry into your mouth, whereas the agrochemical fruit will have been heavily sprayed with herbicides, fungicides, insecticides and slug deterrents. Organic berries are smaller and sweeter than non-organic ones.

Strawberries

From organic growers, strawberries are naturally sweet and delicious. Their flavour is concentrated in smaller, less watery fruit. As with all berries and grapes, they are high in vitamin C. Strawberries are also rich in soluble fibre and beta-carotene and contain phytochemicals that help to ease arthritis.

Below: *Organic strawberries are naturally firm and delicious.*

Above: *Organic blueberries are strong cancer-preventing berries.*

Above: *Cranberries are a good source of vitamins A and C and potassium.*

Blackberries

These high-fibre berries contain a wealth of minerals including iron, magnesium and calcium. They are rich in the bioflavonoids, which act as antioxidants, inhibiting the growth of cancer cells and protecting against cell damage by carcinogens.

Raspberries

These soft and fragrant berries are effective in removing toxins from the body. To make an uncooked purée or coulis, process some raspberries in a food processor or blender until smooth. Sweeten with maple syrup to taste and add a splash of lemon juice to bring out the flavour. For a smooth purée press through a nylon strainer. Store raspberries in the refrigerator for up to two days.

Right: *Raspberries are high in vitamin C.*

Blueberries

These are exciting considerable interest in terms of cancer research, being rich in anthocyanidins, the phytochemicals that give them their blue colour. The consensus is that they can help prevent cancer.

Cranberries

An excellent source of vitamin C, cranberries also provide potassium and vitamin A. Cranberry juice is effective in treating such infections of the urinary tract as cystitis.

Redcurrants

These pretty, delicate berries are rich in antioxidants, carotene and vitamins A and C.

Below: *Redcurrants*

Below: *Blackberries*

GRAPES, MELONS and FIGS

Some of the first fruits ever cultivated, grapes, melons and figs are now available in an enormous range of shapes, colours and sizes. They are excellent sources of essential nutrients.

Grapes

There are hundreds of different kinds of organic grapes available, from the largest black sweet varieties through to tiny seedless white ones. Wine grapes are often incredibly fragrant and remarkably differing in taste, texture, size, consistency and acidity. Semillon grapes are a classic variety from South West France, now grown from Australia to California. They have a delightful honey-like taste. Sauvignon grapes have herbal and melon flavours, with a citrus fruit edge. Friulian grapes are floral and crisply acidic, whereas Marsanne grapes are relatively low in acidity with a smooth nutty tone to their flavour.

Right: Delicious raw, organic figs can also be poached or baked.

Below: Grapes are high in vitamin C and carbohydrates.

Organic grapes are naturally high in antioxidants. They provide the perfect pick-up for convalescents, being a good source of carbohydrates and vitamin C. Grapes are easy to eat and taste delicious. Eat them at any time except after a big meal, as they tend to ferment and upset the stomach if it is full. They are best eaten straight off the bunch, or chopped into fruit salads, and taste excellent in fresh green salads.

Figs

The wonderful squashy texture of organic figs's flesh is the perfect foil for their crispy seeds, and the delicate fruit has a fantastically sweet and toffee-like flavour. Figs can be eaten raw but are also delicious poached or baked. These fruits are a great cure for constipation and, since they are high in iron, figs can help protect the body against anaemia.

Melons

There are two kinds of melons – musk melons and watermelons. Musk melons include the honeydew and Israeli HaOgen varieties. Their flesh is typically sweet and peach coloured. Watermelons include the classic pink-fleshed and deep-green-skinned varieties as well as rare paler versions such as the Early Moonbeam with its yellow flesh and striped green skin.

Agrochemically grown melons are sprayed with particularly noxious chemicals, including lindane and paraquat. The danger of ingesting these chemicals through a melon's skin is low, as only the inside flesh is eaten. However, if a melon plant is sprayed with pesticides and then watered, it is possible that some of the agrochemical will be diluted in the water. Melons are storehouses of the water used to irrigate them. Organic melons are refreshing and cleansing, easing fluid retention and urinary problems. Try serving them cubed on sticks or simply serve a crescent in its skin, decorated with small summer fruits. Melons are also delicious in sweet and savoury salads.

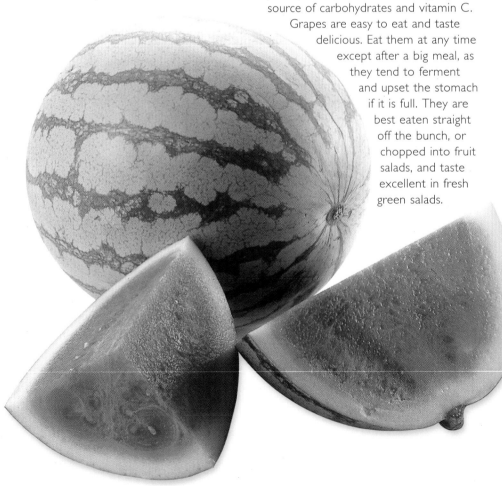

Left: Organic watermelons are filled with the unpolluted water used to irrigate them.

CITRUS FRUITS

Native to every warm to tropical country, citrus fruits are the most ubiquitous of tropical fruits and are enjoyed throughout the globe, from northern Europe to the southern tip of Chile. Oranges, grapefruit, lemons, limes, pomelos, tangerines, satsumas, kumquats and mandarins are all grown organically and should be strongly favoured over cheaper agrochemical alternatives.

Agrochemical citrus fruits are heavily treated with a huge range of powerful agrochemical toxins. Over one hundred different agrochemicals are permitted for use on citrus orchards in the USA, with a potentially higher and more dangerous toxic cocktail applied to citrus crops in the developing world. Organic citrus fruits are not dyed, whereas many agrochemically grown ones are injected with artificial colourings.

All of the members of the organic citrus family benefit from being grown as nature intended. Vitamin and mineral levels are boosted and the fruits are packed with bioflavonoids. The benefits of wax-free citrus peel are obvious to jam makers, with organic marmalade being the best choice by far. All citrus fruits are great for preventing or treating colds and sore throats and generally raising immunity.

Lemons
Smaller and more irregularly shaped than agrochemical lemons, organic lemons are juicy and tart. Although all citrus fruits contain citric acid, lemons have an amazing property that means they work as an alkaline food. When the human body digests lemon juice, a by-product is potassium carbonate. This salt actually neutralizes the digestive system, creating a beneficial balance.

In the kitchen, lemons have limitless uses. From soups to sorbets, there is scarcely a dish that does not benefit from a squeeze of lemon juice or a sprinkling of grated rind. When lemon juice is squirted over cooked meats, fish and vegetables, the lemon juice caramelizes to crisp the main ingredient.

Organic lemons are not dyed and they are sometimes greener than agrochemical ones. Ripe lemons will yield to the touch when you squeeze them lightly. Rolling a lemon firmly over a work surface or in the palms of your hands will help you extract the maximum amount of juice.

Unwaxed, organic lemon rind adds an understated warmth to the dish and contributes bacteria-fighting limonine oils. The juice itself is packed with vitamin C and numerous phytochemicals, supporting the development of general health, and will help the body to build a strong immune system.

Below: Organic oranges

Oranges and Grapefruit
Organic citrus fruits have more vitality – grapefruits are tarter and oranges are rounder in flavour. Like many other agrochemical citrus crops, non-organic oranges and grapefruit are routinely coated with anti-fungal waxes that would contaminate any dishes prepared with citrus rind or peel. If the skin of the fruit is matt, not shiny, this is evidence that it has not been waxed. Both fruits are high in vitamin C and grapefruits offer valuable support for gum health. Try squeezing grapefruit juice into a fruit cocktail to add zest, or simply halve the fruit and eat it with a spoon.

Below: Unwaxed organic lemons

Limes
Once considered an exotic fruit, limes are now a part of every modern cook's kitchen. The juice has a sharper flavour than that of lemons, so use less juice if you substitute limes for lemons in a recipe. Limes are an essential part of organic holistic cancer treatment.

Left: Organic limes

TROPICAL FRUITS

Organic kiwi fruits, pineapples, papaya and mangoes are abundant sources of vitamin C. All of these fruits tend to be smaller than their non-organic equivalents, with denser and sweeter flesh. They also have higher levels of micronutrients, which result in rounded, more intense flavours.

Most tropical fruits are naturally high in sugar, so they should be picked and eaten as soon as they are ripe. As they are often transported vast distances, this creates a temptation for agrochemical growers to pick under-ripe fruit for shipment. Organic farmers, however, allow fruit to ripen naturally for longer, which improves the nutritional content and flavour. When fully ripe, organic mangoes, kiwi fruit and papayas all feel slightly soft when squeezed. Organic tropical fruit should be eaten as soon as it is ripe, because it has a relatively short shelf life.

Left: Kiwi fruit contain as much fibre as pears.

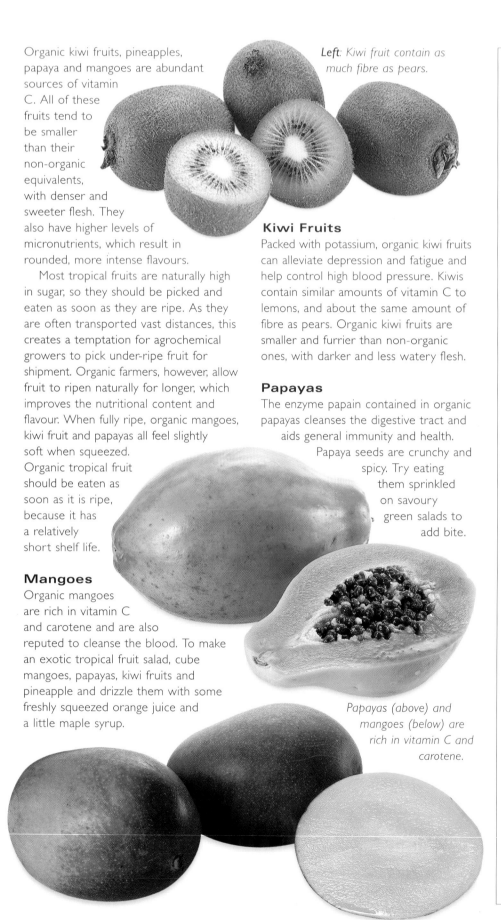

Kiwi Fruits

Packed with potassium, organic kiwi fruits can alleviate depression and fatigue and help control high blood pressure. Kiwis contain similar amounts of vitamin C to lemons, and about the same amount of fibre as pears. Organic kiwi fruits are smaller and furrier than non-organic ones, with darker and less watery flesh.

Papayas

The enzyme papain contained in organic papayas cleanses the digestive tract and aids general immunity and health. Papaya seeds are crunchy and spicy. Try eating them sprinkled on savoury green salads to add bite.

Papayas (above) and mangoes (below) are rich in vitamin C and carotene.

Mangoes

Organic mangoes are rich in vitamin C and carotene and are also reputed to cleanse the blood. To make an exotic tropical fruit salad, cube mangoes, papayas, kiwi fruits and pineapple and drizzle them with some freshly squeezed orange juice and a little maple syrup.

PREPARING A MANGO

1 Place the mango narrow side down on a chopping board. Cut off a thick lengthways slice, keeping the knife as close to the stone as possible. Turn the mango round and repeat on the other side. Cut off the flesh adhering to the stone and scoop the flesh from the mango slices.

2 To make a "hedgehog", prepare the mango as above and then score the flesh on each thick slice with criss-cross lines at 1cm/½in intervals, taking care not to cut through the skin.

3 Carefully turn the mango halves inside out and serve.

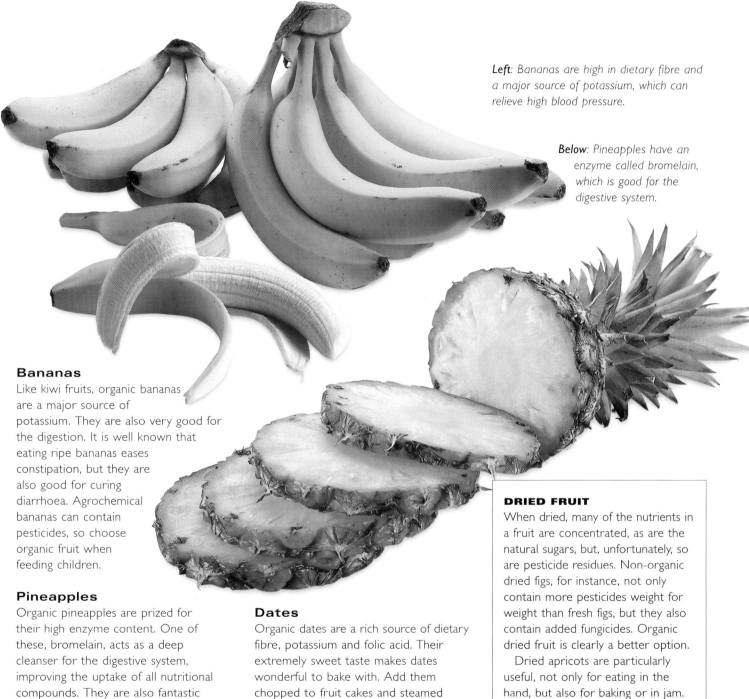

Left: Bananas are high in dietary fibre and a major source of potassium, which can relieve high blood pressure.

Below: Pineapples have an enzyme called bromelain, which is good for the digestive system.

Bananas

Like kiwi fruits, organic bananas are a major source of potassium. They are also very good for the digestion. It is well known that eating ripe bananas eases constipation, but they are also good for curing diarrhoea. Agrochemical bananas can contain pesticides, so choose organic fruit when feeding children.

Pineapples

Organic pineapples are prized for their high enzyme content. One of these, bromelain, acts as a deep cleanser for the digestive system, improving the uptake of all nutritional compounds. They are also fantastic for the complexion, especially when applied topically.

Dates

Organic dates are a rich source of dietary fibre, potassium and folic acid. Their extremely sweet taste makes dates wonderful to bake with. Add them chopped to fruit cakes and steamed puddings, or eat them whole. They can be given to children instead of sweets (candies), and are a useful food for people needing extra energy, including sportsmen and women, pregnant women and the elderly. Non-organic dates are often soaked in syrups and oils, but you will find that organic dates are naturally sweet.

Left: Organic dates are naturally sweet and high in energy.

DRIED FRUIT

When dried, many of the nutrients in a fruit are concentrated, as are the natural sugars, but, unfortunately, so are pesticide residues. Non-organic dried figs, for instance, not only contain more pesticides weight for weight than fresh figs, but they also contain added fungicides. Organic dried fruit is clearly a better option.

Dried apricots are particularly useful, not only for eating in the hand, but also for baking or in jam. They are a rich source of carotenes and, when eaten in quantity, contain useful quantities of vitamin C. As such they are the staple and only protection from scurvy available to many people in remote mountain communities, such as the Himalayan area of Ladakh. Organic dried apricots have also been credited with helping to reduce high blood pressure, protecting against cancer and supporting clear, naturally beautiful skin.

MEAT, POULTRY and GAME

Meat and poultry that has been farmed organically is the prime choice for cooks whose criteria are good quality, fine taste and texture, and whose concerns include basic levels of animal welfare. Intensively produced meat is almost always bland, watery, fatty and laced with unnatural hormones, antibiotics and drugs. Welfare conditions for the animals that provide non-organic meat are often horrific, from their rearing to slaughter. Although there are some excellent small non-organic meat farms, and free-range meat is better than meat from intensively reared animals and birds, choosing organic meat and poultry is the only option that fully addresses the issues.

Organic meat labelled as such by a recognized certifying body is also the only option if you want to avoid genetically modified organisms, because about 99 per cent of all non-organic meat is produced from animals whose feed contains some GMOs.

Above: Animals raised on organic farms enjoy a healthy, stress-free lifestyle.

Farming Methods

Non-organic, intensively farmed animals and birds are taken away from their mothers within a few days of birth and reared in huge herds and flocks. Most of their lives are spent indoors, and they are fed unnatural dried food pellets laced with growth hormones. Antibiotics are used routinely as a safeguard against the diseases and parasites that flourish in the cramped and stressful conditions in which they are kept. Animals and birds are brought to maturity as quickly as possible, by feeding them growth hormones, which speed up the process.

When intensively farmed livestock are ready for slaughter, they generally travel long distances in cramped lorries to the abattoir. In 2001, the European Union exported about 875,000 tonnes of live cows and beef to the rest of the world. At the same time, about 170,000 tonnes of live cows and beef were imported into Europe from Argentina, Botswana, Poland and Brazil. The growth of intensive meat farms has eradicated small local abattoirs, with huge centralized slaughterhouses replacing them for the processors' convenience.

Animal welfare is at the heart of organic animal husbandry. Animals are allowed to feed more freely and grow naturally, resulting in meat and poultry that tastes very much better.

The absolute freedom of game's wild existence means that it cannot be classified as organic. However, truly wild game from unpolluted countryside areas is an excellent choice for anyone who supports animal welfare and freedom. Farmed game that is organically certified is delicious and sustainable.

Biodynamic farming really comes into its own for meat products. Biodynamic animals live extremely comfortable lives, from birth to the abattoir. Many different kinds of heirloom and rare breed animals are free to mingle under cover or outdoors, in scenes reminiscent of an old-fashioned dream of how an animal farm should be. In the UK, regional species of pig such as the Tamworth porker are reared biodynamically, whereas this breed is almost unheard of on commercial intensive meat farms. While organic farm animals, which are unwell, may be treated with chemical medicines if homeopathy and other

complementary treatments do not work, biodynamic animals must be entirely chemical free. Meat is always hung after slaughter, which helps the flavour to develop. While this process occurs with all quality organic and non-organic meats, biodynamic meat is guaranteed to benefit from this traditional treatment.

Buying Organic Meat

Everybody who wants to eat delicious organic meat and poultry is encouraged to experiment with different stores or direct buying schemes. It is convenient to be able to obtain organic meat from the supermarket, but it is worth considering what is on offer at specialist fine organic suppliers and farmers' markets as well as local box schemes.

All organic meat tastes good because the animals are free range and feed on grass. The best organic meat tastes even better, however, because the carcasses are hung in the traditional manner after slaughter. Buying from a local supplier or taking delivery of organic meat from a box scheme will also provide you with cooking tips as part of the service. Another important advantage of buying meat either direct or from a specialist outlet is that the purchaser can often order an old-fashioned cut or ask for meat to be prepared in a particular way.

Organic halal and kosher meat is available in some larger Islamic and Jewish communities through mail order and box schemes. Check local Islamic or Jewish journals or search the Internet for details of a scheme near you.

Biodynamic and organic meats may be more expensive than intensively farmed meat, but this is not necessarily a bad thing. Reducing the quantity of meat we consume is recommended by doctors and nutritionists. When meat becomes an occasional treat, the cost is not so relevant, especially when the quality is first rate. Occasional meat eating is much more in line with man's original diet than daily hamburgers. Enjoyed weekly or fortnightly, organic meat will regain its special place in our diet.

Beef and Veal
Organic beef contains a much better balance of good and bad cholesterol than meat from intensively reared cows. This is because the animals' diet includes a high content of grass, whereas many intensively reared cattle are fed dry food almost exclusively. Some good quality non-organic beef cattle benefit from a free-range, grass-fed existence,

Above: *Organic beef rib is a healthier choice.*

but buying organic beef ensures this happens.

For a classic roast beef, use either sirloin or fore rib. Back rib and topside (pot roast) are both excellent slow roasted. When grilling (broiling) or frying steaks, use sirloin, rib eye, rump or fillet steaks. Neck or clod has an open, slightly sticky texture, and is good for stews, whereas shin (shank), chuck steak and top rump are best for casseroles where whole slices are needed. Pot roast silverside or brisket cuts, as these need to be cooked slowly over a long period. Flank and thin flank are good for making mince (ground beef) for bolognese sauces and cottage pies. Minced (ground) clod and shin are great for hamburgers and steak tartare because they are virtually fat free. Shin makes a good filling for slow-cooked pies.

If you buy veal make sure that it is organic. It will not be as pale as intensively farmed veal but you will have the satisfaction of knowing that it has come from a calf that has been reared with its mother, rather than being removed when only a few days old, which causes both animals great distress. Veal steaks are best simply pan-fried to seal in their flavour.

Above: *Organic lamb is especially tender and full of flavour.*

Mutton and Lamb
Most good supermarkets offer organic lamb, but usually only as chops and mince (ground lamb). Organic lamb is tender and full of flavour. The fat is clearly visible and can be removed easily. Organic mutton can be harder to find but many organic butchers stock it. It is invaluable for many authentic dishes, especially stews with an Arabic flavour. Minced mutton or lamb, which comes from shoulder, belly or leg meat, can be used instead of minced beef.

For a classic roast mutton or roast lamb, use leg, shoulder, saddle or rack. If you like your lamb pink, choose saddle or rack of lamb. Grill (broil) or fry leg steaks, loin or chump chops or cutlets. The rarer the meat, the more tender and flavoursome it will be. Lamb and mutton can both be fatty, but the meat can easily be trimmed. Make kebabs from neck fillet (US shoulder or breast) and butterflied or cubed leg. Casserole middle neck or shoulder meat for classic dishes such as navarin of lamb.

Right: Organic pork loin is a popular cut for roasting.

Pork

There are lots of delicious organic pork products available, including traditional home-made sausages, honey roasted hams, gammon and bacon. Most organic and non-organic bacon is cured with saltpetre. Although this helps to preserve the pinkish colour of the meat, there are some concerns about whether this traditional process is entirely healthy. A few specialist organic and biodynamic pork farms now offer fine-quality pork products that do not contain this ingredient. The meat they sell is darker, with a brown rather than red tinge, but it tastes just as delicious. High-quality organic pork sausages are widely available in supermarkets and delicatessens, but as with all organic meat products, traditional organic farmers' markets and delivery services offer an even more extensive range. Look out for pork sausages with apple, sage or forest fruits, as well as preserved salamis and saucissons.

Pork is a tender meat, which is suitable for all forms of cooking. Leg is a popular cut for roasting, as is blade, which can be roasted on the bone or boned and stuffed. For a truly succulent roast, try spare rib. Perhaps the most popular cut for roasting is loin, which provides the best crackling. To achieve this, score the fat deeply, rub in salt and roast the joint dry. When grilling (broiling) pork chops or steaks, it is essential to watch them carefully. They must be cooked through, as underdone pork can cause infection, but they should not be allowed to dry out.

Pork fillet (tenderloin) and schnitzel steaks are the best choice for frying. For braising, choose pork chops, steaks, spare ribs, blade, loin or belly meat. Hand and spring meat is a large cut which can be cubed and cooked in tender pork casseroles and stews.

Above: Organic chilli and pepper salami (left) and hot salami are all available from specialist organic butchers and organic stores.

Poultry

Organic poultry tends to be less fatty than intensively reared equivalents because the birds have more freedom to exercise and are not fed growth hormones. Because it is less fatty the meat benefits from being cooked slowly.

Organic chicken, duck, goose and turkey are easy to obtain, but goose and turkey tend to be more seasonal, their availability linked to festivals such as Christmas, Easter and Thanksgiving. As well as whole birds, poultry portions and breast fillets are available. They may be on the bone or boneless. Buying whole birds and cutting them up is not difficult, however, and provides the perfect opportunity for making homemade stock.

Above: Barbary ducks are lower in fat than other ducks.

Duck and Goose These are fatty birds with dark meat that has plenty of flavour. The fat helps to keep the meat moist during cooking. Goose is nearly always roasted, though the legs may be added to casseroles. Ducks are generally roasted whole or cut up for frying or casseroling.

American Long Island and British Aylesbury ducks have paler, tender meat with a significant proportion of fat and a rich flavour. Barbary and Nantes ducks have slightly less fat. The barbary, a big bird, provides a good proportion of firm breast meat. The Nantes is smaller, more tender and with a delicate flavour.

Unlike other domesticated poultry, geese have defied all attempts to rear them intensively. They are not prolific layers and are one of the few remaining sources of seasonal food. Goose fat is used in traditional cooking across central and Eastern Europe and in Scandinavia.

Chicken and Turkey Organic birds are raised in humane conditions, fed on a natural and (usually) traditional-style diet. They do not have lurid-coloured skin. The skeleton of an organic bird is bigger and stronger, and the legs are longer. When cooked, the flesh is less uniform in colour and texture; the breast meat is paler and the leg darker. Standards and conditions relating to the scheme or terms by which the birds are classified as organic are usually outlined on the packaging.

As well as whole birds, chicken and turkey are available in a wide choice of portions. Look for birds with a clear, soft skin, with no bruises or blemishes. The tougher the skin, the older the bird.

Organic chicken and turkey need to be cooked slower and longer than non-organic poultry to get the best flavour and texture. When roasting, try stuffing the cavity with grains and herbs, or with fresh fruit and spices, for an aromatic dish. Rub the skin with sea salt and different vinegars for added crispiness and zest. Stock made from the carcase of an organic bird will be incomparably richer in flavour and colour and will set to a firmer jelly.

Game

Some game is farmed organically, including rabbit and venison. In a few parts of the world, other types of game, such as elk and wild boar are seasonally available, either from rural farmers' markets, or specialist suppliers. Animals and birds that are truly wild cannot be classified as organic, as their habitat and diet is not controlled or able to be inspected by an organic certifier. Wild game from areas with low agrochemically managed farmlands is unlikely to be contaminated with chemical pollutants.
Venison The term venison is used not only for meat from deer but also from elk, moose, reindeer, caribou and antelope. Deer are now farmed organically, but the demand for most farmed game animals is still too slow to stimulate a market.

Venison is a dark, close-textured meat with very little fat; what there is should be firm and white. If it is in good condition and a prime cut, such as

haunch, loin, fillet or best end, it will be juicy and tender and is best served rare. Other cuts, such as shoulder, neck and shin, are often marinated and benefit from long and gentle cooking to bring out the flavour of the meat.
Rabbit Fresh rabbit is a delicate well-flavoured meat, pale and mild in colour. It is high in protein, low in cholesterol and particularly low in fat. Organically farmed rabbit may be bought all the year round. It can be grilled (broiled), fried, roasted or stewed. Baste it well so that the meat does not dry out.
Wild Boar The meat of wild boar has a strong taste. It is dark in colour and, as there is little fat, it can be dry and tough, although the flavour is excellent. For this reason wild boar is usually marinated. It should be cooked in the same way as pork.
Game Birds Fresh game birds are only available during the hunting season, which varies from bird to bird and from country to country. In some countries frozen game is stocked all through the year. Simple

Above: Organic turkeys are free to exercise and are not fed growth hormones.

cooking methods are often the best for game birds: plain roasting for tender birds and simple casserole cooking for tougher birds. Organic butchers and direct suppliers will be able to provide useful cooking advice.

Pheasants are the most plentiful game birds and are often sold in a brace: a pair of birds that includes a male and a female. The hen is smaller and more tender than the cock. Organic partridge, grouse and quail are also available. Scottish grouse has a wonderful, rich flavour from feeding on the highland heather of Scotland, where it is native.

There are two types of partridge, the French or red-legged partridge, and the English, or grey-legged partridge. The red-legged bird is bigger but the flavour of the grey bird is often preferred.

Below: Wild boar has a strong taste and little fat.

FISH and SHELLFISH

Organic fish is a delicious source of protein and can be prepared and cooked very easily. Fresh fish is versatile and great for your health. Omega-3 essential fatty acids found naturally in oily fish help to lower cholesterol levels, protecting the heart and circulation system. Eating fish also reduces the risk of developing high blood pressure during pregnancy, and can help to prevent premature births. However, environmentally aware cooks need to shop with care.

Many fish are either caught using deeply environmentally insensitive methods or raised in unsustainable farms. Organic cooks should buy organically farmed fish or wild fish from sustainable farms and fisheries. If you have doubts about the source or sustainability of fish

Below: *Organic fish is farmed using environmentally sensitive methods.*

that you want to buy, write to or e-mail the head office of the retailer or processor to find out more. Every time an organization receives a letter of interest from a consumer, it is more likely to improve the sustainability of its practices. For information on the Internet, visit the web sites of organic certification bodies. You can ask good fishmongers or restaurateurs about the seafood they prepare, or contact a specialist organization such as the Marine Stewardship Council.

Farmed Fish

Organic fish farms are clean and humane. Chemicals are not permitted to be used routinely, although they may occasionally be administered if infection occurs. Many intensive fish farms need to douse their fish regularly in chemicals simply

Above: *Pale, organically farmed salmon*

because they are so intensive. The more fish are crammed into a body of water, the easier diseases such as furunculosis and parasites like fish lice can spread. Organic fish farmers keep numbers lower and the result is a radical reduction in disease and pestilence. There are some non-organic fish farms that do maintain healthier numbers, but buying organically farmed fish is the best way of being sure that the fish have been managed well.

Despite the many advantages, organic fish farming poses great challenges to pioneering organic aquaculture experts. To be certified as organic, fish must be fed fishmeal that is half a by-product of fish for human consumption, and half from sustainable sources. The trouble is, most fish by-products are from white fish such as cod. Farmed fish including salmon do not easily digest this sort of fishmeal, so there can be a lot of wasted food which then pollutes surrounding waters. Also, fishmeal from white fish has relatively low levels of fatty acids, so organically farmed fish can have relatively low levels of Omega-3 oils unless they are very carefully managed by an expert organic fish farmer. On the plus side, organically farmed fish are not permitted to be fed any genetically modified foods, so buying organic fish is the only way you can be certain that your farmed fish dinner is GM free.

Although good-quality non-organic salmon usually has relatively low levels of chemical residues, organically farmed salmon has even less. Organically farmed

Right: *Seawater fish farms produce excellent sea trout.*

fish are generally top class in terms of taste and texture, whereas intensively farmed fish are often bland and fatty. Organically farmed fish also have paler flesh. The stronger colour of non-organic farmed salmon is due to a diet based on fishmeal with added carotenoids. Although these are the same as the beneficial compounds found in carrots, organic cooks will prefer the more natural paler colour of organically farmed salmon.

Salmon, trout and carp taste wonderful grilled (broiled), steamed or fried in olive oil, especially when they are served with a generous squeeze of fresh lemon juice. Smoked in the traditional way, organically farmed fish have incomparable flavour, so different from the bland non-organic product, which is prepared using artificial wood smoke flavouring.

Below: *MSC-certified halibut harvested by methods that protect the seabed.*

Seawater Fish Farms

Organic seawater fish farms are beginning to rear many more breeds of fish. These include organic sea trout, bass, cod, halibut and bream. Humane and causing the minimum impact on the marine environment, organic sea fish farming is still in its infancy. As wild fish stocks come under increasing threat, this area of organic farming is set to grow.

There are currently only a few experimental organic prawn and shrimp farms, but this sector is certain to increase exponentially. Non-organic farmed prawns and shrimp farms tend to be the antithesis of the organic ideal, and have devastated large areas of the tropical world from the Indian Ocean to the mangroves of Honduras. Abusing the rights of local farmers who rear the crop, the prawn and shrimp industry often replaces rural diverse communities with a single polluting monoculture. To avoid adding to this type of situation, do not buy farmed prawns or shrimps unless they are certified as organic.

Such shellfish as cockles, mussels, scallops and oysters are sometimes farmed in enclosures around coastal seawaters. They feed on naturally occurring plankton and are a healthy source of food whose production has a low impact on the environment. Mussels and oysters are also a good source of betaine, a

substance that helps to protect against heart attacks. These shellfish are easy to prepare and make nutritious, high protein meals. Oysters should simply be prised open with a knife and eaten whole, with a squirt of lemon. Clean mussels by scrubbing them in fresh water and pulling off any fibrous "beards" that sprout between the two halves of the shell. Discard any mussels which are open or fail to snap shut when tapped with a knife.

Left: *Organic mussels and other shellfish are increasingly farmed in enclosures around coastal seawaters.*

MAINTAINING STANDARDS

There is no organic standard for wild fish. However, the MSC – Marine Stewardship Council – is a certifying body that is beginning to address the issue. It is a leading voice in the sustainable fishing debate, and offers practical guidance to consumers, fishermen and governments alike.

When certifying a fishery, the MSC looks at three areas of activity. First, the state of the fish stocks in the locality is assessed to determine whether fishing is being carried out sustainably. The fishery's effect on the marine ecosystem is also looked at. One major problem of modern fishing methods is catching fish other than the target species – the "by-catch". The MSC standard is only awarded if levels of by-catch for the fishery are acceptable. Finally, management systems are examined to satisfy the MSC that good practice is being maintained.

Fishermen often work under an umbrella organization, which may be a government body, that regulates the area of the sea they harvest. If good management is in place, their practices can be co-ordinated to ensure sustainable fishing.

Buying MSC-certified Fish

A secondary certification scheme traces all fish certified to the MSC standard from the fishery to the retailer, so consumers can buy wild fish with confidence if it carries the MSC logo. You will find the logo on fresh and frozen fish, convenience products and on menus where restaurants support the scheme.

MSC-certified fish is sold through independent fishmongers, farmers' markets, supermarkets and delicatessens in the UK and Europe, USA and Australia. Fish caught at MSC-certified fisheries are also sold in Canada, New Zealand and South East Asian countries. However, not all these countries use the logo.

Wild Fish

The last major wild food resource, the sea, is under intense threat from over-fishing. Worldwide, sea fish are now so over-exploited that many once abundant stocks are now under threat of extinction. Catching wild fish has become a serious technological pursuit. Wild sea fish are hunted with the aid of radar, planes and submarines and caught with lines or trawler nets, trapping the targeted catch and also other fish, mammals and birds. These wholesale raids do not discriminate between adults and young fish.

Wild fish are increasingly subjected to chemical, biological and hormonal attack from such polluted fresh waters as rivers and lakes. Some intensive fish farms release their waste water, with its cargo of chemicals and germs, into nearby rivers and seas. Fish from these farms often escape and interbreed with wild stocks to produce hybrid mutations. Pesticides and fertilizers from agrochemical crops also flow into rivers and lakes through groundwater. The fertilizers promote algae growth, ruining the delicate balance of water ecosystems, while pesticides simply poison the inhabitants.

Wild salmon spend almost all of their lives in the sea, only returning to fresh water when it is time to spawn. They have incredible homing instincts.

Above: Wild salmon live in the sea, returning to fresh water only when it is time to spawn.

A salmon that has swum hundreds of kilometres away from its birthplace will return to the very creek where its life began. If the water it has to pass through has been contaminated by fish farm, agrochemical farm or factory pollution, this ancient cycle is irrevocably disturbed.

Types of Wild Sea Fish

Wild sea fish fall into two groups: those that live at the bottom of the sea, and those that live in the middle waters or near the surface. Surface fish include common varieties such as sardines, mackerel, anchovies, pilchards, Atlantic herring and swordfish. Fishermen utilize many methods to catch these fish, including traps, lines and drag nets. In Japan, fishermen sometimes lure squid using mechanical jiggers with bright lights. The squid attach themselves to the machinery, so they can be hauled on to the boats easily. Knowledgeable fishermen easily target surface species, ensuring a good percentage of the catch is the target fish. Despite this, many of these species are now fully or over fished.

Fish species from the middle waters include tuna, salmon and herring. These fish are almost always caught with nets.

Tuna are a similar size to dolphins and often associate with them. In the past, this frequently meant that when tuna were caught, so were dolphins. The public outcry that ensued when this became common knowledge has diminished this practice. All tuna sold in the USA and Canada now has to be dolphin friendly, and most other industrialized nations offer dolphin-friendly tuna.

Catching tuna without catching dolphins is very tricky however. One technique that has replaced dolphin-associated tuna fishing is to use floating aggregate devices, or FADs. These float in the sea and attract the tuna because of the cover they provide. Fishermen then net all of the fish below the FAD, including juvenile tuna and other by-catch species. Although dolphin-friendly tuna does save dolphins, it is often at the expense of other species with a less popular public image.

Probably the best way to catch tuna in terms of the ecosystem is with so-called "long lines". These fishing lines with multiple hooks are dragged behind boats and target tuna extremely efficiently. Some successful long-line tuna fisheries use this method, including one in the Maldives that supplies retailers and restaurants around the world.

Below: Wild cockles can be picked by hand.

Fish that live on the bottom of the sea are generally trawled with big nets. Cod, carp, hake, haddock, hoki and Alaskan pollock all live near the seabed, as do flat fish including plaice, halibut and sole. Cephalopods such as squid and octopus are often also trapped in the nets, but offer a valuable source of under-exploited seafood. Trawling the seabed can be extremely destructive, disturbing ancient ecosystems. The Marine Stewardship Council has approved one fishery that trawls responsibly, and more fisheries that use other sustainable harvesting methods for species at the bottom of the sea. Fisheries awarded MSC certification are sustainable, so you can be sure that buying these products will not contribute to bad fishing practices.

Shellfish

Lobsters and crabs also live at the bottom of the sea but they are only harvested in coastal waters. They are usually collected in pots, either using bait or trapdoors. Scallops and oysters, which also live in coastal waters, are traditionally trawled. Today, they are often harvested by divers. This method protects the delicate ecosystems found at the bottom of the sea, while providing top quality seafood for the caring cook. Other shellfish such as wild cockles and mussels are more easily harvested. They can be picked by hand from the bottom of shallower waters. However, most commercially available shellfish are currently farmed.

Intensively farmed prawns and shrimps are bad news for organic consumers. Try to buy wild shellfish. Those from Iceland are particularly acceptable as an alternative to organically farmed prawns and shrimps. Iceland is heavily reliant on its fishing industry, so it has become a benchmark country for sustainable fishing techniques. Most prawns from Iceland are caught by trawling with nets with bigger holes than other fishing nations. The holes allow young prawns to escape, so they can grow and breed.

MOULES MARINIÈRE

1 Chop 1 onion and 2 shallots. Put in a large pan with 25g/1oz/2 tbsp butter and cook over low heat until softened and translucent.

2 Add 300ml/½ pint/1¼ cups white wine, a bay leaf and a sprig of fresh thyme. Bring to the boil. Add 2kg/4½lb cleaned mussels, cover the pan tightly and steam over a high heat for 2 minutes. Shake the pan vigorously and steam for 2 minutes more. Shake again and steam until all the mussels have opened. Discard any closed shells.

3 Stir in 30ml/2 tbsp chopped fresh parsley and serve at once.

DAIRY FOODS and EGGS

Opting for organic products means obtaining the maximum nutrition from whatever dairy foods you consume, without supporting the negative aspects associated with intensive farming methods. Dairy foods are excellent sources of protein and calcium.

On an organic dairy farm, cows have regular access to open fields. Their diet is made up almost exclusively of organic grasses and grains and they are never routinely treated with the hormones that are used on non-organic farms in some countries to boost milk production. Nor are they dosed with antibiotics except as a last resort. If you prefer not to eat any dairy foods, there are some excellent organic alternatives.

Milk

Organic milk is the only kind of milk that is guaranteed to be free of genetically modified ingredients, as many non-organic cows eat GM feed. It is available with varying amounts of cream, from skimmed to full fat. Full fat (whole) milk generally only contains about 2 percent fat, so all milk is a low fat food. Most milk is pasteurized, homogenized or sterilized, but it can also be found raw. Pasteurization is a heating process that helps to control bacteria levels in the milk. Homogenization distributes

Right: *Goat's, cow's, sheep's and soya milk*

the fat content throughout the milk, so there is no need to shake it to mix in the cream. Sterilization extends the shelf life of sealed cartons of milk, so that they do not need to be refrigerated. All these processes are permitted under organic certification laws because they are mechanical processes that do not involve the use of chemicals.

Cow's milk is not the only organic option. Goat's milk has a distinctive, musky flavour, which many people love. It is much easier to digest than cow's milk, so individuals who cannot tolerate cow's milk often find they can drink goat's milk without suffering adverse reactions. Organic sheep's milk is sometimes on sale at the larger farmer's markets or in delicatessens. It doesn't taste as pungent as goat's milk, but contains more of the lactose that can cause dairy intolerance.

Yogurts, Creams and Dairy Desserts

Live yogurt is a natural probiotic. This means it boosts the amount of beneficial bacteria in the intestines of those who eat it. This, in turn, aids the absorption of nutrients, such as calcium, as well as offering some protection from various disorders, including tooth decay and

heart disease. An even better way of improving the levels of good bacteria in your gut is to eat prebiotic foods such as onions, leeks, wheat, oats, bananas and Jerusalem artichokes.

Many of the world's largest non-organic dairy corporations now also offer organic yogurts, creams and dairy desserts. While this ensures improved availability of organic dairy products, the quality is variable. Organic dairy products all have the benefits of humane and environmentally sustainable production, but mass-produced yogurts and dairy desserts are often watery, high in sugar and low in flavour. Whether they are runny or thick, organic creams should always be mouthwateringly rich. The organic connoisseur will choose organic yogurts, desserts and creams from smaller enterprises or companies who are primarily organic.

Butter

Organic butter has a much richer taste than non-organic alternatives. Both types, however, are equally high in saturated fats, which can raise cholesterol levels in the body and contribute to heart disease. Consider organic butter a luxurious, delicious and slightly decadent treat, great for the occasional indulgence, as when making the perfect fried egg, but something to be limited. That said, organic butter is far better for your health than many non-organic margarines and spreads. These will often contain hydrogenated or trans fats, which may be far more damaging to the heart than butter.

Right: *Organic butter*

Cheeses

Organic cheeses are made from organic milk, so they offer all the environmental, humanitarian and healthy eating benefits of other organic dairy products. They come in scores of different varieties, from hard types such as Cheddar, Cheshire, Double Gloucester and Lancashire, through blues like Stilton and Gorgonzola, to soft and creamy Camembert and cottage cheese. Lots of artisan cheesemakers now use organic ingredients. Buying organic cheese is a must if you want to avoid eating genetically modified rennet.

Soya Milk and Other Substitutes

Soya beans have been transformed into nutritious "milks" and dairy alternative foods for thousands of years. There are dozens of versions on the market, including the fresh product, which looks like cow's milk but is slightly thicker and has a nutty taste. More readily available is long-life soya milk, which comes in cartons and does not need to be refrigerated until it is opened. Sweetened versions can also be found, and it is possible to buy soya milk that has been fortified with extra vitamins as well as calcium.

Soya milk is low in calories and contains no cholesterol. Easy to digest, it is a valuable food, particularly for those who cannot tolerate cow's milk. Children who suffer from asthma and eczema often get relief when they switch from cow's milk to a non-dairy alternative such as soya milk.

Soya cream is much thicker and richer than soya milk because it is made with a higher proportion of beans.

Soya beans are not the only ingredient that can be made into nutritious liquid. Other beans can be used in a similar way, as can some nuts and grains. Rice milk is thin and has a delicate taste. Tiger nut milk has a similar consistency and a sweet taste. Oat milk is pleasantly mild, while pale yellow pea milk is quite creamy. Non-dairy milks can be bought from health food shops or made at home. Try them on muesli or other organic cereals or in creamy soups. When using in tea, put non-dairy milk in first and stir the tea thoroughly to prevent curdling. The high acidity in coffee means that curdling is almost inevitable, so try to avoid using non-dairy milks here.

Above: *Organic Stilton and Brie are widely available.*

Eggs

Organic free-range eggs come from hens that have ample access to land free from chemical fertilizers and pesticides. The birds are not routinely debeaked to stop them retaliating when hemmed in by other hens, nor are they given growth promoters. Antibiotics are administered only when unavoidable. It is important to look for labels on eggs that attest to organic certification. Although the term "free range" suggests that hens spend their days out of doors, non-organic free-range birds often have limited access to the open air. Organic eggs are the only eggs that can be guaranteed to be free from yolk colourants.

Look out for other types of eggs at farmers' markets. Duck eggs are a pretty shade of blue, goose eggs are big enough for two and quail's eggs are small and speckled. All can be boiled, fried, scrambled or used in cakes, in the same way as hen's eggs. When soft-boiled, organic eggs are far less likely to contain the salmonella that is often found in eggs from intensive chicken barns. Soft-boiled or lightly poached eggs have the advantage of containing fewer Cholesterol Oxidation Products (COPS), which means they can be beneficial to blood cholesterol levels.

Below: *When farmed organically, quail and duck eggs are guaranteed free from yolk colourants.*

BEANS and PULSES

These staples are a fantastic resource for any organic cook and provide vital protein for vegetarians and vegans. Organic red and white kidney beans, aduki beans, haricot beans, flageolet or cannellini beans, soya beans, mung beans, black-eyed beans (peas) and chickpeas are all available. A good source of B vitamins and many minerals, including iron, selenium and zinc, organic beans are far better for you than the agrochemical equivalents, which are often grown in developing countries where pesticide use is extremely heavy.

Soya beans are particularly good for women, as they are rich in the phytoestrogens that help to prevent osteoporosis and breast cancer, plus folic acid for preconceptual care. Chickpeas are especially high in calcium.

Cooking Beans and Pulses

Most beans and pulses, with the exception of lentils, must be soaked overnight before being cooked. Lentils can be cooked straight from the sieve after rinsing, but will also benefit from being soaked for an hour or more'. Soaking makes

Left: Aduki beans have a nutty flavour.

Left: Chickpeas have a delicious hearty taste and creamy texture.

beans and pulses easier to digest. So does cooking them with a small piece of kombu seaweed. Cooking with salt toughens beans, so only season them once they have been cooked.

Kidney beans, whether organic or not, must be cooked thoroughly to ensure any natural toxins they contain are neutralized. Boil the beans vigorously for about 15 minutes, then change the water and simmer for about 1¾ hours until they are tender.

Cooked beans and pulses taste great in soups, salad, stews and meat-free pâtés, as well as classic Indian dishes such as dhal. A quick dhal soup can be made by boiling equal amounts of red lentils and yellow split

Above: Haricot, red kidney, flageolet and pinto beans

SPROUTING BEANS, SEEDS, GRAINS AND PULSES

When beans, pulses, seeds and grains germinate, their nutritional levels rise dramatically. B vitamins increase by almost 30 per cent and vitamin C by up to 60 per cent. Organic sprouts are easy to grow yourself.

1 Wash 45ml/3 tbsp beans, pulses, seeds or grains thoroughly in water, then place in a large jar. Fill the jar with lukewarm water, cover with a piece of muslin and hold in place with an elastic band. Leave in a warm place to stand overnight.

2 Drain thoroughly the next morning and refill the jar with water. Shake gently, then drain again. Leave the jar on its side in a warm place, away from direct sunlight. In the evening rinse again, draining well.

3 Continue to rinse and drain twice daily until small roots and shoots have emerged. Most sprouts will be ready within a week. Sprinkle on salads, chop into spreads or add to stir-fries or curries.

Below: White and black soya beans form the basis for quick high-protein meals.

peas, then stirring in onion and a chopped tomato, which has been fried with curry spices. For a delicately flavoured salad, mix cooked flageolet beans with arugula (rocket) leaves and add a drizzle of walnut oil.

Beans and pulses should be stored in a cool, dry place. Keep packets tightly closed or decant into sealed tubs. Beans and pulses can be kept for years and still be capable of germinating, but the fresher they are the better, so buy them in small quantities and use quickly.

Soya Bean Products

Highly nutritious soya bean products including tofu and tempeh are ideal for keeping in the refrigerator or freezer to form the basis for quick, high-protein meals. It is vital to ensure that all the soya products you buy are organic. Many non-organic soya products have been made from genetically modified beans, bred for resistance to extremely strong pesticides and herbicides. GM soya beans are able to grow in soil that has been drenched in these harsh chemicals, whereas beans that have not been genetically modified are destroyed by the toxicity. There is no benefit to the consumer in eating GM soya beans; the only advantage is to the farmer who is able to use stronger and stronger chemicals.

Tofu Also known as bean curd, tofu is derived from soya milk, which is curdled using a natural coagulant. The curds are drained and pressed to make tofu, in a process similar to that used when making soft cheese. Firm tofu can be sliced and fried. It is a popular ingredient in stir-fries, especially when it has been marinated in soy sauce to strengthen its somewhat bland flavour. For soups, sauces and creamy desserts, choose silken tofu, which is smooth and light. Smoked, marinated and deep-fried tofu are all available in health-food stores and Oriental stores. Organic tofu can also be bought in long-life cartons.

TVP Many vegetarians rely on soya bean products for their protein, especially in the form of Textured Vegetable Protein or TVP. This highly processed ingredient is widely used in organic processed foods and is also available dried. It can be useful to keep some in the cupboard for making vegetarian burgers or lasagne, but

COOKING TIMES FOR PRESOAKED BEANS AND PULSES

The table below provides a rough guide only, as cooking times may alter according to how long the items have been stored, and the quantity cooked. In most cases, the volume of water should be three times that of the chosen ingredient, except in the case of butter beans, where double the amount of water will be sufficient. Ingredients that need very long cooking times, such as chickpeas, marrowfat peas and soya beans, may need up to four times the amount of water.

Beans	Time (minutes)
Aduki beans	45–60
Black-eyed beans (peas)	60
Butter (lima) beans	6
Chickpeas	180
Dried green (field) beans	45
Flageolet (small cannellini) beans	50
Haricot (navy) beans	60
Kidney beans	120
Lentils – brown	45
Lentils – green	30
Lentils – red	20–30
Mung beans	60
Peas – marrowfat	120
Peas – split	45
Soya beans	200

TVP is low on taste, lacking in texture and offers limited nutrition. Fresh soya bean products such as tofu and tempeh are superior in every way.

Tempeh This Indonesian food is made by fermenting cooked soya beans with a cultured starter. It has a meatier, nuttier flavour than tofu, and the firmer texture means it can be used in pies. Slices of tempeh taste delicious fried in sunflower oil and tamari or soy sauce and served with pitta bread.

Left: Tempeh freezes well, so conveniently keeps for long periods.

GRAINS

Getting to grips with organic grains is not difficult. There is a wide selection available, from wheat in all its various forms to lesser known grains such as the highly nutritious quinoa.

Rice

Organic brown rice is one of the ultimate grains, in terms of taste, nutrition and healing potential. It is very easily digestible, gently soothing the intestinal tract. It is simultaneously comforting and satisfying to eat, particularly when served with crisp and fresh stir-fried organic vegetables.

Above: Bulgur wheat

Above: Brown rice is high in complex carbohydrates, with protein, fibre and B vitamins. It is one of the ultimate grains.

Although organic white rice is a convenient ingredient and has a much shorter cooking time, it is less nutritious, since most of the minerals and vitamins are lost when the bran and germ of the grain is removed in the milling process.

Bulgur Wheat

This pale, sand-coloured grain, made from dried and crushed cooked wheat berries, is nutty in flavour and comes in varying degrees of coarseness. When cooked, by soaking in double its volume of boiling water for 15–20 minutes, bulgur wheat is similar in appearance to couscous but is heavier, and has more flavour. Bulgur is usually served cold. Combined with flat-leaf parsley, mint, tomatoes, cucumber, onion and a lemon and oil dressing, it forms the basis of the Middle Eastern salad, tabbouleh.

Millet

Another under-used but essential grain, organic millet contains all the essential amino acids. It is the only alkaline grain, making it easily digestible. It is also a rich source of silicon, the substance that helps to build collagen for keeping skin, eyes, nails and arteries healthy, vibrant and flexible. Widely eaten in many parts of Africa, the small ground grain is cream in colour, with a pleasant, neutral taste.

Quinoa

Until recently this tiny round grain was little known outside its native Bolivia, but quinoa (pronounced "keen-wah") is becoming increasingly popular, partly because it tastes delicious, but also because it is a very good source of protein, fibre and B group vitamins. Like brown rice, quinoa tastes faintly nutty. Quinoa is useful for making stuffings, pilaffs and cereals.

Above: Millet

Above: Quinoa

COOKING QUINOA

Quinoa is a quick and easy side dish to prepare at home. When cooked, the tiny bead-shaped grains have a mild, slightly bitter taste and firm texture. It contains all eight essential amino acids and is a rich source of vital nutrients. Quinoa is cooked like rice, but the grains quadruple in size, becoming translucent with an unusual white outer ring.

1 Always wash quinoa before cooking to remove the fine, soapy, white powder that coats the grains.

2 Boil in a pan of water for about 20 minutes until the khaki-coloured round grains turn into pretty translucent white spirals. Serve with curries, stir-fries or casseroles as an alternative to boiled rice.

The table below provides a rough guide only, as cooking times may alter according to how long the items have been stored, and the quantity cooked. In most cases, the volume of water should be three times that of the chosen ingredient, except in the case of rolled oats, quinoa and white rice, where double the amount of water will be sufficient. Ingredients that need very long cooking times, such as polenta, may need up to four times the amount of water.

Grains	Time (minutes)
Amaranth	20–25
Barley	80–90
Buckwheat	20
Millet	30
Oats – groats	120
Oats – rolled	10
Polenta – milled corn	25
Quinoa	15
Rice – brown	40–60
Rice – white	15–20
Wheat – whole	90
Wheat – cracked	25
Wild rice	60

Oats

Organic oats are extraordinarily high in soluble fibre and are a fundamental food for heart health. A bowl of porridge or oat-rich muesli (granola) is a great foundation for the day, giving greater stores of energy than high-sugar, non-organic breakfast cereals. Organic oat-based muesli is readily available, but it is also easy to make at home. Simply add chopped organic hazelnuts, linseed (flax), sunflower and pumpkin seeds to an oat base, then sweeten the mixture by stirring in chopped dried fruit. Store the muesli in an airtight container in a dry cupboard, and the muesli will last as long as the nuts – about three months.

Organic breakfast cereals not only retain their micro-nutrients but also tend to contain less refined sugar and salt than non-organic varieties, supporting healthier energy levels and moderating moods throughout the day. For a special treat, make a classic Bircher muesli by soaking equal quantities of oats and milk or dairy-free milk overnight. Stir in an equal quantity of yogurt and honey the next morning, with a freshly grated apple and one other chopped fresh fruit.

Oats are also widely used in baking and are delicious in flapjacks, added to the topping for a fruit crumble or crisp, or sprinkled on homemade breads.

Wheat Berries

These are whole wheat grains with the husks removed. They are packed with concentrated goodness and have a sweet, nutty flavour and chewy texture. Wheat berries are delicious when added to salads. They can be used to add texture to breads and stews, or combined with rice or other grains. They must be soaked overnight, then cooked in boiling water until they are tender. When germinated, the berries sprout into wheatgrass, a powerful cleanser and detoxifier.

Couscous

Although this looks like a grain, couscous is a form of pasta made by steaming and drying cracked durum wheat. When cooked, couscous is light and fluffy in texture. It is a mainstay of Middle Eastern cooking, its fairly bland flavour provides a good foil for spicy dishes. Couscous also tastes great flavoured with ginger or galangal and rose water and served as a traditional accompaniment to a Moroccan tagine.

Left: Couscous

Combining Grains and Pulses

To maximize the amount of protein available from non-animal sources, mix grains and proteins. This is good advice for anyone seeking to eat a well-balanced diet, but it is essential advice for vegans. Divide foods into three groups: grains; beans and pulses; and seeds and nuts. In any meal, choose a combination of two of these groups. Cooks do this quite naturally a lot of the time. Baked beans on toast is one classic dish; while rice and dhal forms another traditional combination.

When cooked, wheat berries make a delicious addition to salads, and they can also be used to add texture to breads and stews.

1 Place the wheat berries in a bowl and cover with cold water. Soak overnight, rinse thoroughly and drain.

2 Place the berries in a large pan and fill with cold water. Bring to the boil, then cover and simmer for 1–2 hours until the wheat berries are tender. Check regularly and replenish the water when necessary.

FLOUR and PASTA

Organic food companies produce many different kinds of milled grains, more so than non-organic flour companies. In addition to wheat flour, there are flours made from buckwheat, rice, rye and maize, as well as quinoa and spelt. Organic pastas are also common and come in every shape and colour, from spaghetti to spirals. Japanese pastas such as udon and soba, are also readily available in organic form.

These products have an important part to play in the organic kitchen, particularly for people who wish to

Right: Udon noodles are high in complex carbohydrates and will provide energy over a long period.

Below: Spelt flour and grain

eliminate wheat and other high-gluten grains, such as rye, barley and oats, from their diet because they are allergic to gluten. Consult a qualified nutritionist if you have this allergy.

Many of us rely too heavily on wheat for carbohydrates – eating wheat-based cereals for breakfast, sandwiches for lunch, biscuits or cakes for tea and pasta for supper. Rather than cutting out wheat entirely, assess your average daily intake and make sure that you eat a good spread of different organic grains.

Wheat Flours

Depending on the degree of processing, wheat flour may be either wholemeal (whole-wheat) or white. Stoneground wholemeal flour is the best for you since

it retains all its valuable nutrients, but white flour is often better in baking. Most pasta and noodles are made of plain durum wheat or wholemeal flour. High in complex carbohydrates, pasta and noodles provide energy over a long period. Wholewheat versions are richer in vitamins, minerals and fibre, and often have a preferable texture. There is a wide choice of organic wheat noodles including Japanese udon noodles, thin, white somen noodles, egg noodles and ramen.

Above: From back to front, hemp spaghetti, gluten-free corn spaghetti and spiralina tagliatelle

Non-wheat Flours

Spelt is one of the most ancient grains and is rich in vitamins and minerals. It is the ancestor to modern wheat, but many people with gluten intolerance are able to digest spelt flour. Flours that do not contain gluten, such as rice, soya, buckwheat, quinoa and millet flours, have different cooking properties. Buckwheat is used to make blinis in Russia, soba noodles in Japan and pasta in Italy. Buckwheat pancakes are popular in parts of the USA and France. Rice flour is used in sticky Asian cakes and sweets, and to thicken sauces. Opaque-white rice noodles are popular in many South-east Asian countries.

BREAD and BAKED GOODS

All organic breads are better for you than the non-organic equivalent because the grains contain more nutrients and fewer agrochemical toxins. Unless bread is organic, it is likely to have had chemical flour improvers, flour extenders and preservatives added, as well as conditioners and flavourings, and invariably contains excess salt.

Some organic loaves are better than others, however, and it is important to seek out a good supplier whose loaves freeze well, so that you can stock up if necessary. A good organic loaf will have been made in the traditional manner, with enough yeast to ensure an even, close texture, and will taste delicious.

Factory-made Breads

Alongside some excellent organic factory-made breads, there are some inferior loaves. Factory-made organic bread is sometimes made by the flash-baking method. This uses excessive amounts of yeast to make the dough rise rapidly. These breads have a spongy texture, mediocre flavour and are not as nutritional as organic loaves made by hand in the traditional way and allowed to rise slowly. The flash-baking method is cheaper for the manufacturer, but bread made this way is contributing to the current yeast intolerance boom.

Below: Organic white baguette, wheatfree loaf and naturally leavened campagne (at back).

Baking Bread

If you want to be absolutely certain of the quality of your organic loaf, bake your own. This is much easier than many people appreciate. Bread can be made by hand and baked in the oven or with the aid of an electric bread-maker, which mixes, kneads, rises and bakes the bread in one easy hands-free operation.

Wheat is the easiest type of flour to use for conventional yeast-based breads, as it contains plenty of gluten, the sticky substance that keeps dough stretchy and helps it to rise. Use wholemeal (whole-wheat) flour for preference for its fibre content. Quality flours also provide protein and vitamins, especially the B vitamins, and useful amounts of zinc and magnesium, which help to harmonize moods, improve the condition of the skin and promote healing.

Below: Carrot and raisin cake, gluten-free almond cakes and choc chip hazelnut cookies.

Making bread with other flours is more of a challenge, as the gluten content of different grains varies considerably. Rice flour, buckwheat flour, corn meal and oatmeal, which contain little or no gluten, must either be mixed with wheat flour in a yeast loaf, leavened with bicarbonate of soda (baking soda) or used to make flat breads such as rice cakes.

Cakes and Biscuits

Commercially baked organic biscuits (cookies) and cakes are almost always superior to non-organic ones because they contain more vitamins and fewer additives. However, some organic sweet products still include too much refined sugar, both in terms of health and taste. To ensure the biscuits and cakes you buy are the best on the shelf, check the ingredients. Better still, bake your own. Experiment with the different organic flours on offer, add sweetness by using chopped dried fruit or flavour with grated orange rind, organic cocoa powder or a pinch of cinnamon or mixed spice.

THE ORGANIC STORE CUPBOARD

A well stocked store cupboard is a valuable asset for any cook, but it is absolutely essential for the organic cook, who may not be able to obtain every ingredient at the last minute by simply popping down to the local store.

It is worth spending a bit of time sourcing organic food. There is already a lot of it out there, and with more and more products becoming available all the time, switching to organic ingredients is relatively easy. You don't have to do it all at once; simply replace non-organic oils, vinegars, jams, nuts, seasonings and other items in your store cupboard with organic alternatives when they run out. A good organic stockist with a rapid turnover is a good place to start, and the Internet can be handy, too.

Sugars and Honeys

Organic sugars are beneficial because they do not cause the pollution to developing countries that agrochemically grown versions often do. Refined and unrefined organic versions of all standard sugars except refined white are readily available, from demerara (raw) to soft brown. Unrefined organic sugars have far fewer vitamins and nutrients stripped out of them during processing than

Below: Molasses is a great source of iron.

refined sugars, and for this reason they have a slightly better flavour, too. That said, organic sugar still has a high empty calorie value, so it should always be used sparingly for a healthy balanced diet.

Rapadura This exciting alternative to refined sugar is only available in organic form. Similar in colour and texture to soft brown sugar, it has a much more interesting flavour and nutrient profile because it is made by simply sun-drying organic sugar cane juice, so all the beneficial vitamins and minerals of this natural product are retained. Rapadura is suitable for any style of cooking that calls for sugar, including jam-making and meringues. It is also known as jaggery, the Hindi name for this product.

Above: Rapadura is an excellent organic alternative to refined sugar.

Molasses Another excellent natural sweetener derived from sugar cane is molasses. Organic molasses has all the minerals in sugar cane in concentrated form, and is a great source of iron. The most nutritionally valuable type is thick and very dark blackstrap molasses. The powerful taste of molasses makes it a good choice for treacly biscuits, cakes, puddings and sauces.

Honey The most popular alternative to refined sugar is honey. Organic honey must come from unpolluted areas if it is to retain its purity. Most non-organic honey comes from bees fed on liquid sugar rather than collecting pollen. It is inferior to the organic version, both in its blandness and its lack of nutrition.

There are some wonderful organic honeys, each reflecting the flavours of the flowering plants visited by the bees. From Australian manuka honey to Zimbabwean forest honey, the choices range from powerful dark solid honeys to delicate golden liquid honeys. It is worth tasting a selection to discover your personal favourite, and familiarizing yourself with each variety so you can select the ideal match when cooking. Try using honey instead of syrup or sugar in cakes, or giving a hint of sweetness to salad dressings and hot sauces.

Honey has long been highly valued for its medicinal and healing properties. Mixed with lemon juice and hot water, it has antiseptic properties and can relieve sore throats. It is also thought to be helpful in treating diarrhoea and asthma.

Left: Organic farmers' markets are a good place to seek out unusual and homemade organic jams, marmalades, honeys, pickles and preserves.

Above: Fruit syrups are natural sweeteners, which can be used in place of sugar.

Other Natural Sweeteners

There are lots of other sweetening options for the organic cook to explore including organic maple syrup, maple sugar and a wide range of fruit products.

Maple Syrup and Sugar Made by tapping the sap of the maple tree, organic maple syrup and sugar are not over-processed, so retain their richness. Drizzled over hot pancakes, maple, with its buttery tones, is the ultimate syrup. A small amount, added to a savoury batter, tantalizes the palate. Maple syrup is sweeter than sugar so less is required in cooking.

Fruit Syrups and Pastes Concentrated organic fruit syrups also make great sweeteners, whether you choose the liquid form or the solid paste. They contain none of the pesticides found in agrochemical versions and no added sugar or preservatives. They are just as popular with children as with adults. Concentrates are made from many types of organic fruit, including apples, pears, grapes, dates, peaches, blackcurrants and oranges. Apple and date versions add most sweetness, so can be used more sparingly than some other types. Their flavours are also not particularly dominant, so they will not overwhelm other ingredients. Pastes can also be used in cooking, but will need to be dissolved in water first. On their own, fruit pastes taste delicious when spread on bread. Most organic outlets sell concentrated fruit syrups and pastes. They can be stored in a refrigerator for 2–3 months.

Puréed dried fruits such as prunes, figs, dates and apricots can also be used to sweeten pies, crumbles and cakes. To make spiced apricot purée, place some apricots in a pan with enough water to cover, add a cinnamon stick, two cloves and a little freshly grated nutmeg, and simmer for 20 minutes until the apricots are plump. Leave to cool then purée in a food processor until smooth. Add more water if the mixture seems a little thick.

Above: Organic chocolate comes in dark, white and milk varieties.

Cocoa and Chocolate

Agrochemical cocoa is the most heavily sprayed food crop, and is often unfairly traded, too. By buying organic cocoa and chocolate products you ensure that you are not supporting agrochemical pollution in developing countries.

Organic chocolate products are usually higher in cocoa and lower in sugar than the non-organic equivalent, and are free from hydrogenated fats, emulsifiers and other chemical additives. Organic cocoa is naturally high in tannins and antioxidant flavonoids, plus B vitamins and iron. This means that eating organic chocolate in moderation can do you good, as it is thought to offer some protection against heart attacks.

The darker the chocolate, the higher the percentage of cocoa solids and the more intense the taste. Chocolate with 70 per cent cocoa solids has a proportionally higher nutritional content.

Organic chocolate comes in a wide array of products, from specialist hand-made pralines to slabs of dark (bittersweet), milk and white and flavoured chocolates. They all keep well and can be stored in the refrigerator, so there is no need to eat all the chocolate at once.

Above: A selection of organic honeys

Nuts and Seeds

Organic nuts and seeds are little powerhouses that would grow into new plants or mighty trees if sown and allowed to germinate. This makes them an incredibly rich source of nutrients. High in plant oils and protein, they also yield B complex vitamins, potassium, magnesium, calcium, phosphorus and iron. The fat they contain is largely monounsaturated or polyunsaturated (only coconuts and brazil nuts contain saturated fat) and they are the richest vegetable source of vitamin E, which has been credited with reducing the risk of heart disease, strokes and certain cancers.

Many people equate a healthy diet with a low fat diet, but this is not true. It is important that we eat a balanced diet, including proteins, carbohydrates and fats. While saturated and hydrogenated fats are undesirable, unrefined polyunsaturated fats are essential. They provide energy and help to prevent heart disease, eczema, ulcers and arthritis when eaten as part of a healthy diet and combined with a balanced lifestyle. The best way of obtaining polyunsaturated fats is to eat nuts and seeds, since these also provide the antioxidants necessary to optimise the value of these fats.

Seeds are very good for you for many other reasons, too. Sunflower seeds are rich in many minerals, including zinc, which aids skin regeneration and helps to heal cuts and minor abrasions. The

Walnuts (above) and hazelnuts (below) are a good source of protein.

seeds also contain B vitamins and will ease fatigue, irritability and depression. Flax (linseed) seeds are gentle healers for the intestinal tract. Sesame seeds are a good source of protein, zinc and iron, so are good for sexual health. Pumpkin seeds have similar nutrients, plus calcium and B vitamins.

Cooking With Organic Nuts And Seeds

Health reasons aside, organic nuts and seeds taste great. You can add chopped nuts and seeds to salads, savoury roasts, breads and cakes. Roasting nuts and seeds in a dry, non-stick frying pan for

MAKING NUT BUTTER

Nut butters don't have to contain just one type of nut. Make your own wholesome nut butter using a combination of organic peanuts, hazelnuts and cashew nuts.

1 Place 75g/3oz/½ cup shelled nuts in a food processor or blender and process until finely ground.

2 Pour 15–30ml/1–2 tbsp sunflower oil into the processor or blender and process to a coarse paste. Spread on toast or stir into stir-fries to produce a rich, creamy sauce. Store in an airtight container.

Above: Peanuts

Right: Organic chestnuts are sweet and starchy.

Above: Pumpkin seeds make a perfect organic snack food.

NUT NOTES

The perfect snack food, nuts provide plenty of nutrients, too.

• Brazil nuts are a good source of protein, with lots of vitamin B₁ and magnesium to aid concentration and support the nervous system.

• Walnuts contain as much protein as eggs, plus potassium, zinc and iron.

• Pecan nuts, walnuts and hemp seeds are a source of linoleic acid, which has anti-inflammatory properties. Smokers who have kicked the habit find it soothes lungs irritated by the free radicals in cigarette smoke. These nuts and seeds are also a first line of defence against other forms of cancer, because of their high vitamin E content, plus the fact that they are the only known sources of an antioxidant group called avenanthramides. People who eat walnuts or pecans five times a week have been discovered to lower their risk of developing coronary heart disease by 35 per cent.

• Pine nuts are the richest source of protein of any nut, with a deliciously buttery flavour that makes them great in salads.

• Peanuts are a good source of both iron and protein.

• Hazelnuts have a sweet flavour but are relatively low in calories.

• Chestnuts are sweet and starchy, and help to bind other ingredients, in nut roasts or stuffings, for instance.

a few minutes greatly improves the flavour. Watch them carefully and toss frequently so that they don't scorch.

Store-bought non-organic nut butters, including peanut butter, often contain unwanted hydrogenated oil and can be loaded with sugar, so buy organic nut or seed butters. Alternatively, make your own by processing your favourite nuts and seeds through a masticating juicer or in a food processor or blender.

Tahini, made by grinding sesame seeds, is especially good. Stir tahini or nut butter into a stir-fry for an instant sauce. When used in this way, nut and seed butters become favourite seasonings. When spread on toast, they make nutritious and very tasty toppings.

Oils

Cold pressed organic oils retain almost all the health and taste benefits of the raw nuts and seeds from which they are made. This is not the case with most agrochemical oils, which are extracted at high temperatures. In the process the natural antioxidants, minerals and other vitamins in the oil are destroyed. Non-organic oil is then further processed with solvents to lessen the colour and tone down the taste of the final product. Cold-pressed organic oils are prized for these very characteristics.

Olive oil is a firm favourite. In terms of colour and taste, it is a wonderful addition to any meal. It is a versatile food that can be eaten alone on bread instead of butter, added to salads or used for cooking, and is the perfect partner for organic food. It is the most digestible oil, and is universally acknowledged as being highly effective in preventing heart disease and treating liver disorders. Many nut oils make delicious salad dressings when whisked with lemon juice or vinegar. Organic sunflower and safflower oils are rich in polyunsaturates that are great for heart health. Use them in dishes that require a lighter taste than olive oil, such as in oriental cooking and cake baking.

Storing Nuts, Seeds and Oils

Buy nuts in the shell, if possible, and eat them as soon as possible after shelling. If you must store them, put them in airtight bags and keep them in a cool place or the refrigerator. Store seeds in the same way. Buy cold pressed organic oils in small quantities, so that they can be used quickly, and store in a cool place. Never allow them to be exposed to heat during storage. Do not store nuts, seeds or oils for more than a few months, or the oil they contain may become rancid.

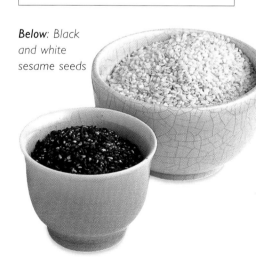

Below: Black and white sesame seeds

Above: Cold-pressed organic sunflower and safflower oils

SEASONINGS

If you are new to organic cooking, you may find you need to rethink your approach to seasonings of all kinds. Organic ingredients taste so good that to mask their flavours would be a sin. Use spices, condiments and strong flavourings such as vinegar with care, choosing always the organic option.

Spices

Over sixty different kinds of spices are regularly used in cooking around the world. About twenty of these are easily available organically grown. Try to find organic spices where you can, because non-organic ones have often been heavily sprayed with pesticides. Most of these plants are grown in developing countries where non-organic farming practices can undermine farmers' health and the environment. Until recently dried spices with organic certification were quite difficult to track down. Now they are much more readily available, in good organic stores, direct from the packers or through mail order companies.

Spices are almost always used dried when their flavours are condensed. However, fresh versions of chillies and ginger are also popular. Organic dried chillies are a useful store-cupboard ingredient. They come whole, powdered or in flakes and tend to be hotter than fresh chillies. Especially valuable chillies include fruity, mild anchos, chipotles and hot habaneros.

Below: Fresh organic root ginger has an intense fiery flavour.

Above: Organic dried chillies are free from harmful pesticide residues.

Fry dried spices before adding them to a dish. Heat a pan with or without oil and fry or toast the spices for about 1 minute, until they release their aroma. Shake the pan often to prevent them from sticking. Most spices should be toasted whole, then crushed with a pestle in a mortar or whizzed in a coffee blender. However such spices as nutmeg and cinnamon are too large or bulky to be heated whole. Crush cinnamon bark or grate whole nutmeg just before toasting it. These spices retain more flavour when they are stored whole.

Fresh organic root ginger is smaller and has a more intense flavour than the swollen and sometimes watery non-organic spice. Ginger and galangal add a hot yet refreshing flavour to sweet and savoury dishes, including marinades, stir-fries, fresh vegetables, poached fruit and cakes and bakes.

The five spices most often used in Indian cooking are coriander, cumin, turmeric, pepper and chilli. Many other spices are used alongside this quintet, including star anise and fenugreek. Try adding nutmeg to savoury dishes such as pumpkin soup and baked fish as well as more traditional sweet dishes such as Christmas pudding or rice pudding. The powerful essential oils in this spice have slightly euphoric properties, so they lift the spirits. No wonder nutmeg is a popular spice in mulled wine and other festive Christmas treats. Add caraway seeds to sauerkraut or bean stews, as they help to ease flatulence. Coriander seeds can help to cool an otherwise hot and spicy dish, as well as adding their distinctive flavour. Chilli powder acts like cornflour (cornstarch), thickening stews and curries, and pepper adds accent to almost everything, including strawberries.

Salt

The main flavouring used in cooking throughout the world is salt. At one time this was guaranteed to be a natural product extracted from seawater. Table salt is now almost exclusively over-refined, with magnesium carbonate

---

PREPARING FRESH GINGER

1 You don't need to peel fresh organic root ginger. Using a small, sharp paring knife, simply chop to the size specified in the recipe.

2 Alternatively, grate ginger finely. Special bamboo graters can be found in many Asian stores, but an ordinary box grater will do the job equally well. Freshly grated ginger can be squeezed with the fingers to release the juice, if required.

Left: Sea salt contains a variety of minerals and salts.

Right: Wholegrain organic mustard.

added to ensure it flows freely. Sea salt, whether organically certified or not, has a much broader spectrum of taste because it contains a variety of different minerals and salts alongside the sodium chloride that is its main component. Keep your salt usage low, as using too much of this mineral compound can lead to high blood pressure. One benefit of using good-quality salt is that it has a stronger flavour, so you do not need to use as much salt. Organically certified salts are particularly delicious and it is most reassuring to know that such salts are routinely inspected by the certifier whose logo they bear.

Right: Organic light and dark shoyu (soy sauce) adds flavour.

Soy Sauces

Many organic cooks use organic soy sauces such as tamari and shoyu to add saltiness and depth to their meals. These products will enhance the flavour of most savoury dishes, but should be added in moderation, at the end of the cooking process. High temperatures destroy the delicate proteins and enzymes that are so beneficial in these products.

Vinegars

Organic vinegars are made by fermenting ingredients such as organic apples and grapes. Over time, these fine ingredients will develop into zesty condiments to be drizzled over fish or added to salad dressings, pickles and marinades. There

are plenty of organic varieties, including balsamic and Japanese mirin rice vinegar.

Some non-organic vinegars are good-quality products, with fine flavours and good fragrances. However, many non-organic vinegars are horrible. The vinegar in most of England's famous fish and chip shops bears little resemblance to good, old-fashioned malt vinegar.

At the opposite end of the spectrum is organic cider vinegar. This raw, unfiltered, non-distilled, undiluted product is aged in wooden barrels and contains no preservatives, and has superb health benefits. It is antibacterial, antiseptic, anti-inflammatory and detoxifying. It also helps to keep blood thin, which is useful for people who eat meat and dairy products.

Other Condiments

Many condiments contain vinegar as a major ingredient, including mustard, prepared salad dressings, mayonnaise, chutneys, pickles and olives. The benefits of buying organic versions of these products are obvious, since you can be sure that a good vinegar has been used as a base. Other ingredients will be organic, too, so whatever you buy is likely to be flavoursome and of good quality. The eggs in organic mayonnaise will have come from free-range organic chickens. Vegan organic mayonnaise is also readily available, made from soy or pea protein. The taste of some organic full grain mustards puts regular non-organic mustards to shame. While many non-organic commercial salad dressings threaten to drown your healthy leaves in refined, sugary oils, organic salad dressings have been known to outshine a home-made mixture. Although the best chutneys and pickles are made in your kitchen, there are plenty of excellent ones available in supermarkets, farmers' markets and good organic stores.

Above: Cider vinegar is antibacterial.

DRINKS

Over the past decade or so, the demand for organic drinks has grown enormously. From a niche market, the beverage industry has burgeoned, producing drinks that are often so delicious that even those who are not yet fully committed to the organic ideal seek them out. From table water to gin, an organic certification mark on the bottle is a sign of fine quality and sustainable ingredients.

Below, left to right: Organic biodynamic white and red wines and elderflower wine.

Wine

Organic wine is an explosion of flavours. Very often produced by small artisan vineyards, the organic grapes used in organic wines are much more diverse than those found in the majority of standard non-organic wines. Hangovers are usually caused by sulphites, which can also provoke asthma and migraines. Levels of sulphur are much lower in organic wines, so you really can feel the difference the next day. Organic vineyards recycle their waste grape skins by

composting them, and they often plant flowering plants among the vines to attract pollinating insects and predators.

Prizewinning organic and biodynamic red and white wines are produced all over the world, including in France, Italy, Australia and California. Red wine is full of health-promoting antioxidants, so it is good for preventing heart disease as well as relieving stress if drunk in moderation.

To find a good supplier of organic wine, contact an independent wine dealer. The Internet is an invaluable tool for finding such retailers; simply make a search for organic wine dealers and look for one in your area. Alternatively, buy the wines direct from the vineyard.

Fruit wines can also be delicious. Organic stores sell several varieties, but the best way to investigate the many delights of elderberry, elderflower and blackcurrant wine is to make your own. Home wine-making kits can be used with organic ingredients to produce excellent results.

Store organic wine on its side in a cool, dark place to keep the cork moist. Try adding your favourite wines to sauces and fruit salads, or organic sherry and port to trifles and cakes.

Spirits

Wines are not the only prizewinning organic drinks. Some incredible spirits are available, including industry award winners such as Del Meguey mezcal. This organic mezcal is produced by traditional artisans in Mexico who have had the craft passed down to them through countless generations. Del Meguey produce five kinds of organic mezcal, with their top-of-the-range product achieving international status as one of the finest spirits in the world.

Organic gin and vodka have also reached a fine quality now, with Juniper Green gin and UK5 vodka made in London, England. Distilled from organic raw ingredients, you will find that these spirits have a clean, round taste, with lots of warm flavours in the gin. You can also buy organic Scotch whisky, plus more unusual spirits including Grappa and Calvados.

Beer and Cider

Organic beer and lager microbreweries have sprung up and begun to flourish all over the world, from North America to Belgium and Germany. The intensity that organic hops impart to the flavour of organic beers and lagers has encouraged the general trend towards high quality traditional brews. There are dark stouts and light lagers, bronze bitters and extra strong Belgian beers. There is even a German hemp beer, Cannabia, based on an ancient Roman recipe.

Organic ciders are made from organic apples, and often contain much less added sulphur dioxide than non-organic ciders. This makes them less likely to provoke hangovers in the morning. The largest range of organic cider is currently produced in England, but they are also brewed commercially in France.

Serve cider cold with a hot pork dinner or ham lunch. Alternatively, add a little to the pan when roasting lamb for additional flavour and acidity.

Water

The ultimate soft drink is water. Essential for human health, it is undeniably the most thirst-quenching drink of them all. Add a squeeze of lemon juice or a sprig of fresh mint, and it becomes even more enjoyable. Although bottled water cannot be certified as organic, the label can state that it was sourced from organically farmed land. This is important if you want to avoid pesticides that may have run off agrochemical farmland into the water table beneath.

Tap water quality varies hugely between regions, depending on the geology of the area and its filtration capabilities. At best, it is pure and full of beneficial minerals such as calcium. At worst, it can contain pesticides, hormones and heavy metals.

Water Filters The best way to ensure that the water you drink is as pure as possible is to invest in a good-quality water filter. There are many variations on three basic types. The most common is the carbon filter, which is good at cleaning most impurities, including fluoride. An even better version incorporates a built-in reverse osmosis system that guarantees absolute purity from all heavy metals and other pollutants. Distillers are

Above: *Fresh organic lemonade.*

also available, but the water they produce must be supplemented carefully with minerals from foods or supplements. Choosing organic drinks is a good way of avoiding additives, but drinking pure water is even better.

Fizzy Drinks

If you want to enjoy fizzy drinks or sodas as part of an organic diet it is essential that the drinks you buy are also organic. Non-organic colas are universally bad for your health. Although it is usual for both organic and non-organic fizzy drinks to contain a very high proportion of sugar, the non-organic drinks are full of artificial chemical additives that are seriously undermining. The phosphoric acid in colas is directly related to loss of calcium in bone. This can lead to osteoporosis, a disease that is becoming more common throughout the industrialized world.

Non-organic diet drinks usually contain synthetic sweeteners such as aspartame and saccharine. These artificial additives are strictly banned in organic foods, with very good reason. Aspartame is a neurotoxin that affects the appetite control centres in the brain. As a result, serotonin levels in the brain drop, often leading to depression. Consumers of artificially sweetened drinks often have difficulty dieting.

Left to right: *Organic Juniper Green gin, made in London and German hemp beer, Cannabia.*

Fruit Cordials

Not only are organic cordials better than non-organic ones in terms of taste and sweetness, but they are also more nutritious. They contain no artificial colourings or flavourings, refined sugars or artificial sweeteners. Made from real fruit juices, they taste much more like the fruit pictured on the label than the highly processed alternatives. However, many organic cordials are still high in sugar, so check the ingredients, especially if you are preparing the drink for a child. Organic sugar is almost as unhealthy as non-organic sugar, and just as destructive to teeth.

Fruit and Vegetable Juices

Commercially available organic juices vary considerably in terms of flavour, but all score over non-organic ones because they are free of pesticide residues. It takes a lot of fruit and vegetables to make a relatively small amount of juice. If the produce contains pesticide residues, these will be concentrated when the fruit or vegetable is juiced. Drinking organic juice means that you are getting more concentrated vitamins, minerals and phytonutrients instead.

If you buy fruit or vegetable juices, try to ensure that they come from freshly pressed

Right: Organic fruit and vegetable juices are a fabulous source of vitamins, minerals and phytonutrients.

Right: Vanilla spice tea leaves, fair-trade breakfast and Japanese nagata kukicha teas

produce rather than concentrates. Minimal processing results in a more natural taste and higher nutrient content. Some juices now include natural healers and energizers such as ginseng, chlorophyl-rich spirulina and wheatgrass.

Juicing The best juices are freshly made, either squeezed manually from citrus fruits or processed with the aid of a juice machine, or juicer. Most juicers are based on the centrifugal system. The fresh produce is grated and sieved at high speed to separate the juice from the pulp. Other juicers work by effectively "chewing" the produce. The juice that is released comes from between the plant's cell walls and is extremely high in nutrients and

flavour. These machines are called masticating juicers, and although expensive, they are the best on the market. Hard and soft fruits and vegetables, leafy greens and fresh herbs can all be juiced in machines.

If you do not own a juicer, make fruit juices in a food processor or blender. Peel, stone (pit), core or seed the fruit before blending. Juices made in this way tend to be thicker and have a higher fibre content than regular juices because the pulp has not been removed. Soft fruits, such as melon and grapes, are ideal for blended juices.

Teas, Fruit Teas and Tisanes

Organic teas are grown with respect for the land and the people who tend it. The teas are generally fairly traded, with communities far away from the end beverage gaining real benefits whenever a packet is sold. Pesticide residues are at issue here. Although these are not high in agrochemically grown teas, the crop is generally sprayed intensively throughout its growth. This pollutes the land and poses a serious health threat to the workers. Organic teas are full of flavour, and are readily available in lots of different varieties, including loose leaves and tea bags containing either single estate varieties or blends. Flavoured or spiced teas are also on sale. All these products contain vitamins and minerals as well as powerful antioxidants that protect the heart and help to prevent cancer. When you buy organic, even the tea bags are better for the environment, because unlike non-organic tea bags, they have to be chlorine-free.

There are hundreds of organic fruit teas, spice teas and herbal tisanes available, generally with much better flavour than the non-organic equivalents.
Fruit Teas Organic fruit teas rely on natural fruit for their flavour and colour, whereas non-organic fruit teas are often boosted with synthetic and "nature-identical" flavourings and colours. This results in overpoweringly strong rather than less subtle tastes.
Herbal Tisanes and Spice Teas These have direct healing benefits as well as delicate flavours. The herbs and spices they contain are often pharmacoepial grade, meaning that they are of the same quality as herbs prescribed by herbalists.

Some blends are available specifically formulated for medicinal purposes as well as flavour, including mixes to help you sleep, to aid digestion, to ward off colds or to ease stress.

Lavender, hyssop, thyme and marjoram infused together are taken as a remedy for cold symptons. Hops, chamomile and lime flower are used to beat insomnia. Rosemary is said to stimulate the circulation and improve concentration while thyme boosts the immune system and helps fight infections. Elderflower tisane can ease painful sinuses and bronchial conditions.

Almost any herb and its flowers can be used to make tea, and the method is generally the same. Place several sprigs of the freshly picked herb in a cup and pour over hot, but not boiling, water and leave for several minutes to infuse. Strain the liquid to remove the leaves and drink it hot or cold with honey, lemon or sugar to taste. Spices require

Above: *Organic drinking chocolate powder*

greater heat to extract the constituents, so they need to be placed in a pan of cold water, heated and simmered for 10 to 15 minutes.

Coffee and Cocoa

Organic coffee and cocoa are grown in hot, tropical, mountainous regions such as South and Central America, East Africa and Indonesia. It is essential to have faith in the producer's trading practices. The cultivation of agrochemical coffee often involves heavy pesticide use, especially in developing countries. There are health and safety concerns, too, about conditions for workers on the plantations. The confidence that comes from buying organically grown, fairly traded coffee doubles the pleasure of drinking this beverage. Look out for organic instant coffee granules or powder as well as ground coffee or whole roasted beans. Store whole or ground beans in the refrigerator and they will retain their freshness for longer.

Organic drinking chocolate is available as an instant powder. Although organic coffee and drinking chocolate powder are not the healthiest organic products, organic drinking chocolate is much better for you than the non-organic version because it contains only natural ingredients, including antioxidant-rich organic cocoa. Intensively produced non-organic drinking chocolate contains dried non-organic milk, hydrogenated fats, refined sweeteners and artificial flavourings.

Above: *Buying and grinding fair-traded organic coffee beans can double the pleasure of drinking coffee.*

SPRING

As the days start to get a little longer and the weather gets warmer, the fresh organic ingredients traditionally associated with this time of year – such as tender young vegetables and new season lamb – start to appear in the shops and farmers' markets.

The season's vegetables require little cooking to bring out their sweet flavour: try asparagus with a tangy lemon sauce, or sweet young carrots and leeks or Escalopes of Chicken with new potatoes. Brightly coloured spring vegetables also look and taste good when served with pasta, or when added to soups.

Light fish dishes are a popular choice now after long, dark winter days – Salmon Fish Cakes or Fillets of Sea Bream in Filo Pastry, served simply with spring vegetables, are a real treat. And this is the time of year to enjoy organic lamb, in dishes such as Lamb Stew, Herb-crusted Rack of Lamb with Puy Lentils, and Lamb Burgers. For dessert, nothing tastes better than tender spring rhubarb served with ginger ice cream, or made into a meringue pie.

CHICKEN, AVOCADO and SPRING ONION SOUP

Organic avocados ripen naturally over a longer period of time than non-organic, producing really rich-flavoured fruit. Combined here with chicken and spring onions they add a creaminess to this delicious soup.

SERVES SIX

1.5 litres/2½ pints/6¼ cups chicken stock
½ fresh chilli, seeded
2 skinless, boneless chicken breast fillets
1 avocado
4 spring onions (scallions), finely sliced
400g/14oz can chickpeas, drained
sea salt and freshly ground black pepper

1 Pour the chicken stock into a large pan and add the chilli. Bring to the boil, add the whole chicken breast fillets, then lower the heat and simmer for about 10 minutes, or until the chicken is cooked.

COOK'S TIP
Handle chillies with care as they can irritate the skin and eyes. It is advisable to wear rubber gloves when preparing them.

2 Remove the pan from the heat and lift out the chicken breasts with a slotted spoon. Leave to cool a little, then, using two forks, shred the chicken into small pieces. Set the shredded chicken aside.

3 Pour the chicken stock into a food processor or blender and add the chilli. Process the mixture until smooth, then return to the pan.

4 Cut the avocado in half, remove the skin and stone (pit), then slice the flesh into 2cm/¾in pieces. Add it to the stock, with the spring onions and chickpeas.

5 Return the shredded chicken to the pan, with salt and pepper to taste, and heat gently. When the soup is heated through, spoon into warmed and serve

PASTA and CHICKPEA SOUP

A simple, country-style soup. The shapes of the pasta and the beans complement one another beautifully. Look out for really large pasta shells, which you can find in farmers' markets and good organic stores.

SERVES FOUR TO SIX

1 onion
2 carrots
2 celery sticks
60ml/4 tbsp olive oil
400g/14oz can chickpeas, rinsed
    and drained
200g/7oz can cannellini beans,
    rinsed and drained
150ml/¼ pint/⅔ cup passata (bottled
    strained tomatoes)
120ml/4fl oz/½ cup water
1.5 litres/2½ pints/6¼ cups chicken stock
2 fresh or dried rosemary sprigs
200g/7oz dried giant conchiglie
sea salt and ground black pepper
freshly grated Parmesan cheese or
    premium Italian-style vegetarian
    cheese, to serve

1 Chop the onion, carrots and celery sticks finely, either in a food processor or by hand.

2 Heat the olive oil in a large pan, add the chopped vegetable mixture and cook over a low heat, stirring frequently, for 5 minutes, or until the vegetables are just beginning to soften.

3 Add the chickpeas and cannellini beans, stir well to mix, then cook for 5 minutes. Stir in the passata and water, then cook, stirring, for 2–3 minutes.

4 Add 475ml/16fl oz/2 cups of the stock and one of the rosemary sprigs. Bring to the boil, cover, then simmer gently, stirring occasionally, for 1 hour.

5 Pour in the remaining stock, add the pasta and bring to boil, stirring. Lower the heat slightly and simmer, stirring frequently, until the pasta is *al dente*: 7–8 minutes or according to the instructions on the packet.

6 When the pasta is cooked, taste the soup for seasoning. Remove the rosemary and serve the soup hot in warmed bowls, topped with grated cheese and a few rosemary leaves from the rosemary sprig.

COOK'S TIP
Organic passata is a must for this recipe as most non-organic tomato products contain genetically modified tomatoes.

TAPENADE with QUAIL'S EGGS and CRUDITÉS

This olive-based spread or dip makes a sociable start to a meal. Serve the tapenade
with hard-boiled quail's eggs or small organic hen's eggs and a selection of mixed spring
vegetable crudités and let everyone help themselves.

SERVES SIX

225g/8oz/2 cups pitted black olives
2 large garlic cloves, peeled
15ml/1 tbsp salted capers, rinsed
6 canned or bottled anchovy
    fillets, drained
50g/2oz good-quality canned tuna
5–10ml/1–2 tsp Cognac (optional)
5ml/1 tsp chopped fresh thyme
30ml/2 tbsp chopped fresh parsley
30–60ml/2–4 tbsp extra virgin olive oil
a dash of lemon juice
30ml/2 tbsp crème fraîche or
    fromage frais (optional)
12–18 quail's eggs
ground black pepper

For the crudités
bunch of spring onions (scallions),
    halved if large
bunch of radishes, trimmed
bunch of baby fennel, trimmed and halved
    if large, or 1 large fennel bulb, cut into
    thin wedges

To serve
French bread
unsalted (sweet) butter or olive oil and
    sea salt to dip

1 Process the olives, garlic cloves, capers, anchovies and tuna in a food processor or blender. Transfer to a mixing bowl and stir in the Cognac, if using, the thyme, parsley and enough olive oil to make a paste. Season to taste with pepper and a dash of lemon juice. Stir in the crème fraîche or fromage frais, if using, and transfer to a serving bowl.

2 Place the quail's eggs in a pan of cold water and bring to the boil. Cook for only 2 minutes, then immediately drain and plunge the eggs into iced water to stop them from cooking any further and to help make them easier to shell.

3 When the eggs are cold, carefully part-shell them.

4 Serve the tapenade with the eggs and crudités and offer French bread, unsalted butter or oil and sea salt to accompany them.

COOK'S TIPS
• Crème fraîche or fromage frais softens the distinctive flavour of the olives for a milder tapenade.
• In Provence, where tapenade comes from, it is traditional to serve it with crudités of celery, fennel and tomato.
• Tapenade is also delicious spread on toast and served with pre-dinner drinks.

OYSTERS ROCKEFELLER

This is the perfect dish for those who prefer to eat their oysters lightly cooked. As a cheaper alternative, for those who are not "as rich as Rockefeller", give mussels or clams the same treatment; they will also taste delicious.

SERVES SIX

450g/1lb/3 cups coarse sea salt,
   plus extra to serve
24 oysters, opened
115g/4oz/½ cup butter or
   non-hydrogenated margarine
2 shallots, finely chopped
500g/1¼lb spinach leaves, finely chopped
60ml/4 tbsp chopped fresh parsley
60ml/4 tbsp chopped celery leaves
90ml/6 tbsp fresh white or wholemeal
   (whole-wheat) breadcrumbs
10–20ml/2–4 tsp vodka
cayenne pepper
sea salt and ground black pepper
lemon wedges, to serve

COOK'S TIP
If you prefer a smoother stuffing, whizz it to a paste in a food processor or blender at the end of step 3.

1 Preheat the oven to 220°C/425°F/ Gas 7. Make a bed of coarse salt on two large baking sheets. Set the oysters in the half-shell in the bed of salt to keep them steady. Set aside.

2 Melt the butter or margarine in a frying pan. Add the chopped shallots and cook them over a low heat for 2–3 minutes until they are softened. Stir in the spinach and let it wilt.

3 Add the parsley, celery leaves and breadcrumbs to the pan and fry gently for 5 minutes. Season with salt, pepper and cayenne pepper.

4 Divide the stuffing among the oysters. Drizzle a few drops of vodka over each oyster, then bake for about 5 minutes until bubbling and golden brown. Serve on a heated platter on a shallow salt bed with lemon wedges.

LEEK and MUSSEL TARTLETS

Wild mussels are easily harvested and are simply gathered off rocks in shallow water by hand. Serve these vividly coloured little tarts as a first course, with a few salad leaves, such as watercress, rocket and frisée.

3 Preheat the oven to 190°C/375°F/ Gas 5. Roll out the pastry and line six 10cm/4in tartlet tins (quiche pans). Prick the bases and line the sides with foil. Bake for 10 minutes. Remove the foil and bake for 5–8 minutes. Reduce the temperature to 180°C/350°F/Gas 4.

4 Soak the saffron in 15ml/1 tbsp hot water for 10 minutes. Fry the leeks in the oil in a pan over a medium heat for 6–8 minutes. Add the peppers and cook for 2 minutes.

SERVES SIX

large pinch of saffron threads
2 large leeks, sliced
30ml/2 tbsp olive oil
2 large yellow (bell) peppers, halved, seeded, grilled (broiled), peeled and cut into strips
900g/2lb mussels
2 large eggs
300ml/½ pint/1¼ cups single (light) cream or soya cream
30ml/2 tbsp finely chopped fresh parsley
sea salt and ground black pepper
salad leaves, to serve

For the pastry
225g/8oz/2 cups plain (all-purpose) flour
115g/4oz/½ cup chilled butter, diced
45–60ml/3–4 tbsp chilled water

1 To make the pastry, sift the flour into a mixing bowl and add the butter. Rub the butter in with your fingertips until the mixture resembles fine breadcrumbs.

2 Sprinkle 45ml/3 tbsp of the water over and mix with a round-bladed knife until the mixture comes together and a soft dough is formed. Add more water if necessary. Wrap the dough in clear film (plastic wrap) and chill for 30 minutes.

COOK'S TIP
Use soya cream instead of the single cream and soya margarine instead of butter for a non-dairy option.

5 Bring 2.5cm/1in depth of water to the boil in a large pan and add 10ml/2 tsp salt. Scrub the mussels and remove the beards. Discard any mussels that stay open when tapped, then throw the rest into the pan. Cover and cook over a high heat, shaking the pan occasionally, for 3–4 minutes, or until the mussels open. Discard any unopened mussels. Shell the remainder.

6 Beat the eggs, cream and saffron liquid together. Season with salt and pepper and whisk in the parsley. Arrange the leeks, peppers and mussels in the cases, add the egg mixture and bake for 20–25 minutes. Serve with salad leaves.

DEEP-FRIED TOFU BALLS

Tofu is a wonderfully healthy and versatile ingredient and is flavoured to perfection in this Japanese dish, known as hiryozu, *which means flying dragon's head. The tangy lime sauce provides a lovely contrast to the savoury tofu balls.*

SERVES FOUR

2 × 285g/10¼oz packets firm tofu
20g/¾oz carrot, peeled
40g/1½oz green beans
2 large (US extra large) eggs, beaten
30ml/2 tbsp sake
10ml/2 tsp mirin
5ml/1 tsp sea salt
10ml/2 tsp shoyu
pinch of unrefined caster (superfine) sugar
    or rapadura
sunflower oil, for deep-frying

For the lime sauce
45ml/3 tbsp shoyu
juice of ½ lime
5ml/1 tsp rice vinegar or mirin

To garnish
300g/11oz mooli (daikon), peeled
2 dried red chillies, halved and seeded
4 chives, finely chopped

1 Drain the tofu and wrap in a dishtowel or kitchen paper. Set a chopping board on top and leave for 2 hours, or until it loses most of its liquid.

2 Cut the mooli for the garnish into about 4cm/1½in thick slices. Make 3–4 small holes in each slice with a skewer or chopstick and insert chilli pieces into the holes. Leave for 15 minutes, then grate the daikon and chilli finely.

3 To make the tofu balls, chop the carrot finely. Trim and cut the beans into 5mm/¼in lengths. Cook both vegetables for 1 minute in boiling water.

4 In a food processor, blend the tofu, eggs, sake, mirin, salt, shoyu and sugar until smooth. Transfer to a bowl and mix in the carrot and beans.

5 Fill a wok or pan with oil 4cm/1½in deep, and heat to 185°C/365°F.

6 Soak a piece of kitchen paper with a little vegetable oil, and lightly moisten your hands with it. Scoop 40ml/2½ tbsp of the mixture in one hand and shape into a ball between your hands.

7 Carefully slide the ball into the oil and deep-fry until crisp and golden brown. Drain on kitchen paper. Repeat with the remaining mixture.

8 Arrange the tofu balls on a plate and sprinkle with chives. Put 30ml/2 tbsp grated mooli in each of four bowls. Mix the lime sauce ingredients in a small serving bowl. Serve the hot tofu balls with the lime sauce to be mixed with grated daikon by each guest.

ASPARAGUS with LEMON SAUCE

This is a good spring dish as the asparagus gives the immune system a kick start to help detoxify after winter. The sauce has a light, fresh taste and brings out the best in asparagus.

SERVES FOUR AS A FIRST COURSE

675g/1½lb asparagus, tough ends removed, and tied in a bundle
15ml/1 tbsp cornflour (cornstarch)
10ml/2 tsp unrefined sugar or rapadura
2 egg yolks
juice of 1½ lemons
sea salt

COOK'S TIP
Use tiny asparagus spears for an elegant appetizer for a special dinner party.

1 Cook the bundle of asparagus in boiling salted water for 7–10 minutes.

2 Drain the asparagus well (reserving 200ml/7fl oz/scant 1 cup of the cooking liquid) and arrange the spears attractively in a serving dish. Set aside.

3 Blend the cornflour with the cooled, reserved cooking liquid and place in a small pan. Bring to the boil, stirring all the time with a wooden spoon, then cook over a gentle heat until the sauce thickens slightly. Stir in the sugar, then remove the pan from the heat and allow to cool slightly.

4 Beat the egg yolks thoroughly with the lemon juice and stir gradually into the cooled sauce. Cook the sauce over a very low heat, stirring all the time, until it thickens. Be careful not to overheat the sauce or it may curdle. Once the sauce has thickened, remove the pan from the heat and continue stirring for 1 minute. Season with salt or sugar if necessary. Allow the sauce to cool slightly.

5 Stir the cooled lemon sauce, then pour a little over the cooked asparagus. Cover and chill for at least 2 hours before serving accompanied by the rest of the lemon sauce.

BRAISED LEEKS with CARROTS

Sweet carrots and leeks go well together and are delicious finished with a little chopped mint or chervil. This is an easy accompaniment to roast lamb for a spring Sunday lunch.

4 Add seasoning, the wine and half the chopped herb. Heat until simmering, then cover and cook gently for 5–8 minutes until the leeks are tender, but not collapsed.

5 Uncover the leeks and turn them in the buttery juices. Increase the heat slightly, then boil the liquid rapidly until reduced to a few tablespoons.

6 Add the carrots to the leeks and reheat them gently, then swirl in the remaining butter or oil. Adjust the seasoning, if necessary. Transfer to a warmed serving dish and serve sprinkled with the remaining chopped herb.

SERVES SIX

65g/2½oz/5 tbsp butter or
   75ml/5 tbsp olive oil
675g/1½lb carrots, thickly sliced
2 fresh bay leaves
75ml/5 tbsp water
675g/1½lb leeks, cut into 5cm/
   2in lengths
120ml/4fl oz/½ cup white wine
30ml/2 tbsp chopped fresh mint
   or chervil
sea salt and ground black pepper

1 Heat 25g/1oz/2 tbsp of the butter or 30ml/2 tbsp of oil in a pan and cook the carrots gently for 4–5 minutes.

2 Add the bay leaves, seasoning and the water to the pan. Bring to the boil, cover lightly and cook for 10–15 minutes until the carrots are tender. Uncover, then boil the cooking juices until they have all evaporated, leaving the carrots moist and glazed.

3 Meanwhile, heat another 25g/1oz/ 2 tbsp of the remaining butter or 30ml/2 tbsp of oil in a deep frying pan or wide pan that will take the sliced leeks in a single layer. Add the leeks and fry them very gently in the melted butter over a medium to low heat for 4–5 minutes, without allowing them to turn brown.

VARIATION
Braised leeks in tarragon cream
Cook 900g/2lb leeks in 40g/1½oz/3 tbsp butter or 45ml/3 tbsp olive oil as above. Season, add a pinch of sugar, 45ml/3 tbsp tarragon vinegar, 6 fresh tarragon sprigs and 60ml/4 tbsp white wine. Cover and cook as above. Add 150ml/¼ pint/⅔ cup double (heavy) cream or soya cream and allow to bubble and thicken. Season and sprinkle with chopped fresh tarragon.

PARSLEY and ROCKET SALAD

This salad is light but full of flavour, and makes a tasty first course, ideal for a spring dinner party. Shavings of rich-tasting cheese ensure that this salad is special.

SERVES SIX AS A FIRST COURSE

1 garlic clove, halved
115g/4oz good white bread, cut into
   1cm/½in thick slices
45ml/3 tbsp olive oil, plus extra for
   shallow frying
75g/3oz rocket (arugula) leaves
75g/3oz baby spinach
25g/1oz flat leaf parsley, leaves only
45ml/3 tbsp salted capers,
   rinsed and dried
40g/1½oz Parmesan cheese or premium
   Italian-style vegetarian cheese,
   pared into shavings

For the dressing
25ml/1½ tbsp black olive paste
1 garlic clove, finely chopped
5ml/1 tsp smooth organic mustard
75ml/5 tbsp olive oil
10ml/2 tsp balsamic vinegar
ground black pepper

1 First make the dressing. Whisk the black olive paste, garlic and mustard together in a mixing bowl. Gradually whisk in the olive oil, then the vinegar. Adjust the seasoning to taste with black pepper – the dressing should be sufficiently salty already and not need any additional salt.

2 Preheat the oven to 190°C/375°F/ Gas 5. Rub the halved garlic clove over the bread and cut or tear the slices into bitesize croûtons. Toss them in the olive oil and place on a small baking tray. Bake in the oven for 10–15 minutes, stirring once, until golden brown. Cool on kitchen paper.

3 Mix the rocket, baby spinach and flat leaf parsley in a large salad bowl.

4 Heat a shallow layer of olive oil in a frying pan. Add the capers and fry briefly until crisp. Scoop out straight away and drain on kitchen paper.

5 Toss the dressing and croûtons into the salad and divide it among six individual bowls or plates.

6 Scatter the cheese shavings and the fried capers over the top of the salad and serve immediately.

COOK'S TIP
Use a swivel-action or fixed-blade potato peeler to cut thin shavings from a block of Parmesan or premium Italian-style vegetarian cheese.

BEETROOT and RED ONION SALAD

There is a wide variety of organic beetroots available – this salad looks especially attractive when made with a mixture of red and yellow. Try it with rich meats such as roast beef or cooked ham.

SERVES SIX

500g/1¼lb small red and yellow
   beetroot (beet)
75ml/5 tbsp water
60ml/4 tbsp olive oil
90g/3½oz/scant 1 cup walnut or
   pecan halves
5ml/1 tsp unrefined caster (superfine)
   sugar or rapadura, plus a little extra
   for the dressing
30ml/2 tbsp walnut oil
15ml/1 tbsp balsamic vinegar
5ml/1 tsp soy sauce
5ml/1 tsp grated orange rind
2.5ml/½ tsp ground roasted
   coriander seeds
5–10ml/1–2 tsp orange juice
1 red onion, halved and very
   thinly sliced
15–30ml/1–2 tbsp chopped
   fresh fennel
75g/3oz watercress or mizuna leaves
handful of baby red chard or beetroot
   (beet) leaves (optional)
sea salt and ground black pepper

1 Preheat the oven to 180°C/350°F/ Gas 4. Place the beetroot in a shallow ovenproof dish just large enough to hold them in a single layer, and add the water. Cover the dish tightly with a close-fitting lid or foil and bake for about 1–1½ hours, or until the beetroot are just cooked and tender.

2 Allow the beetroot to cool. Once cooled, peel the beetroot, then slice them or cut them into strips and toss with 15ml/1 tbsp of the olive oil. Transfer to a large bowl and set aside.

3 Meanwhile, heat 15ml/1 tbsp of the olive oil in a small frying pan and cook the walnuts or pecans until they begin to brown. Add the sugar and cook, stirring, until the nuts begin to caramelize. Season with 2.5ml/½ tsp salt and lots of ground black pepper, then turn the nuts out on to a plate and leave to cool.

4 In a jug (pitcher) or small bowl, whisk together the remaining olive oil, the walnut oil, vinegar, soy sauce, orange rind and ground roasted coriander to make the dressing. Season with salt and pepper to taste and add a pinch of caster sugar. Whisk in orange juice to taste.

5 Separate the red onion slices into half-rings and add them to the slices or strips of beetroot. Add the dressing and toss thoroughly to mix.

6 When ready to serve, toss the salad with the fennel, watercress or mizuna and red chard or beetroot leaves, if using. Transfer to individual bowls or plates and sprinkle with the caramelized nuts. Serve immediately.

ASSORTED SEAWEED SALAD

This salad is a fine example of the traditional Japanese idea of eating: look after your appetite and your health at the same time. Seaweed is a nutritious, alkaline food which is rich in fibre. Its unusual flavours are a great complement to fish and tofu dishes.

SERVES FOUR

5g/⅛oz each dried wakame, dried arame
    and dried hijiki seaweeds
about 130g/4½oz enokitake mushrooms
2 spring onions (scallions)
a few ice cubes
½ cucumber, cut lengthways
250g/9oz mixed salad leaves

For the marinade
15ml/1 tbsp rice vinegar
6.5ml/1¼ tsp salt

For the dressing
60ml/4 tbsp rice vinegar
7.5ml/1½ tsp toasted sesame oil
15ml/1 tbsp shoyu
15ml/1 tbsp water with a pinch
    of dashi-no-moto (dashi
    stock granules)
2.5cm/1in piece fresh root ginger,
    finely grated

1 First rehydrate the seaweeds. Soak the dried wakame seaweed for 10 minutes in one bowl of water and, in a separate bowl of water, soak the dried arame and hijiki seaweeds together for 30 minutes.

2 Trim the hard end of the enokitake mushroom stalks, then cut the bunch in half and separate the stems.

3 Slice the spring onions into thin, 4cm/1½in long strips, then soak the strips in a bowl of cold water with a few ice cubes added to make them curl up. Drain. Slice the cucumber into thin, half-moon shapes.

4 Cook the wakame and enokitake in boiling water for 2 minutes, then add the arame and hijiki for a few seconds. Immediately remove from the heat. Drain and sprinkle over the vinegar and salt while still warm. Chill until needed.

5 Mix the dressing ingredients in a bowl. Arrange the mixed salad leaves in a large bowl with the cucumber on top, then add the seaweed and enokitake mixture. Decorate the salad with spring onion curls and serve with the dressing.

MARINATED SALMON with AVOCADO SALAD

Use only the freshest of salmon for this delicious salad. The marinade of lemon juice and dashi-konbu "cooks" the salmon, which is then served with avocado, toasted almonds and salad leaves, accompanied by a miso mayonnaise.

SERVES FOUR

2 very fresh salmon tails, skinned and
    filleted, 250g/9oz total weight
juice of 1 lemon
10cm/4in dashi-konbu seaweed, wiped with
    a damp cloth and cut into 4 strips
1 ripe avocado
4 shiso or basil leaves, stalks removed and
    cut in half lengthways
about 115g/4oz mixed leaves such as
    lamb's lettuce, frisée or rocket (arugula)
45ml/3 tbsp flaked (sliced) almonds,
    toasted in a dry frying pan until
    just slightly browned

For the miso mayonnaise
90ml/6 tbsp good-quality mayonnaise
15ml/1 tbsp miso paste
ground black pepper

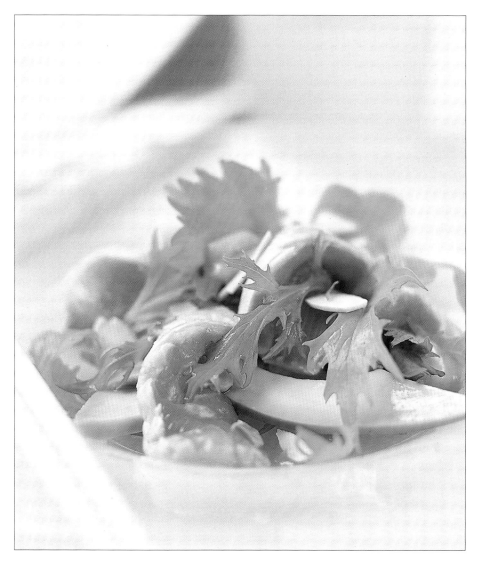

1 Cut the first salmon fillet in half crossways at the tail end where the fillet is not wider than 4cm/1½in. Next, cut the wider part in half lengthways. This means the fillet from one side is cut into three. Cut the other fillet into three pieces, in the same way.

2 Pour the lemon juice into a wide, shallow plastic container and add two of the dashi-konbu pieces. Lay the salmon fillets in the base of the container and sprinkle with the rest of the dashi-konbu. Marinate for about 15 minutes, then turn the salmon and leave for a further 15 minutes. The salmon should change to a pink "cooked" colour. Remove the salmon from the marinade and wipe with kitchen paper.

3 Holding a very sharp knife at an angle, cut the salmon into 5mm/¼in thick slices against the grain.

4 Halve the avocado and sprinkle with a little of the remaining salmon marinade. Remove the avocado stone (pit) and skin, then carefully slice to the same thickness as the salmon.

5 Mix the miso mayonnaise ingredients in a small bowl. Spread about 5ml/1 tsp on to the back of each of the shiso or basil leaves, then mix the remainder with 15ml/1 tbsp of the remaining marinade to loosen the mayonnaise.

6 Arrange the salad leaves on four plates. Add the avocado, salmon, shiso leaves and almonds and toss lightly. Drizzle over the remaining mayonnaise and serve immediately.

VARIATION
Alternatively, build a tower of avocado and salmon. For each serving, place an eighth of the avocado slices in the centre of a plate, slightly overlapping. Add a shiso or basil leaf, miso-side down. Then place an eighth of the salmon on top, slightly overlapping. Repeat the process. Arrange the salad and almonds, and spoon over the mayonnaise.

GARGANELLI with SPRING VEGETABLES

Fresh, brightly coloured spring vegetables both look and taste good when served with pasta. A light sauce of dry white wine, extra virgin olive oil and fresh herbs is used to marry the two together for a delicious flavour.

SERVES FOUR

1 bunch asparagus, about 350g/12oz
4 young carrots
1 bunch spring onions (scallions)
130g/4½oz shelled fresh peas
350g/12oz/3 cups dried garganelli
60ml/4 tbsp dry white wine
90ml/6 tbsp extra virgin olive oil
a few sprigs fresh flat leaf parsley, mint and
    basil, leaves stripped and chopped
sea salt and ground black pepper
freshly grated Parmesan cheese or premium
    Italian-style vegetarian cheese, to serve

1 Trim off and discard the woody part of each asparagus stem, then cut off the tips on the diagonal. Cut the stems on the diagonal into 4cm/1½in pieces. Cut the carrots and spring onions on the diagonal into similar-size pieces.

2 Plunge the carrots, peas, asparagus stems and tips into a large pan of salted boiling water. Bring back to the boil, then reduce the heat and simmer for 8–10 minutes, until tender.

3 Meanwhile, cook the pasta in salted boiling water for 10–12 minutes, or according to the instructions on the packet, until just tender.

4 Drain the asparagus, carrots and peas and return them to the pan. Add the white wine, olive oil and salt and black pepper to taste, then gently toss over a medium to high heat until the wine has reduced and the vegetables glisten with the olive oil.

5 Drain the garganelli and tip it into a warmed large bowl. Add the vegetables, spring onions and sprigs of fresh herbs and toss well. Divide the pasta among four warmed individual plates and serve immediately, with freshly grated cheese.

COOK'S TIP
Garganelli are rolled short pasta shapes made with pasta dough enriched with egg. If you can't get garganelli, use another short shape, such as penne.

PENNE with CREAM and SMOKED SALMON

This modern classic uses just three essential ingredients, which combine together beautifully to make a quick and easy dish. Accompany with a green salad, ciabatta bread and sparkling wine for a simple but nutritious and tasty meal.

SERVES FOUR

350g/12oz/3 cups dried penne or
    other pasta tubes
115g/4oz thinly sliced smoked salmon
2–3 fresh thyme sprigs
30ml/2 tbsp extra virgin olive oil
150ml/¼ pint/⅔ cup extra-thick
    single (light) cream or
    soya cream
sea salt and ground black pepper

1 Cook the dried pasta in a large pan of lightly salted boiling water for 10 minutes until it is just tender, or according to the instructions on the packet.

2 Meanwhile, using sharp kitchen scissors, cut the smoked salmon slices into thin strips, about 5mm/¼in wide. Strip the leaves from the thyme sprigs and rinse them thoroughly in cold water.

3 Drain the pasta and return it to the pan. Add the oil and heat gently, then stir in the cream with about one-quarter of the smoked salmon and thyme leaves, then season with pepper. Heat gently for 3–4 minutes, stirring all the time. Check the seasoning. Divide the pasta among four warmed bowls, top with the remaining salmon and thyme leaves and serve immediately.

VARIATION
Although white penne is the traditional pasta to serve with this sauce, it also goes very well with fresh wholemeal penne or ravioli stuffed with spinach and ricotta cheese.

CHICKEN and ASPARAGUS RISOTTO

Use fairly thick asparagus in this classic springtime risotto, as fine spears tend to overcook. The thick ends of the asparagus are full of flavour and they become beautifully tender in the time it takes for the rice to absorb the stock.

SERVES FOUR

75ml/5 tbsp olive oil
1 leek, finely chopped
115g/4oz/1½ cups oyster or brown cap
    (cremini) mushrooms, sliced
3 skinless, boneless chicken breast
    fillets, cubed
350g/12oz asparagus
250g/9oz/1¼ cups risotto rice
900ml/1½ pints/3¾ cups simmering
    chicken stock
sea salt and ground black pepper
fresh Parmesan or premium
    Italian-style vegetarian cheese curls,
    to serve

1 Heat the olive oil in a pan. Add the finely chopped leek and cook gently until softened, but not coloured. Add the sliced mushrooms and cook for 5 minutes. Remove the vegetables from the pan and set aside.

2 Increase the heat and cook the cubes of chicken until golden on all sides. Do this in batches, if necessary, and then return them all to the pan.

3 Meanwhile, discard the woody ends from the asparagus and cut the spears in half. Set the tips aside. Cut the thick ends in half and add them to the pan. Return the leek and mushroom mixture to the pan and stir in the rice.

4 Pour in a ladleful of boiling stock and cook gently, stirring occasionally, until the stock is completely absorbed. Continue adding the stock a ladleful at a time, simmering until it is absorbed, the rice is tender and the chicken is cooked.

COOK'S TIP
To thoroughly remove all the soil from organic leeks, slice in half along their length and rinse under running water.

5 Add the asparagus tips with the last ladleful of boiling stock for the final 5 minutes and continue cooking the risotto very gently until the asparagus is tender. The whole process should take about 25–30 minutes.

6 Season the risotto to taste with salt and freshly ground black pepper and spoon it into individual warm serving bowls. Top each bowl with curls of cheese, and serve.

ESCALOPES of CHICKEN with VEGETABLES

This is a quick and light dish — ideal as the weather starts to warm up and easy meals become the order of the day. Flattening the chicken breasts thins and tenderizes the meat and also speeds up the cooking time.

SERVES FOUR

4 skinless, boneless chicken breast fillets,
    each weighing 175g/6oz
juice of 1 lime
120ml/4fl oz/½ cup olive oil
675g/1½lb mixed small new season
    potatoes, carrots, fennel (sliced
    if large), asparagus and peas
sea salt and ground black pepper
sprigs of fresh flat leaf parsley, to garnish

For the tomato mayonnaise
150ml/¼ pint/⅔ cup mayonnaise
15ml/1 tbsp sun-dried tomato
    purée (paste)

1 Lay the chicken fillets between sheets of clear film (plastic wrap) or baking parchment and use a rolling pin to beat them until they are evenly thin. Season the chicken and sprinkle with the lime juice.

2 Heat 45ml/3 tbsp of the oil in a frying pan or griddle and cook the chicken escalopes for 10–12 minutes on each side, turning frequently.

3 Meanwhile, put the new potatoes and carrots in a small pan with the remaining oil and season with sea salt. Cover and cook over a medium heat for 10–15 minutes, stirring frequently.

4 Add the fennel and cook for a further 5 minutes, stirring frequently. Finally, add the asparagus and peas and cook for 5 minutes more, or until all the vegetables are tender and cooked.

5 To make the tomato mayonnaise, mix together the mayonnaise and sun-dried tomato purée in a small bowl. Spoon the vegetables on to a warmed serving platter or individual plates and arrange the chicken on top. Serve the tomato mayonnaise with the chicken and vegetables. Garnish with sprigs of flat leaf parsley.

COOK'S TIP
Any combinations of baby vegetables can be used. The weight specified is for prepared vegetables. Adjust the cooking time or the order in which they are added to the pan according to how long the chosen vegetables take to cook, for example add root vegetables first, before quick-cooking ones such as courgettes (zucchini), mangetouts (snow peas) or green beans.

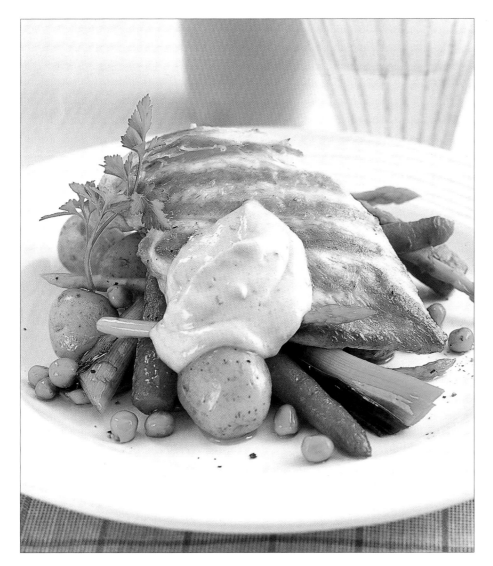

ROAST LEG of LAMB

Tender young organic lamb is available only in the springtime, and is often served with a sauce using the first sprigs of mint of the year and early new potatoes. If you buy organic young lamb you can be happy in the knowledge that countryside seasons are being utilized and respected, and that the meat is fresh.

SERVES SIX

1.5kg/3¼lb leg of lamb
4 garlic cloves, sliced
2 fresh rosemary sprigs
30ml/2 tbsp light olive oil
300ml/½ pint/1¼ cups red wine
5ml/1 tsp honey
45ml/3 tbsp redcurrant jelly
sea salt and ground black pepper
spring vegetables, to serve

For the roast potatoes
45ml/3 tbsp olive oil
1.3kg/3lb potatoes, such as Desirée, peeled and cut into chunks

For the mint sauce
about 15g/½oz fresh mint
10ml/2 tsp unrefined caster (superfine) sugar or rapadura
15ml/1 tbsp boiling water
30ml/2 tbsp white wine vinegar

1 Preheat the oven to 220°C/425°F/ Gas 7. Make small slits into the lamb all over the joint. Press a slice of garlic and a few rosemary leaves into each slit, then place the joint in a roasting pan and season well. Drizzle the oil over the lamb and roast for about 1 hour.

COOK'S TIP
To make a quick and tasty gravy from the pan juices, add about 300ml/½ pint/ 1¼ cups red wine, stock or water and boil, stirring occasionally, until reduced and well-flavoured. Season to taste, then strain into a sauce boat to serve.

2 Meanwhile, mix the wine, honey and redcurrant jelly in a small pan and heat, stirring, until the jelly melts. Bring to the boil, then reduce the heat and simmer until reduced by half. Spoon this glaze over the lamb and return it to the oven for 30–45 minutes.

3 To make the potatoes, put the oil in a roasting pan on the shelf above the meat. Boil the potatoes for 5–10 minutes, then drain them and fluff up the surface of each with a fork.

4 Add the prepared potatoes to the hot oil and baste well, then roast them for 45 minutes, or until they are crisp.

5 While the potatoes are roasting, make the mint sauce. Place the mint on a chopping board and scatter the sugar over the top. Chop the mint finely, then transfer to a bowl.

6 Add the boiling water and stir until the sugar has dissolved. Add 15ml/1 tbsp vinegar and taste the sauce before adding the remaining vinegar. (You may want to add slightly less or more than the suggested quantity.) Leave the mint sauce to stand until you are ready to serve the meal.

7 Remove the lamb from the oven, cover it loosely with foil and set it aside in a warm place to rest for 10–15 minutes before carving. Serve with the crisp roast potatoes, mint sauce and a selection of seasonal spring vegetables.

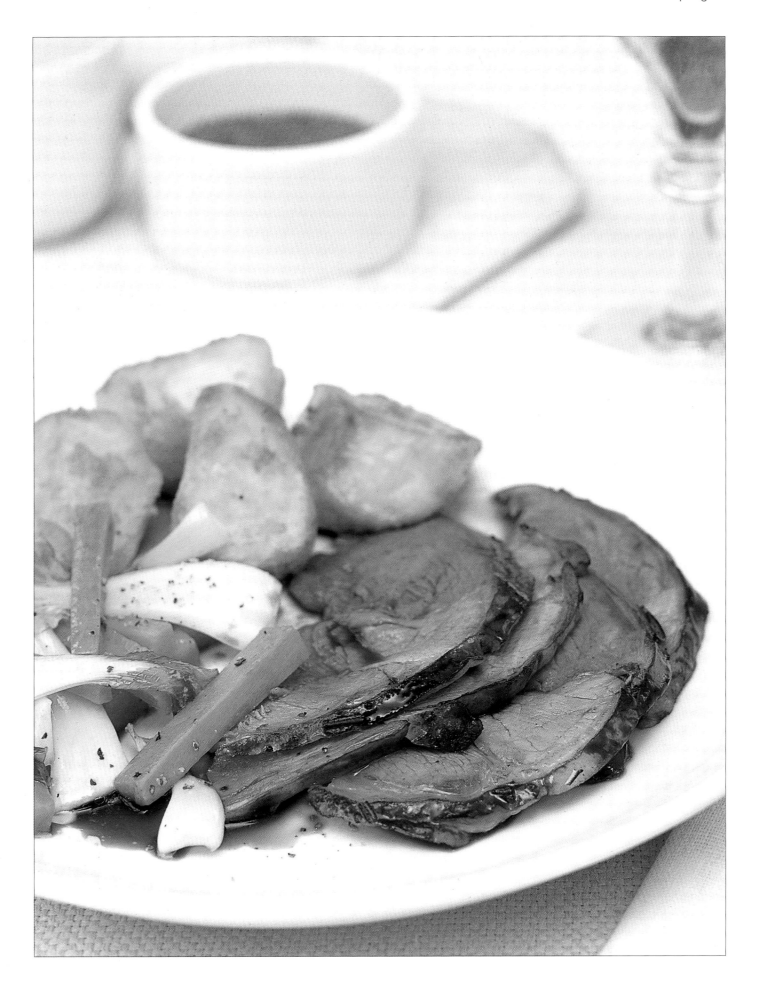

HERB-CRUSTED RACK of LAMB with PUY LENTILS

This lamb roast is quick and easy to prepare but looks impressive when served – it is the perfect choice when entertaining. Puy lentils are a favourite ingredient in the south of France. Their delicate flavour is the perfect complement to the rich meat.

SERVES FOUR

2 × 6-bone racks of lamb, chined
50g/2oz/1 cup fresh white or wholemeal (whole-wheat) breadcrumbs
2 large garlic cloves, crushed
90ml/6 tbsp chopped mixed fresh herbs, plus extra sprigs to garnish
50g/2oz/¼ cup butter, melted or 50ml/3½ tbsp olive oil
sea salt and ground black pepper
new potatoes, to serve

For the Puy lentils
1 red onion, chopped
30ml/2 tbsp olive oil
400g/14oz can Puy lentils, rinsed and drained
400g/14oz can chopped tomatoes
30ml/2 tbsp chopped fresh flat leaf parsley

1 Preheat the oven to 220°C/425°F/ Gas 7. Trim any excess fat from the lamb, and season with salt and pepper.

2 Mix together the breadcrumbs, garlic, herbs and butter or oil, and press on to the fat-sides of the lamb. Place in a roasting pan and roast for 25 minutes. Cover with foil; stand for 5 minutes before carving.

3 Cook the onion in the olive oil until softened. Add the lentils and tomatoes and cook gently for 5 minutes, or until the lentils are piping hot. Stir in the parsley and season to taste.

4 Cut each rack of lamb in half and serve with the lentils and new potatoes. Garnish with herb sprigs.

LAMB BURGERS with RED ONION and TOMATO RELISH

A sharp-sweet red onion relish works well with burgers based on Middle Eastern style lamb. Serve with pitta bread and tabbouleh for an authentic taste, though baked potatoes and a crisp green salad are also good.

SERVES FOUR

25g/1oz/3 tbsp bulgur wheat
500g/1¼lb lean minced (ground) lamb
1 small red onion, finely chopped
2 garlic cloves, finely chopped
1 green chilli, seeded and finely chopped
5ml/1 tsp ground toasted cumin seeds
2.5ml/½ tsp ground sumac (optional)
15g/½oz/¼ cup chopped fresh flat
    leaf parsley
30ml/2 tbsp chopped fresh mint
olive oil, for frying
sea salt and ground black pepper

For the relish
2 red (bell) peppers, halved and seeded
2 red onions, cut into 5mm/¼in thick slices
75–90ml/5–6 tbsp extra virgin olive oil
350g/12oz cherry tomatoes, chopped
½–1 fresh red or green chilli, seeded
    and finely chopped (optional)
30ml/2 tbsp chopped fresh mint
30ml/2 tbsp chopped fresh parsley
15ml/1 tbsp chopped fresh oregano
    or marjoram
2.5–5ml/½–1 tsp each ground toasted
    cumin seeds
2.5–5ml/½–1 tsp sumac (optional)
juice of ½ lemon
unrefined caster (superfine) sugar
    or rapadura, to taste

1 Pour 150ml/¼ pint/⅔ cup hot water over the bulgur wheat in a mixing bowl and leave to stand for 15 minutes, then drain the wheat in a sieve and squeeze out the excess moisture.

2 To make the relish, grill (broil) the peppers, skin side up, until the skin chars and blisters. Place in a bowl, cover and leave to stand for 10 minutes. Peel off the skin, dice the peppers finely and place in a bowl.

3 Brush the onions with 15ml/1 tbsp oil and grill for 5 minutes on each side, until browned. Leave to cool.

4 Place the bulgur in a bowl and add the minced lamb, onion, garlic, chilli, cumin, sumac, if using, parsley and mint. Mix the ingredients thoroughly together by hand, then season with 2.5ml/½ tsp salt and plenty of black pepper and mix again. Form the mixture into eight small burgers.

5 Chop the onions for the relish. Add with the tomatoes, chilli to taste, herbs and 2.5ml/½ tsp each of the cumin and sumac, if using, to the peppers. Stir in 60ml/4 tbsp of the remaining oil and 15ml/1 tbsp of the lemon juice. Season with salt, pepper and sugar and leave to stand for 20–30 minutes.

6 Heat a heavy frying pan over a high heat and grease lightly with olive oil. Cook the burgers for about 5–6 minutes on each side, or until just cooked at the centre.

7 While the burgers are cooking, taste the relish and adjust the seasoning, adding more pepper, sugar, oil, chilli, cumin, sumac, if using, and lemon juice to taste. Serve the burgers with the relish.

LAMB STEW with NEW POTATOES and SHALLOTS

This fresh lemon-seasoned stew is finished with an Italian mixture of chopped garlic, parsley and lemon rind known as gremolata, the traditional topping for osso bucco.

SERVES SIX

1kg/2¼lb boneless shoulder of lamb,
    trimmed of fat and cut into
    5cm/2in cubes
1 garlic clove, finely chopped
finely grated rind of ½ lemon and
    juice of 1 lemon
90ml/6 tbsp olive oil
45ml/3 tbsp wholemeal (whole-wheat) flour
1 large onion, sliced
5 anchovy fillets in olive oil, drained
2.5ml/½ tsp unrefined caster (superfine)
    sugar or rapadura
300ml/½ pint/1¼ cups fruity white wine
475ml/16fl oz/2 cups lamb stock or half
    stock and half water
1 fresh bay leaf
fresh rosemary sprig
fresh parsley sprig
500g/1¼lb small new potatoes
250g/9oz shallots, peeled but left whole
45ml/3 tbsp double (heavy) cream or
    soya cream (optional)
sea salt and ground black pepper

For the gremolata
1 garlic clove, finely chopped
finely shredded rind of ½ lemon
45ml/3 tbsp chopped fresh flat leaf parsley

1 Mix the lamb with the garlic and the rind and juice of ½ lemon in a non-metallic container. Season with pepper and mix in 15ml/1 tbsp olive oil, then leave to marinate in the refrigerator for 12–24 hours.

2 Drain the lamb carefully, reserving the marinade, and pat the lamb dry with kitchen paper. Preheat the oven to 180°C/350°F/Gas 4.

COOK'S TIP
A mezzaluna (double-handled, half-moon shaped, curved chopping blade) makes a very good job of chopping gremolata ingredients. If using a food processor or electric chopper, take care not to over-process the mixture as it is easy to mince the ingredients to a paste.

3 Heat 30ml/2 tbsp olive oil in a large, heavy frying pan. Season the flour with salt and pepper and toss the drained, dried lamb in it to coat it lightly, shaking off any excess flour. Add the lamb to the pan, in small batches, and seal it on all sides in the hot oil stirring constantly with a wooden spoon.

4 As each batch of lamb becomes brown, transfer it to an ovenproof pan or flame-proof casserole. You may need to add an extra 15ml/1 tbsp olive oil to the pan.

5 Reduce the heat, add another 15ml/1 tbsp oil to the pan and cook the sliced onion gently over a very low heat, stirring frequently, for 10 minutes until softened and golden but not browned. Add the drained anchovy fillets and the sugar, and cook, mashing the anchovies into the onion with a wooden spoon.

6 Add the reserved marinade, increase the heat a little and cook for 1–2 minutes, then pour in the fruity white wine and lamb stock or lamb stock and water, and bring to the boil. Simmer the sauce gently for about 5 minutes, then pour the sauce over the lamb in the pan or casserole.

7 Tie the bay leaf, rosemary and parsley together to make a bouquet garni and add to the lamb. Season the stew, then cover tightly and cook in the oven for 1 hour. Add the potatoes to the stew and stir well, then return the stew to the oven and cook for a further 20 minutes.

8 Meanwhile, to make the gremolata, chop the garlic, lemon rind and parsley together finely. Place in a dish, then cover and set aside.

9 Heat the remaining olive oil in a frying pan and brown the shallots on all sides, then stir them into the lamb stew. Cover and cook the stew for a further 30–40 minutes until the lamb is tender. Transfer the lamb and vegetables to a warmed serving dish and keep hot. Discard the bunch of herbs.

10 Boil the remaining cooking juices to reduce, then add the double cream or soya cream, if using, and simmer for 2–3 minutes. Adjust the seasoning, adding a little lemon juice to taste if liked. Pour this sauce over the lamb, scatter the gremolata mixture over the top and serve immediately.

SALMON FISH CAKES

The secret of a good fishcake is to make it with freshly prepared fish and potatoes, home-made breadcrumbs and plenty of fresh herbs, such as dill and parsley or tarragon. Serve simply with rocket leaves and lemon wedges.

SERVES FOUR

450g/1lb cooked salmon fillet
450g/1lb freshly cooked potatoes, mashed
25g/1oz/2 tbsp butter, melted or
   30ml/2 tbsp olive oil
10ml/2 tsp wholegrain mustard
15ml/1 tbsp each chopped fresh dill and
   chopped fresh parsley or tarragon
grated rind and juice of ½ lemon
15g/½oz/2 tbsp wholemeal
   (whole-wheat) flour
1 egg, lightly beaten
150g/5oz/2 cups dried breadcrumbs
60ml/4 tbsp sunflower oil
sea salt and ground black pepper
rocket (arugula) leaves and chives, to garnish
lemon wedges, to serve

1 Flake the cooked salmon, discarding any skin and bones. Put it in a bowl with the mashed potato, melted butter or oil and wholegrain mustard, and mix well. Stir in the herbs and the lemon rind and juice. Season to taste with plenty of sea salt and ground black pepper.

2 Divide the mixture into eight portions and shape each into a ball, then flatten into a thick disc. Dip the fish cakes first in flour, then in egg and finally in breadcrumbs, making sure that they are evenly coated with crumbs.

3 Heat the oil in a frying pan until it is very hot. Fry the fish cakes in batches until golden brown and crisp all over. As each batch is ready, drain on kitchen paper and keep hot. Garnish with rocket and chives and serve with lemon wedges.

COOK'S TIP
Any fresh white or hot-smoked fish is suitable. Always buy organically farmed fish, or sustainably caught wild fish.

FILLETS of SEA BREAM in FILO PASTRY

Any firm fish fillets can be used for this dish – bass, grouper and red mullet or snapper are particularly good – and, as the number of organic seawater fish farms grows, an increasing variety of breeds is becoming available. Each parcel is a meal in itself and can be prepared several hours in advance.

3 Thinly slice the potatoes lengthways. Brush a baking sheet with a little of the oil. Lay a sheet of filo pastry on the sheet, brush it with oil, then lay a second sheet crossways over the first. Repeat with two more pastry sheets. Arrange a quarter of the sliced potatoes in the centre, season and add a quarter of the shredded sorrel. Lay a bream fillet on top, skin-side up. Season.

4 Loosely fold the filo pastry up and over to make a neat parcel. Make three more parcels; place on the baking sheet. Brush with half the melted butter or oil. Bake for about 20 minutes until the filo is puffed up and golden brown.

SERVES FOUR

8 small waxy salad potatoes,
   preferably red-skinned
200g/7oz sorrel, stalks removed
30ml/2 tbsp olive oil
16 filo pastry sheets, thawed if frozen
4 sea bream fillets, about 175g/6oz each,
   scaled but not skinned
50g/2oz/¼ cup butter, melted or
   60ml/4 tbsp olive oil
120ml/4fl oz/½ cup fish stock
250ml/8fl oz/1 cup whipping cream
   or soya cream
sea salt and ground black pepper
finely diced red (bell) pepper and
   salad leaves, to garnish

VARIATION
Use small spinach leaves or baby chard in place of the sorrel.

1 Preheat the oven to 200°C/400°F/Gas 6. Cook the potatoes in a pan of lightly salted boiling water for about 20 minutes, or until just tender. Drain and leave to cool.

2 Set about half the sorrel leaves aside. Shred the remaining leaves by piling up six or eight at a time, rolling them up like a fat cigar and slicing them.

5 Meanwhile, make the sorrel sauce. Heat the remaining butter or oil in a pan, add the reserved sorrel and cook gently for 3 minutes, stirring, until it wilts. Stir in the stock and cream. Heat almost to boiling point, stirring so that the sorrel breaks down. Season to taste and keep hot until the fish parcels are ready. Serve garnished with red pepper and salad leaves. Hand round the sauce separately.

SEARED SCALLOPS with CHIVE SAUCE on LEEK and CARROT RICE

Scallops are one of the most delicious shellfish. Organically farmed scallops feed on naturally occurring plankton and are a healthy food whose cultivation has a low environmental impact.

SERVES FOUR

12–16 shelled scallops
45ml/3 tbsp olive oil
50g/2oz/⅓ cup wild rice
65g/2½oz/5 tbsp butter or
  75ml/5 tbsp olive oil
4 carrots, cut into long thin strips
2 leeks, cut into thick, diagonal slices
1 small onion, finely chopped
115g/4oz/⅔ cup long grain rice
1 fresh bay leaf
200ml/7fl oz/scant 1 cup white wine
450ml/¾ pint/scant 2 cups fish stock
60ml/4 tbsp double (heavy) cream or
  soya cream
a little lemon juice
25ml/1½ tbsp chopped fresh chives
30ml/2 tbsp chervil sprigs
sea salt and ground black pepper

1 Lightly season the shelled scallops, brush with 15ml/1 tbsp of the olive oil and set aside.

2 Cook the wild rice in a pan in plenty of boiling water for about 30 minutes or according to the packet instructions, until tender, then drain.

3 Heat half the butter or oil in a small frying pan and cook the carrot strips fairly gently for 4–5 minutes. Add the leek slices and fry for another 2 minutes. Season with sea salt and black pepper and add 30–45ml/2–3 tbsp water, then cover and cook the vegetables for a few minutes more. Uncover the pan and cook until the liquid has reduced. Set aside off the heat.

4 Melt half the remaining butter with 15ml/1 tbsp of the remaining oil in a heavy pan. Add the onion and fry for 3–4 minutes, until softened but not browned.

5 Add the long grain rice and bay leaf to the pan and cook, stirring constantly, until the rice looks translucent and the grains are coated with oil.

6 Pour in half the wine and half the stock. Season to taste with salt and bring to the boil. Stir, then cover and cook very gently for 15 minutes, or until the liquid is absorbed and the rice is cooked and tender.

7 Reheat the carrots and leeks gently, then stir them into the long grain rice with the wild rice. Taste and adjust the seasoning, if necessary.

8 Meanwhile, pour the remaining wine and stock into a small pan and boil it rapidly until reduced by half.

COOK'S TIP
Choose fresh rather than frozen scallops as the frozen ones tend to exude water on cooking. Have the pan very hot as scallops need only the briefest cooking at high heat – just until they turn opaque and brown on each side.

VARIATION
Use organic brown rice instead of the white long grain rice – it has a longer cooking time so check the packet for instructions.

9 Heat a heavy frying pan over a high heat. Add the remaining butter or oil. Add the scallops, and lightly sear them for 1–2 minutes on each side, then set aside and keep warm.

10 Pour the reduced stock and wine into the pan and heat until bubbling, then add the cream and boil until thickened. Season with lemon juice, sea salt and plenty of ground black pepper. Stir in the chopped chives and seared scallops.

11 Stir the chervil sprigs into the mixed rice and vegetables and pile it on to individual serving plates. Arrange the scallops on top and spoon the sauce over the rice. Serve immediately.

FROZEN CLEMENTINES

*These pretty, sorbet-filled fruits store well in the freezer, so make them well in advance
and they will be perfect for an impromptu dinner party. Organic citrus fruit has a matt
skin – evidence that they have not been coated with shiny anti-fungal wax.*

MAKES TWELVE

16 large clementines or small oranges
175g/6oz/scant 1 cup unrefined caster
 (superfine) sugar or rapadura
105ml/7 tbsp water
juice of 2 lemons
a little fresh orange juice (if necessary)
fresh mint leaves, to decorate

1 Carefully slice the tops off 12 of the clementines to make lids. Place the lids on a baking sheet. Loosen the clementine flesh with a sharp knife then carefully scoop it out into a mixing bowl, keeping the shells intact. Scrape out as much of the membrane from the shells as possible. Place the shells on the baking tray and place the tray in the freezer.

2 Put the sugar and water in a heavy pan and heat gently, stirring until the unrefined caster sugar or rapadura dissolves. Boil for 3 minutes without stirring, then leave the syrup to cool. Stir in the lemon juice.

3 Grate the rind from the remaining four clementines. Squeeze the fruits and add the juice and rind to the lemon syrup.

4 Process the clementine flesh in a food processor or blender, then press it through a sieve placed over a bowl to extract as much juice as possible. Add this to the syrup. You need about 900ml/ 1½ pints/3¾ cups of liquid. Make up to the required amount with fresh orange juice if necessary.

5 If making by hand, pour the mixture into a shallow plastic container and freeze for 3–4 hours, beating twice as the sorbet thickens to break up the ice crystals. If using an ice cream maker, churn the mixture until it holds its shape.

6 Gently pack the citrus sorbet into the clementine shells, mounding them up slightly in the centre. Position the lids on top and return the fruit to the freezer for several hours, or until the sorbet is frozen solid.

7 Transfer the frozen clementines to the refrigerator about 30 minutes before serving, to allow the sorbet to soften a little. Serve on individual plates and decorate with fresh mint leaves.

RHUBARB and GINGER ICE CREAM

The tangy combination of gently poached rhubarb and chopped ginger is blended with mascarpone to create this pretty blush-pink ice cream. Look for tender slim stalks of forced rhubarb in spring – it has a delicate pink colour and a delicious flavour.

SERVES FOUR TO SIX

5 pieces of preserved stem ginger
450g/1lb trimmed rhubarb, sliced
115g/4oz/generous ½ cup unrefined
    caster (superfine) sugar or rapadura
30ml/2 tbsp water
150g/5oz/⅔ cup mascarpone cheese
150ml/¼ pint/⅔ cup whipping cream
    or soya cream
wafer baskets, to serve (optional)

1 Using a sharp knife, roughly chop the preserved stem ginger and set it aside. Put the rhubarb slices into a pan and add the sugar and water. Bring to the boil, then cover and simmer for about 5 minutes until the rhubarb is just tender and still bright pink.

2 Tip the mixture into a food processor or blender, process until smooth, then leave to cool. Chill if time permits.

3 If making by hand, in a bowl, mix together the mascarpone, cream and stem ginger with the rhubarb purée. Pour the mixture into a plastic tub and freeze for 6 hours, or until firm, beating the mixture once or twice during the freezing time to break up the ice crystals.

COOK'S TIP

Rapadura is an alternative to refined sugar. It is made by sun-drying organic sugar cane juice and has a similar colour and texture to soft brown sugar, but has more flavour and is more nutritious.

4 If using an ice cream maker, churn the purée for 15–20 minutes until it is thick. Put the mascarpone into a bowl, soften it with a wooden spoon, then beat in the cream. Add the stem ginger, then churn in the ice cream maker until firm. Serve scoops of the ice cream in bowls or wafer baskets.

BANANA and APRICOT CARAMEL TRIFLE

Organic bananas are an excellent source of potassium and very good for the digestion – making this an irresistible dessert for a special occasion. Ginger cake makes an ideal base, adding sharpness to the creamy flavours.

SERVES SIX TO EIGHT

300ml/½ pint/1¼ cups milk or
    soya milk
1 vanilla pod (bean), or 4–5 drops
    vanilla essence (extract)
45ml/3 tbsp unrefined caster (superfine)
    sugar or rapadura
20ml/4 tsp cornflour (cornstarch)
3 egg yolks
60ml/4 tbsp apricot conserve (jam)
175–225g/6–8oz ginger cake, cubed
3 bananas, sliced, with one reserved
    for topping
115g/4oz/generous ½ cup granulated sugar
    or rapadura
300ml/½ pint/1¼ cups double (heavy)
    cream or soya cream
a few drops of lemon juice

1 Pour the milk into a small pan. Carefully split the vanilla pod (if using) down the middle and scrape the tiny seeds into the pan.

2 Add the vanilla pod, or vanilla essence, to the milk and bring just to the boil, then remove the pan from the heat and set aside. When the milk has cooled slightly, remove the vanilla pod.

VARIATION
For an adult-only version of this trifle, substitute a plainer sponge cake for the ginger cake and moisten the sponge with a little apricot brandy and a small glass of sweet dessert wine in step 6.

3 Whisk together the sugar, cornflour and eggs until pale and creamy. Whisk in the milk and return the mixture to the pan. Heat to simmering point, stirring all the time, and cook gently over a low heat until the custard coats the back of a wooden spoon thickly.

4 Leave to cool, covered tightly with clear film (plastic wrap). Ensure the clear film is pressed against the surface of the custard to prevent a skin forming.

5 Put the apricot conserve and 60ml/ 4 tbsp water in a pan and heat gently for 2–3 minutes, stirring.

COOK'S TIP
Use whatever type of cake you prefer in the base of the trifle. Leftover Madeira cake, with its tangy citrus flavour, makes a perfect choice. Choose a jam or conserve with flavours that complement those of your chosen cake: strawberry and raspberry conserve are good with lemon cake, or try peach conserve with a chocolate sponge.

6 Put the cubed cake in a deep serving bowl or dish and pour on the apricot preserve. Cover with sliced bananas, then the custard. Chill for 1–2 hours.

7 Melt the sugar in a small pan with 60ml/4 tbsp water and, when it has dissolved, cook until it is just turning golden. Immediately pour on to a sheet of foil and leave to harden, then break the caramel into pieces.

8 Whip the cream until it forms soft peaks and spread it evenly over the custard. Chill the trifle for 2–3 hours, then top with the remaining sliced banana, dipped into lemon juice, and the cracked caramel pieces.

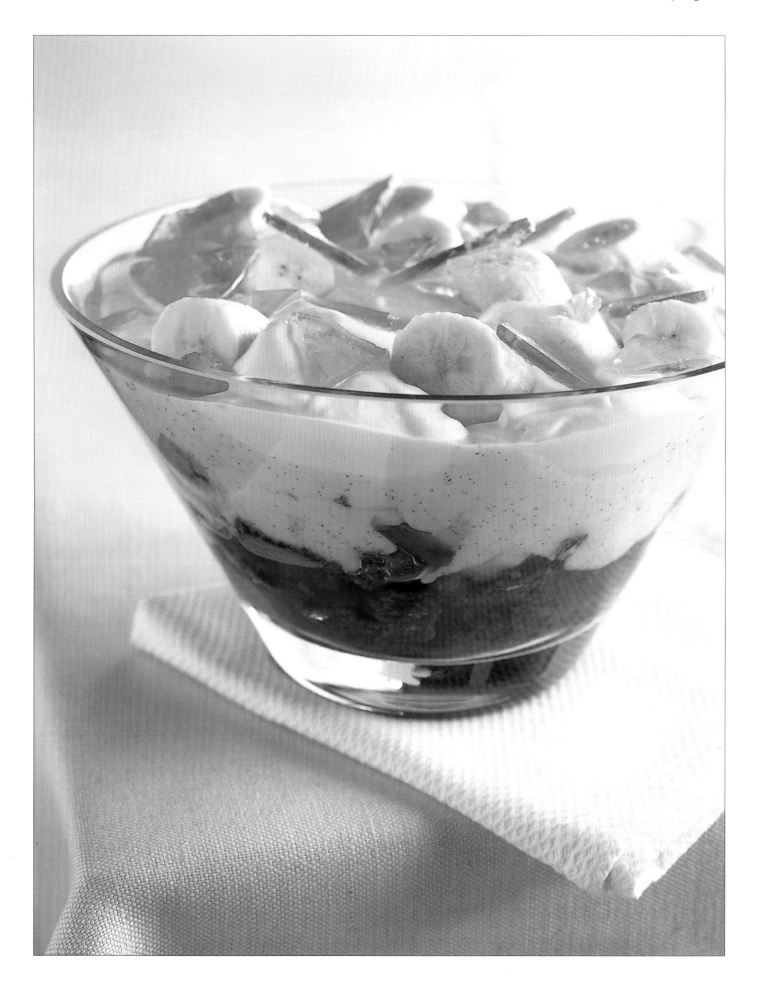

CITRUS and CARAMEL CUSTARDS

Make these Spanish-style custards with organic milk as it is the only type of milk guaranteed to be free of GMOs and excess added antibiotics and hormones. Wonderfully smooth, the custards are delicately scented with tangy citrus flavours and aromatic cinnamon.

2 Preheat the oven to 160°C/325°F/ Gas 3. Whisk the egg yolks, cornflour and sugar together. Remove the rinds and cinnamon from the hot milk and cream and discard. Whisk the hot milk and cream into the egg yolk mixture.

3 Add the grated citrus rind to the custard mixture and stir through. Pour into four individual dishes, each 13cm/ 5in in diameter. Place in a roasting pan and pour warm water into the pan to reach three-quarters of the way up the sides. Bake for 25 minutes, or until the custards are just set. Remove the dishes from the water; leave to cool, then chill.

4 Preheat the grill (broiler) to high. Sprinkle the custards liberally with icing sugar and place under the grill until the tops turn golden brown and caramelize.

COOK'S TIPS
• Prepare the grated rind first, then cut a few strips of rind from the ungrated side using a swivel-bladed vegetable peeler.
• You can use a special cook's blowtorch or salamander to caramelize the tops instead of grilling (broiling) them.

SERVES FOUR

450ml/¾ pint/scant 2 cups milk or soya milk
150ml/¼ pint/⅔ cup single (light) cream
    or soya cream
1 cinnamon stick, broken in half
thinly pared rind of ½ lemon
thinly pared rind of ½ orange
4 egg yolks
5ml/1 tsp cornflour (cornstarch)
40g/1½oz/3 tbsp unrefined caster
    (superfine) sugar or rapadura
grated rind of ½ lemon
grated rind of ½ orange
unrefined icing (confectioner's) sugar,
    to dust

1 Place the milk and cream in a pan. Add the cinnamon stick halves and the strips of pared lemon and orange rind. Bring to the boil, then reduce the heat and simmer for 10 minutes.

RICOTTA CHEESECAKE

This Sicilian-style cheesecake makes good use of ricotta's firm texture. Here, the cheese is enriched with eggs and cream and enlivened with the unwaxed grated rind of organic orange and lemon producing an irresistible, tangy dessert cheesecake filling.

SERVES EIGHT

450g/1lb/2 cups ricotta cheese
120ml/4fl oz/½ cup double (heavy) cream
 or soya cream
2 eggs
1 egg yolk
75g/3oz/6 tbsp unrefined caster (superfine)
 sugar or rapadura
finely grated rind of 1 orange and 1 lemon,
 plus extra to decorate

For the pastry
175g/6oz/1½ cups plain (all-purpose) flour
45ml/3 tbsp unrefined caster (superfine)
 sugar or rapadura
115g/4oz/½ cup chilled butter, diced
1 egg yolk

1 To make the pastry, sift the flour and sugar on to a cold work surface. Make a well in the centre and add the butter and egg yolk. Work the flour into the butter and egg yolk.

2 Gather the dough together, reserve a quarter of it and press the rest into a 23cm/9in fluted flan tin (quiche pan) with a removable base, and chill.

3 Preheat the oven to 190°C/375°F/ Gas 5. Put the cheese, cream, eggs and egg yolk, sugar and citrus rinds in a large bowl and beat well.

4 Prick the bottom of the pastry case, then line with foil and fill with baking beans. Bake for 15 minutes, transfer to a wire rack, remove the foil and beans and allow the pastry to cool in the tin.

5 Spoon the cheese and cream filling into the pastry case and level the surface. Roll out the reserved dough and cut into long, even strips. Arrange the strips on the top of the filling in a lattice pattern, sticking them in place with water.

6 Bake the cheesecake for 30–35 minutes until golden and set. Transfer to a wire rack and leave to cool, then carefully remove the side of the tin. Use a palette knife (metal spatula) to transfer the tart to a serving plate. Decorate with citrus rind before serving.

VARIATIONS
• Add 50g/2oz/⅓ cup plain chocolate chips to the filling in step 3.
• Scatter 75g/3oz sultanas (golden raisins) into the pastry case before adding the filling.

RHUBARB MERINGUE PIE

The sharp tang of tender forced rhubarb with its sweet meringue topping will really tantalize the taste buds. This pudding is delicious hot or cold with cream or vanilla ice cream.

SERVES SIX

200g/7oz/1¾ cups plain (all-purpose) flour, plus extra for flouring
25g/1oz/¼ cup ground walnuts
115g/4oz/½ cup chilled butter or non-hydrogenated magarine, diced
275g/10oz/generous 1½ cups unrefined caster (superfine) sugar or rapadura
4 egg yolks
675g/1½lb rhubarb, cut into small pieces
grated rind and juice of 3 oranges
75ml/5 tbsp cornflour (cornstarch)
3 egg whites
whipped cream or soya cream, to serve

1 Sift the flour into a bowl and add the ground walnuts. Rub in the butter until the mixture resembles fine breadcrumbs. Stir in 30ml/2 tbsp of the sugar with 1 egg yolk beaten with 15ml/1 tbsp water. Mix to a firm dough. Turn out on to a floured surface and knead. Wrap in a plastic bag and chill for 30 minutes.

2 Preheat the oven to 190°C/375°F/ Gas 5. Roll out the pastry on a floured surface and use to line a 23cm/9in fluted flan tin (quiche pan). Prick the base with a fork. Line with foil and fill with baking beans. Bake for 15 minutes.

3 Put the rhubarb, 75g/3oz/6 tbsp of the remaining sugar and the orange rind in a pan. Cover and cook gently until the rhubarb is tender.

4 Remove the foil and beans from the pastry case, then brush with a little of the remaining egg yolk. Bake for 10–15 minutes until the pastry is crisp.

5 Blend together the cornflour and the orange juice in a small bowl. Remove from the heat, stir the cornflour mixture into the cooked rhubarb, then bring back to the boil, stirring constantly until thickened. Cook for a further 1–2 minutes. Allow the mixture to cool slightly, then beat in the remaining egg yolks. Pour into the cooked pastry case, spreading it evenly.

6 Whisk the egg whites in a large mixing bowl until they form soft peaks, then gradually whisk in the remaining sugar, 15ml/1 tbsp at a time, whisking well after each addition.

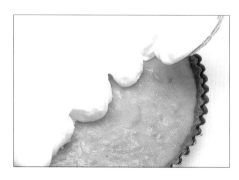

7 Spoon the meringue over the filling to cover completely. Bake for 25 minutes until golden. Serve warm, or leave to cool for about 30 minutes and serve with whipped cream.

TUSCAN CITRUS SPONGE

*This tangy cake comes from the little Tuscan town of Pitigliano. It is a light and airy
whisked sponge made with matzo and potato flours rather than traditional wheat flour.*

SERVES SIX TO EIGHT

12 eggs, separated
300g/11oz/1½ cups unrefined caster
   (superfine) sugar or rapadura
120ml/4fl oz/½ cup fresh orange juice
grated rind of 1 orange
grated rind of 1 lemon
50g/2oz/½ cup potato flour, sifted
90g/3½oz/¾ cup fine matzo meal or
   matzo meal flour, sifted
unrefined icing (confectioner's) sugar,
   for dusting
orange juice and segments of orange,
   to serve

1 Preheat the oven to 160°C/325°F/
Gas 3. Whisk the egg yolks until pale
and frothy, then whisk in the sugar,
orange juice, orange rind and lemon rind.

2 Fold the sifted flours or flour and
meal into the egg and sugar mixture. In
a clean bowl, whisk the egg whites until
stiff, then fold into the egg yolk mixture.

VARIATION
Omit the lemon and replace the orange
with two blood oranges for a really
fruity flavour.

3 Pour the cake mixture into a deep,
ungreased 25cm/10in cake tin (pan) and
bake for about 1 hour, or until a cocktail
stick (toothpick), inserted in the centre,
comes out clean. Leave to cool in the tin.

4 When cold, turn out the cake and
invert on to a serving plate. Dust with
a little icing sugar and serve in wedges
with orange segments, moistened with a
little fresh orange juice.

COOK'S TIPS
• When testing to see if the cake is
cooked, if you don't have a cocktail stick to
hand, use a strand of raw dried spaghetti
instead — it will work just as well.
• If you cannot find organic matzo meal,
try fine polenta instead.

RUSSIAN POPPY SEED CAKE

This plain and simple cake is based on my mother's recipe. Flavoured with lemon and vanilla, and studded with tiny black organic poppy seeds, it has a nutty, distinctive taste that is utterly delicious.

SERVES ABOUT EIGHT

130g/4½oz/generous 1 cup self-raising
   (self-rising) flour
5ml/1 tsp baking powder
2 eggs
225g/8oz/generous 1 cup unrefined caster
   (superfine) sugar or rapadura
5–10ml/1–2 tsp vanilla essence (extract)
200g/7oz/scant 1½ cups poppy
   seeds, ground
15ml/1 tbsp grated lemon rind
120ml/4fl oz/½ cup milk or soya milk
130g/4½oz/generous ½ cup unsalted
   (sweet) butter or non-hydrogenated
   margarine, melted and cooled
30ml/2 tbsp sunflower oil
unrefined icing (confectioners') sugar,
   sifted, for dusting
whipped cream or soya cream, to serve

1 Preheat the oven to 180°C/350°F/ Gas 4. Grease a deep 23cm/9in round springform cake tin (pan). Sift together the flour and baking powder.

2 Using an electric whisk, beat together the eggs, sugar and vanilla essence for 4–5 minutes until pale and fluffy. Stir in the poppy seeds and the lemon rind.

VARIATION
To make a poppy seed tart, pour the cake mixture into a par-cooked pastry crust, then bake for 30 minutes, or until the filling is firm and risen.

3 Gently fold the sifted ingredients into the egg and poppy seed mixture, in three batches, alternating with the milk, then fold in the melted butter or margarine and sunflower oil.

4 Pour the mixture into the tin and bake for 40 minutes, or until firm. Cool in the tin for 15 minutes, then invert on to a wire rack. Leave until cold, dust with icing sugar and serve with cream.

DOUBLE-GINGER CAKE

Preserved stem ginger and organic root ginger, which is smaller and has a more intense flavour than the non-organic variety, are used in this tasty tea bread.

SERVES EIGHT TO TEN

3 eggs
225g/8oz/generous I cup unrefined caster
    (superfine) sugar or rapadura
250ml/8fl oz/I cup sunflower oil
5ml/I tsp vanilla essence (extract)
I5ml/I tbsp syrup from a jar of preserved
    stem ginger
225g/8oz courgettes (zucchini), grated
2.5cm/I in piece fresh root ginger, peeled
    and finely grated
350g/I2oz/3 cups unbleached plain
    (all-purpose) flour
5ml/I tsp baking powder
5ml/I tsp ground cinnamon
2 pieces preserved stem ginger, drained
    and finely chopped
I5ml/I tbsp unrefined demerara (raw)
    sugar or rapadura
butter, to serve (optional)

I Preheat the oven to 190°C/375°F/ Gas 5. Beat together the eggs and sugar until light and fluffy. Slowly beat in the oil until the mixture forms a batter. Mix in the vanilla essence and ginger syrup, then stir in the grated courgettes and fresh ginger.

2 Sift together the flour and baking powder into a large bowl. Add the cinnamon and mix well, then stir the dried ingredients into the courgette mixture.

COOK'S TIP
There is no need to peel fresh organic root ginger. Special bamboo graters can be found in many Asian stores, but a simple box grater will do the job equally well.

3 Lightly grease a 900g/2lb loaf tin (pan) and pour in the courgette mixture, making sure it fills the corners. Smooth and level the top.

4 Mix together the chopped stem ginger and demerara sugar in a small bowl, then sprinkle the mixture evenly over the surface of the courgette mixture.

5 Bake for I hour, or until a skewer comes out clean when inserted into the centre. Leave the cake to cool in the tin (pan) for 20 minutes, then turn out on to a wire rack and leave to cool completely. Serve in slices with butter, if you like.

SUMMER

The abundance of fresh produce at this time of year makes summer a wonderful time for any cook. With hot, sunny days and long, balmy evenings for picnics and barbecues, summer eating is a sheer delight. Chilled dishes are easy to prepare in advance: choose the classic Vichyssoise or the popular Japanese dish, Cold Somen Noodles. Or take your pick from the wide selection of colourful salads, including Tabbouleh and Country Pasta Salad, to make the most of the dazzling array of organic fruit and vegetables available now. If you fancy cooking outside, try barbecueing Marinated Beef with Onion Rings, and accompany them with organic bread and a green salad for a simple meal. With a wide selection of mouthwatering juicy fruits in season, summer desserts really are special. Try a refreshing Watermelon Granita or, if you want something really indulgent, Coffee Crêpes with Peaches and Cream, or Blueberry Frangipane Flan. Summer is also the beginning of the preserving season and you just can't beat home-made strawberry jam served with freshly baked scones and cream – delicious!

VICHYSSOISE

This classic, chilled summer soup is based on the flavourful combination of leeks and potatoes, made luxuriously velvety by adding dairy or soya cream.

SERVES FOUR TO SIX

50g/2oz/¼ cup unsalted (sweet) butter or
    50ml/3½ tbsp olive oil
450g/1lb leeks, white parts only, sliced
3 large shallots, sliced
250g/9oz floury potatoes (such as
    Maris Piper), peeled and cut
    into chunks
1 litre/1¾ pints/4 cups light chicken stock
    or water
300ml/½ pint/1¼ cups double (heavy)
    cream or soya cream
a little lemon juice (optional)
sea salt and ground black pepper
fresh chives, to garnish

1 Heat the butter or oil in a heavy pan. Add the leeks and shallots and cook gently, covered, for 15–20 minutes, stirring once or twice, until soft but not browned.

2 Add the potato chunks to the pan and cook, uncovered, for a few minutes, stirring occasionally.

3 Stir in the light chicken stock or water, 5ml/1 tsp sea salt and ground pepper to taste. Bring to the boil, then reduce the heat and partly cover the pan. Simmer for 15 minutes, or until the potatoes are soft.

4 Cool, then process the soup until smooth in a food processor or blender. Pour the soup into a bowl and stir in the cream. Season to taste.

5 Chill the soup for at least 4 hours or until very cold. Taste the chilled soup for seasoning and add a squeeze of lemon juice, if required. Pour the soup into bowls and garnish with chives.

COLD SOMEN NOODLES

At the height of summer, cold somen noodles served immersed in ice cold water
and accompanied by sauces and relishes make a refreshing and exotic meal.

SERVES FOUR

300g/11oz dried somen or soba noodles

For the dipping sauce
105ml/7 tbsp mirin
2.5ml/½ tsp sea salt
105ml/7 tbsp shoyu
20g/¾oz kezuri-bushi
400ml/14fl oz/1⅔ cups water

For the relishes
2 spring onions (scallions), trimmed and
    finely chopped
2.5cm/1in fresh root ginger, peeled and
    finely grated
2 shiso or basil leaves, finely
    chopped (optional)
30ml/2 tbsp toasted sesame seeds

For the garnishes
10cm/4in cucumber
5ml/1 tsp sea salt
ice cubes or a block of ice
ice-cold water
115g/4oz cooked, peeled small
    prawns (shrimp)
orchid flowers or nasturtium flowers
    and leaves (optional)

1 To make the dipping sauce, put the mirin in a pan and bring to the boil to evaporate the alcohol. Add the salt and shoyu and shake the pan gently to mix. Add the kezuri-bushi and mix with the liquid. Add the water to the pan and bring to the boil. Cook over a vigorous heat for 3 minutes without stirring. Remove from the heat and strain through a muslin bag. Leave to cool, then chill for at least an hour.

2 Prepare the cucumber garnish. If the cucumber is bigger than 4cm/1½in in diameter, cut in half and scoop out the seeds, then slice thinly. For a smaller cucumber, first cut into 5cm/2in lengths, then use a vegetable peeler to remove the seeds and make a hole in the centre. Slice thinly. Sprinkle with the salt and leave in a sieve for 20 minutes, then rinse in cold water and drain.

3 Bring at least 1.5 litres/2½ pints/ 6¼ cups water to the boil in a large pan. Meanwhile, untie the bundle of somen. Have 75ml/2½fl oz/⅓ cup cold water to hand. Somen only take 2 minutes to cook. Put the somen in the rapidly boiling water. When it foams again, pour the glass of water in. When the water boils again, the somen are ready. Drain into a colander. Rinse under cold running water, and rub the somen with your hands to remove the starch. Drain well.

4 Put some ice cubes or a block of ice in the centre of a chilled, large glass bowl, and add the somen. Gently pour on enough ice-cold water to cover the somen, then arrange cucumber slices, prawns and flowers, if using, on top.

5 Prepare all the relishes separately in small dishes or small sake cups.

6 Divide approximately one-third of the dipping sauce among four small cups. Put the remaining sauce in a jug (pitcher) or gravy boat.

7 Serve the noodles cold with the relishes. The guests are invited to put any combination of relishes into their dipping-sauce cup. Hold the cup over the somen bowl, pick up a mouthful of somen, then dip them into the sauce and eat. Add more dipping sauce from the jug and more relishes as required.

PROVENÇAL AIOLI with SMOKED HADDOCK

This substantial salad is a meal on its own and perfect for summer entertaining. Choose organic vegetables and vary them according to what is in season as the summer progresses.

SERVES SIX

1kg/2¼lb smoked haddock
bouquet garni
18 small new potatoes, scrubbed
1 large or 2 small fresh mint sprigs, torn
225g/8oz French (green) beans, trimmed
225g/8oz broccoli florets
6 eggs, hard-boiled
12 baby carrots, with leaves if possible, scrubbed
1 large red (bell) pepper, seeded and cut into strips
2 fennel bulbs, cut into strips
18 red or yellow cherry tomatoes
sea salt
6 large whole cooked prawns (shrimp) or langoustines, in the shell, to garnish (optional)

For the aioli
600ml/1 pint/2½ cups home-made or good-quality bought mayonnaise
2 fat garlic cloves (or more if you prefer), crushed
cayenne pepper

1 Put the smoked haddock into a sauté pan and pour in enough water to barely cover the fish. Add the bouquet garni. Bring the water to the boil, then cover and poach very gently for about 10 minutes until the fish flakes quite easily when tested with the tip of a sharp knife. Drain the fish, discard the bouquet garni and set aside until required.

2 Cook the potatoes with the mint in a pan of lightly salted boiling water until just tender. Drain and set aside.

3 Cook the beans and broccoli in separate pans of lightly salted boiling water for about 5 minutes. They should still be very crisp. Refresh the vegetables under cold water and drain again, then set aside.

4 Remove the skin from the haddock and break the flesh into large flakes. Shell the eggs and halve them lengthways.

5 Pile the haddock in the middle of a large serving platter and arrange the eggs and all the vegetables round the edges or randomly. Garnish with the prawns or langoustines if you are using them.

6 To make the aioli, put the mayonnaise in a bowl and stir in the crushed garlic and cayenne pepper to taste. Serve in individual bowls or one large bowl to hand round.

GRILLED SKEWERED CHICKEN

Organic chicken has a superb flavour and these fabulous little skewers make great finger food. Cook on the barbecue or grill and serve sizzling hot.

SERVES FOUR

8 chicken thighs with skin, boned
8 large, thick spring onions (scallions),
    trimmed
oil, for greasing
lemon wedges, to serve

For the yakitori sauce
60ml/4 tbsp sake
75ml/5 tbsp shoyu
15ml/1 tbsp mirin
15ml/1 tbsp unrefined caster (superfine)
    sugar or rapadura

1 First, make the *yakitori* sauce. Mix all the ingredients together in a small pan. Bring to the boil, then reduce the heat and simmer for 10 minutes.

2 Cut the chicken into 2.5cm/1in cubes. Cut the spring onions into 2.5cm/1in long sticks.

3 To cook the chicken on a barbecue, soak eight bamboo skewers overnight in water. This prevents the skewers from burning during cooking. Prepare the barbecue. Thread about four pieces of chicken and three spring onion pieces on to each of the skewers. Place the *yakitori* sauce in a small bowl and have a brush ready.

4 Cook the skewered chicken on the barbecue. Keep the skewer handles away from the fire, turning them frequently. Brush the chicken with sauce. Return to the coals and repeat this process twice more until the chicken is well cooked.

5 Alternatively, to grill (broil), preheat the grill (broiler) to high. Oil the wire rack and spread out the chicken cubes on it. Grill both sides of the chicken until the juices drip, then dip the pieces in the sauce and put back on the rack. Grill for 30 seconds on each side, repeating the dipping process twice more.

6 Set aside and keep warm. Gently grill the spring onions until soft and slightly brown outside. Do not dip. Thread the chicken and spring onion pieces on to skewers as above.

7 Arrange the skewered chicken and spring onions on a serving platter and serve accompanied by lemon wedges.

COURGETTE FRITTERS with PISTOU

A wide variety of different organic courgettes are available, ranging in colour from pale yellow to deep green. The pistou sauce, made with fresh basil, provides a lovely contrast in flavour, but you could substitute other sauces, such as a tomato and garlic one or a herb dressing.

SERVES FOUR

450g/1lb courgettes (zucchini), grated
75g/3oz/⅔ cup plain (all-purpose) or
    wholemeal (whole-wheat) flour
1 egg, separated
15ml/1 tbsp olive oil
oil for shallow frying
sea salt and ground black pepper

For the pistou sauce
15g/½oz/½ cup basil leaves
4 garlic cloves, crushed
90g/3½oz/1 cup finely grated
    Parmesan cheese or premium
    Italian-style vegetarian cheese
finely grated rind of 1 lemon
150ml/¼ pint/⅔ cup olive oil

1 To make the pistou sauce, crush the basil leaves and garlic in a mortar with a pestle to make a fine paste. Transfer the paste to a bowl and stir in the grated cheese and lemon rind. Gradually blend in the oil, a little at a time, until combined, then transfer to a serving dish.

2 To make the fritters, put the grated courgettes in a sieve over a bowl and sprinkle with plenty of salt. Leave for 1 hour then rinse thoroughly. Dry well on kitchen paper.

3 Sift the flour into a bowl and make a well in the centre, then add the egg yolk and oil. Measure 75ml/5 tbsp water and add a little to the bowl.

4 Whisk the egg yolk and oil, gradually incorporating the flour and water to make a smooth batter. Season and set aside for 30 minutes.

5 Stir the grated, rinsed courgettes into the batter. Whisk the egg white until stiff, then fold into the batter.

6 Heat 1cm/½in of oil in a frying pan. Add dessertspoons of batter to the oil and fry for about 2 minutes until golden brown and crispy. Remove from the pan, using a slotted spoon. Place the fritters on kitchen paper and keep warm while frying the rest. Serve the hot fritters with the pistou sauce.

GRILLED AUBERGINE PARCELS

This is a great organic recipe – little Italian bundles of tomatoes, mozzarella cheese and basil, wrapped in slices of aubergine. The parcels are naturally low in saturated fat, sugar and salt but are indulgent and delicious, too.

SERVES FOUR

2 large, long aubergines (eggplant)
225g/8oz buffalo mozzarella cheese
2 plum tomatoes
16 large basil leaves
30ml/2 tbsp olive oil
sea salt and ground black pepper

For the dressing
60ml/4 tbsp olive oil
5ml/1 tsp balsamic vinegar
15ml/1 tbsp sun-dried tomato purée (paste)
15ml/1 tbsp lemon juice

For the garnish
30ml/2 tbsp toasted pine nuts
torn basil leaves

1 Remove the stalks from the aubergines and then cut the aubergines lengthways into thin, even slices – the aim is to get 16 slices in total (each about 5mm/¼in thick), disregarding the first and last slices.

2 Bring a large pan of water to the boil and cook the aubergine slices for 2 minutes. Drain, then dry on kitchen paper.

3 Cut the mozzarella cheese into eight slices. Cut each tomato into eight slices, not counting the first and last slices.

4 Take two aubergine slices and place on a flameproof tray, in a cross. Place a slice of tomato in the centre, season lightly, add a basil leaf, then a slice of mozzarella, another basil leaf, a slice of tomato and more seasoning.

5 Fold the ends of the aubergine slices around the mozzarella and tomato filling to make a parcel. Repeat with the rest of the ingredients to make eight parcels. Chill the parcels for 20 minutes.

6 To make the tomato dressing, whisk together all the ingredients and season to taste with salt and pepper.

7 Preheat the grill (broiler). Brush the parcels with oil and cook for 5 minutes on each side. Serve hot, with the dressing, sprinkled with pine nuts and basil.

TABBOULEH

This is a wonderfully refreshing, tangy salad of soaked bulgur wheat and masses of fresh organic mint and parsley. Increase the amount of fresh herbs for a greener salad.

SERVES FOUR TO SIX

250g/9oz/1½ cups bulgur wheat
1 large bunch spring onions (scallions),
    thinly sliced
1 cucumber, finely chopped or diced
3 tomatoes, chopped
1.5–2.5ml/¼–½ tsp ground cumin
1 large bunch fresh flat leaf
    parsley, chopped
1 large bunch fresh mint, chopped
juice of 2 lemons, or to taste
60ml/4 tbsp extra virgin olive oil
cos or romaine lettuce leaves
olives, lemon wedges, tomato wedges,
    cucumber slices and mint sprigs,
    to garnish (optional)
natural (plain) yogurt, to serve (optional)

1 Pick over the bulgur wheat to remove any dirt. Place it in a bowl, cover with cold water and leave to soak for about 30 minutes. Tip the bulgur wheat into a sieve and drain well, shaking to remove any excess water, then return it to the bowl.

2 Add the spring onions to the bulgur wheat, then mix and squeeze together with your hands to combine.

3 Add the cucumber, tomatoes, cumin, parsley, mint, lemon juice and oil to the bulgur wheat and toss well.

4 Heap the tabbouleh on to a bed of lettuce leaves and garnish with olives, lemon wedges, tomato, cucumber and mint sprigs, if you like. Serve with a bowl of natural yogurt, if you like.

VARIATION
Use couscous soaked in boiling water in place of the bulgur wheat and use fresh coriander (cilantro) instead of parsley.

TOMATO and MOZZARELLA SALAD

Sweet naturally ripened organic tomatoes and fresh basil capture the essence of summer in this simple salad. Choose plum or beefsteak tomatoes for this dish.

SERVES FOUR

5 ripe tomatoes
2 × 225g/8oz buffalo mozzarella cheeses, drained and sliced
1 small red onion, chopped

For the dressing
½ small garlic clove, peeled
15g/½oz/½ cup fresh basil leaves
30ml/2 tbsp chopped fresh flat leaf parsley
25ml/1½ tbsp small salted capers, rinsed
2.5ml/½ tsp mustard
75–90ml/5–6 tbsp extra virgin olive oil
5–10ml/1–2 tsp balsamic vinegar
ground black pepper

For the garnish
fresh basil leaves
fresh parsley sprigs

1 First make the dressing. Put the garlic, basil, parsley, half the capers and the mustard in a food processor or blender and process briefly to chop. Then, with the motor running, gradually pour in the olive oil through the feeder tube to make a smooth purée with a dressing consistency. Add the balsamic vinegar to taste and season with plenty of ground black pepper.

2 Slice the tomatoes. Arrange the tomato and mozzarella slices on a plate. Scatter the onion over and season with a little ground black pepper.

3 Drizzle the dressing over the salad, then scatter a few basil leaves, parsley sprigs and the remaining capers on top as a garnish. Leave for 10–15 minutes before serving.

SUMMER SALAD

*Ripe organic tomatoes, mozzarella and olives make a good base for a fresh and tangy
pasta salad that is perfect for a light summer lunch.*

SERVES FOUR

350g/12oz/3 cups dried penne
150g/5oz packet buffalo mozzarella,
    drained and diced
3 ripe tomatoes, diced
10 pitted black olives, sliced
10 pitted green olives, sliced
1 spring onion (scallion), thinly sliced on
    the diagonal
1 handful fresh basil leaves

For the dressing
90ml/6 tbsp extra virgin olive oil
15ml/1 tbsp balsamic vinegar or
    lemon juice
sea salt and ground black pepper

COOK'S TIP
Mozzarella made from buffalo milk
has more flavour than the type made
with cow's milk. Look for *mozzarella de
buffalo* in your organic store.

1 Cook the pasta for 10–12 minutes,
or according to the instructions on the
packet. Tip it into a colander and rinse
briefly under cold running water, then
shake the colander to remove as much
water as possible and leave to drain.

VARIATION
Make the salad more substantial by adding
sliced peppers, flaked tuna, anchovy fillets
or diced ham. Always choose sustainably
caught tuna and anchovies.

2 Make the dressing. Whisk the olive oil
and balsamic vinegar or lemon juice in a
jug (pitcher) with a little salt and pepper
to taste.

3 Place the pasta, mozzarella, tomatoes,
olives and spring onion in a large bowl,
pour the dressing over and toss together
well. Taste for seasoning before serving,
sprinkled with basil leaves.

COUNTRY PASTA SALAD

*Colourful, tasty and nutritious, this is the ideal pasta salad for a summer picnic. A variety
of organic pasta is available – any medium-size shapes are suitable for this salad.*

SERVES SIX

300g/11oz/2¾ cups dried fusilli
150g/5oz fine green beans,
    trimmed and cut into
    5cm/2in lengths
1 potato, about 150g/5oz, diced
200g/7oz cherry tomatoes, halved
2 spring onions (scallions),
    finely chopped
90g/3½oz/scant 1¼ cups Parmesan
    cheese or premium Italian-style
    vegetarian cheese, coarsely shaved
6–8 pitted black olives, cut into rings
15–30ml/1–2 tbsp capers, to taste

For the dressing
90ml/6 tbsp extra virgin olive oil
15ml/1 tbsp balsamic vinegar
15ml/1 tbsp chopped fresh flat leaf parsley
sea salt and ground black pepper

1 Cook the pasta according to the
instructions on the packet. Drain it into
a colander, rinse under cold running
water until cold, then shake the colander
to remove as much water as possible.
Leave to drain and dry.

2 Cook the beans and diced potato in a
pan of boiling water for 5–6 minutes or
steam for 8–10 minutes. Drain and let cool.

3 To make the dressing, put all the
ingredients in a large bowl with a little
sea salt and ground black pepper to
taste and whisk well to mix.

4 Add the tomatoes, spring onions,
Parmesan, olive rings and capers to the
dressing then stir in the cold pasta, beans
and potato. Toss well to mix. Cover and
leave to stand for about 30 minutes.
Taste for seasoning before serving.

VARIATIONS
Use other pasta shapes, such as penne or
conchigli, instead of fusilli. Try wholemeal
pasta shapes for a nuttier taste. Other
summer vegetables – steamed courgettes
(zucchini) or mangetouts (snow peas), or
roasted red (bell) peppers – all taste
wonderful in this salad.

THAI BEEF SALAD

Meat does not need to dominate a meal, as this light Thai salad shows. Especially when cooking with good-quality organic meat, a little adds a lot of flavour.

SERVES FOUR

675g/1½lb fillet (tenderloin) or rump (round) beef steak
30ml/2 tbsp olive oil
2 small mild red chillies, seeded and sliced
225g/8oz/3¼ cups shiitake mushrooms, finely sliced

For the dressing
3 spring onions (scallions), finely chopped
2 garlic cloves, finely chopped
juice of 1 lime
15–30ml/1–2 tbsp fish or oyster sauce, to taste
5ml/1 tsp unrefined soft light brown sugar or rapadura
30ml/2 tbsp chopped fresh coriander (cilantro)

To serve
1 cos or romaine lettuce, torn into strips
175g/6oz cherry tomatoes, halved
5cm/2in piece cucumber, peeled, halved and thinly sliced
45ml/3 tbsp toasted sesame seeds

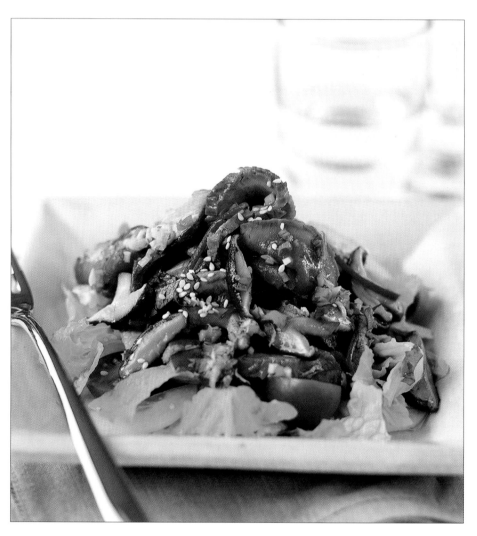

1 Preheat the grill (broiler) until hot, then cook the steak for 2–4 minutes on each side depending on how well done you like steak. (In Thailand, the beef is traditionally served quite rare.) Leave the beef to cool for at least 15 minutes.

2 Use a very sharp knife to slice the meat as thinly as possible and place the slices in a bowl.

VARIATION
If you can find them, yellow chillies make a colourful addition to this dish. Substitute one for one of the red chillies.

3 Heat the olive oil in a small frying pan. Add the seeded and sliced red chillies and the sliced mushrooms and cook for 5 minutes, stirring occasionally. Turn off the heat and add the grilled steak slices to the pan, then stir well to coat the beef slices in the cooked chilli and mushroom mixture.

4 Stir all the ingredients for the dressing together, then pour it over the meat mixture and toss gently.

5 Arrange the salad ingredients on a serving plate. Spoon the warm steak mixture in the centre and sprinkle the sesame seeds over. Serve at once.

FRESH TUNA SALAD NIÇOISE

This classic colourful salad is transformed into something really special by using fresh tuna. When buying tuna make sure it is line-caught tuna that is certified as sustainably caught by the Marine Stewardship Council (MSC).

SERVES FOUR

4 tuna steaks, about 150g/5oz each
30ml/2 tbsp olive oil
225g/8oz fine green beans, trimmed
1 small cos or romaine lettuce or
　2 little gem lettuces
4 new potatoes, boiled
4 ripe tomatoes, or 12 cherry tomatoes
2 red (bell) peppers, seeded and cut
　into thin strips
4 hard-boiled eggs, sliced
8 drained anchovy fillets in oil,
　halved lengthways (optional)
16 large black olives
sea salt and ground black pepper
12 fresh basil leaves, to garnish

For the dressing
15ml/1 tbsp red wine vinegar
90ml/6 tbsp olive oil
1 fat garlic clove, crushed

1 Brush the tuna on both sides with a little olive oil and season. Heat a ridged griddle or the grill (broiler) until very hot, then grill the tuna steaks for 1–2 minutes on each side; the flesh should be pink and juicy in the middle.

2 Cook the beans in a pan of lightly salted boiling water for 4–5 minutes, or until crisp-tender. Drain, refresh under cold water and drain again.

COOK'S TIP
To intensify the flavour of the peppers, grill (broil) them until the skins are charred, place in a bowl and cover with kitchen paper. Leave for 10–15 minutes, then rub off the skins.

3 Separate the lettuce leaves and rinse them thoroughly under cold running water and dry them on kitchen paper. Arrange them on four individual serving plates. Slice the cooked potatoes and tomatoes, if large (leave cherry tomatoes whole or halve them) and divide them among the plates. Arrange the beans and red pepper strips over the potatoes and tomatoes.

4 Shell the hard-boiled eggs and cut them into thick slices. Place a few slices of egg on each plate with the anchovy fillets, if using, and olives.

5 To make the dressing, whisk together the vinegar, olive oil and garlic and season to taste. Drizzle over the salads, arrange the tuna steaks on top, scatter over the basil and serve.

SPICED VEGETABLE COUSCOUS

This tasty vegetarian main course is easy to make and can be prepared with any number of seasonal organic vegetables such as spinach, peas, broad beans or corn.

SERVES SIX

45ml/3 tbsp olive oil
1 large onion, finely chopped
2 garlic cloves, crushed
15ml/1 tbsp tomato purée (paste)
2.5ml/½ tsp ground turmeric
2.5ml/½ tsp cayenne pepper
5ml/1 tsp ground coriander
5ml/1 tsp ground cumin
225g/8oz/1½ cups cauliflower florets
225g/8oz baby carrots, trimmed
1 red (bell) pepper, seeded and diced
225g/8oz courgettes (zucchini), sliced
400g/14oz can chickpeas, drained
    and rinsed
4 beefsteak tomatoes, skinned and sliced
45ml/3 tbsp chopped fresh coriander
    (cilantro)
sea salt and ground black pepper
coriander sprigs, to garnish

For the couscous
2.5ml/½ tsp sea salt
450g/1lb/2⅔ cups couscous
50g/2oz/¼ cup butter or
    50ml/3½ tbsp sunflower oil

1 Heat 30ml/2 tbsp oil in a large pan, add the onion and garlic and cook until soft and translucent. Stir in the tomato purée, turmeric, cayenne, coriander and cumin. Cook, stirring, for 2 minutes.

2 Add the cauliflower, baby carrots and pepper, with enough water to come halfway up the vegetables. Bring to the boil, then lower the heat, cover and simmer for 10 minutes.

3 Add the courgettes, chickpeas and tomatoes to the pan and cook for 10 minutes. Stir in the fresh coriander and season. Keep hot.

4 To cook the couscous, bring about 475ml/16fl oz/2 cups water to the boil in a large pan. Add the remaining olive oil and the salt. Remove from the heat and add the couscous, stirring. Allow to swell for 2 minutes.

5 Add the butter or sunflower oil, and heat through gently, stirring to separate the grains.

6 Turn the couscous out on to a warm serving dish, and spoon the cooked vegetables on top, pouring over any liquid. Garnish with coriander and serve immediately.

GRILLED VEGETABLE PIZZA

*You really can't go too far wrong with this classic mixture of Mediterranean grilled vegetables
on home-made pizza dough. It is filling and healthy, and is a favourite with children.*

3 Place the pizza dough on a sheet of
baking parchment on a baking sheet and
roll or gently press it out to form a
25cm/10in round, making the edges
slightly thicker than the centre.

4 Lightly brush the pizza dough with
any remaining oil, then spread the
chopped plum tomatoes evenly over
the dough.

SERVES SIX

1 courgette (zucchini), sliced
2 baby aubergines (eggplant) or
    1 small aubergine, sliced
30ml/2 tbsp olive oil
1 yellow (bell) pepper, seeded and sliced
115g/4oz/1 cup corn meal
50g/2oz/½ cup potato flour
50g/2oz/½ cup soya flour
5ml/1 tsp baking powder
2.5ml/½ tsp sea salt
50g/2oz/¼ cup non-hydrogenated margarine
about 105ml/7 tbsp milk
4 plum tomatoes, skinned and chopped
30ml/2 tbsp chopped fresh basil
115g/4oz buffalo mozzarella cheese, sliced
sea salt and ground black pepper
fresh basil sprigs, to garnish

1 Preheat the grill (broiler). Brush the
courgette and aubergine slices with a
little oil and place on a grill rack with the
pepper slices. Cook under the grill until
lightly browned, turning once.

2 Meanwhile, preheat the oven to
200°C/400°F/Gas 6. Place the corn meal,
potato flour, soya flour, baking powder
and salt in a mixing bowl and stir to mix.
Lightly rub in the margarine until the
mixture resembles coarse breadcrumbs,
then stir in enough of the milk to make
a soft but not sticky dough.

VARIATION
Top the pizza with 115g/4oz sliced goat's
cheese instead of the mozzarella for a
creamy alternative.

5 Sprinkle with the chopped basil and
season with salt and pepper. Arrange the
grilled vegetables over the tomatoes and
top with the cheese.

6 Bake for 25–30 minutes until crisp and
golden brown. Garnish the pizza with
fresh basil sprigs and serve immediately,
cut into slices.

COOK'S TIP
This recipe uses a combination of
different types of flours to give an
interesting flavour and texture to the
base. If you prefer, use 225g/8oz/2 cups
of plain (all-purpose) flour or a
combination of half plain and half
wholemeal (whole-wheat) flours.

OLIVE OIL ROASTED CHICKEN with SUMMER VEGETABLES

This is a delicious alternative to a traditional roast chicken. Organic chicken can be so much tastier and more tender than intensively reared poultry, especially if the birds are raised biodynamically.

SERVES FOUR

1.8–2kg/4–4½lb roasting chicken
150ml/¼ pint/⅔ cup extra virgin olive oil
½ lemon
few sprigs of fresh thyme
450g/1lb small new potatoes
1 aubergine (eggplant), cut into
    2.5cm/1in cubes
1 red (bell) pepper, seeded and quartered
1 fennel bulb, trimmed and quartered
8 large garlic cloves, unpeeled
coarse sea salt and ground black pepper

1 Preheat the oven to 200°C/400°F/ Gas 6. Rub the chicken all over with olive oil and season with pepper. Place the lemon half inside the bird, with a sprig or two of thyme. Put the chicken breast side down in a large roasting pan. Roast for about 30 minutes.

2 Remove the chicken from the oven and season with salt. Turn the chicken right side up, and baste. Surround the bird with the potatoes, roll them in the pan juices, and return to the oven.

3 After 30 minutes, add the aubergine, red pepper, fennel and garlic cloves to the pan. Drizzle with the remaining oil, and season with salt and pepper. Add any remaining thyme to the vegetables. Return to the oven, and cook for about 40 minutes more, basting and turning the vegetables occasionally.

4 To find out if the chicken is cooked, push the tip of a sharp knife between the thigh and breast. If the juices run clear, it is done. The vegetables should be tender and just beginning to brown. Serve the chicken and vegetables from the pan, or transfer the vegetables to a serving dish, joint the chicken and place it on top. Serve the skimmed juices in a gravy boat.

VARIATION
Serve rosemary potato wedges with the chicken. Heat 60ml/4 tbsp olive oil for 10 minutes in a roasting pan in an oven preheated to 200°C/400°F/Gas 6. Cut the potatoes into wedges and add to the oil. Sprinkle over 10ml/2 tsp dried rosemary. Season and bake for 50–60 minutes.

GRIDDLED CHICKEN with TOMATO SALSA

This simple meal is a great way to enjoy the flavour, colour and health benefits of organic ingredients. For the best result, marinate the chicken overnight.

SERVES FOUR

4 boneless, skinless chicken breast fillets,
   about 175g/6oz each
30ml/2 tbsp fresh lemon juice
30ml/2 tbsp olive oil
10ml/2 tsp ground cumin
10ml/2 tsp dried oregano
15ml/1 tbsp coarse black pepper

For the salsa
1 green chilli
450g/1lb plum tomatoes, seeded
   and chopped
3 spring onions (scallions), chopped
15ml/1 tbsp chopped fresh parsley
30ml/2 tbsp chopped fresh coriander
   (cilantro)
30ml/2 tbsp fresh lemon juice
45ml/3 tbsp olive oil

1 With a meat mallet, pound the chicken between two sheets of clear film (plastic wrap) until thin.

2 In a shallow dish, combine the lemon juice, oil, cumin, oregano and pepper. Add the chicken and turn to coat. Cover and leave to marinate for at least 2 hours, or in the refrigerator overnight.

3 To make the salsa, char the chilli skin either over a gas flame or under the grill (broiler). Leave to cool for 5 minutes. Carefully rub off the charred skin, taking care to wash your hands afterwards. For a less hot flavour, discard the seeds.

4 Chop the chilli very finely and place in a bowl. Add the seeded and chopped tomatoes, the chopped spring onions, chopped fresh parsley and coriander, lemon juice and olive oil and mix well. Set aside until ready to serve.

5 Remove the chicken from the marinade. Heat a ridged griddle. Add the chicken fillets and cook on one side until browned, for about 3 minutes. Turn over and cook for a further 4 minutes. Serve with the chilli salsa.

COOK'S TIP
The hottest part of the chilli is the white membrane that connects the seeds to the flesh. By charring the flesh, the natural sweetness is released and the heat is moderated.

MARINATED BEEF with ONION RINGS

Mexican chillies combine well with garlic in this marinade for grilled steak. Organic beef is tastier and has a better balance of cholesterol than the non-organic kind.

SERVES FOUR

20g/¾oz large mild dried red chillies
 (such as mulato or pasilla)
2 garlic cloves, plain or smoked,
 finely chopped
5ml/1 tsp ground toasted cumin seeds
5ml/1 tsp dried oregano
60ml/4 tbsp olive oil
4 × 175–225g/6–8oz beef steaks, rump
 (round) or rib-eye
sea salt and ground black pepper

For the onion rings
2 onions, sliced into rings
250ml/8fl oz/1 cup milk or soya milk
75g/3oz/¾ cup coarse corn meal
2.5ml/½ tsp dried red chilli flakes
5ml/1 tsp ground toasted cumin seeds
5ml/1 tsp dried oregano
sunflower or safflower oil,
 for deep-frying

1 Cut the stalks from the dried red chillies and discard the seeds. Toast the chillies in a dry frying pan over a high heat, stirring constantly, for 2–4 minutes, until they give off their aroma. Place the chillies in a bowl, cover with warm water and leave them to soak for 20–30 minutes. Drain the chillies and reserve the soaking water.

2 Process the soaked, drained chillies to a paste with the finely chopped garlic, toasted cumin seeds, oregano and oil in a food processor. Add a little of the soaking water, if needed. Season with ground black pepper.

3 Wash and dry the steaks, place them in a non-metallic container, rub the chilli paste all over them and leave to marinate in the refrigerator for up to 12 hours.

4 To make the onion rings, soak the onion slices in the milk for 30 minutes. Mix the corn meal, chilli, cumin and oregano, and season with salt and pepper.

5 Heat the oil for deep-frying in a deep pan to 160–180°C/325–350°F, or until a cube of day-old bread turns brown in about a minute.

6 Drain the onion rings and dip each one into the corn meal mixture, coating it thoroughly. Fry for 2–4 minutes until browned and crisp. Do not overcrowd the pan, but cook in batches. Lift the onion rings out of the pan with a slotted spoon and drain on kitchen paper.

7 Heat a barbecue or cast-iron griddle. Season the steaks with salt and cook for about 4 minutes on each side for a medium result; reduce or increase this time according to how rare or well done you like steak. Serve the steaks with the onion rings.

MOROCCAN FISH TAGINE with COUSCOUS

Fish is a staple food for the organic cook, with its balance of amino acids and oils. Always ensure that it is either organically farmed or sustainably caught in the wild.

SERVES EIGHT

1.3kg/3lb firm fish fillets such as monkfish or
   hoki, skinned and cut into 5cm/2in cubes
60ml/4 tbsp olive oil
4 onions, chopped
1 large aubergine (eggplant), cut into
   1cm/½in cubes
2 courgettes (zucchini), cut into
   1cm/½in cubes
400g/14oz can chopped tomatoes
400ml/14fl oz/1⅔ cups passata (bottled
   strained tomatoes)
200ml/7fl oz/scant 1 cup fish stock
1 preserved lemon, chopped
90g/3½oz/scant 1 cup olives
60ml/4 tbsp chopped fresh coriander (cilantro)
sea salt and ground black pepper
couscous, to serve
coriander sprigs, to garnish

For the harissa
3 large fresh red chillies, seeded and chopped
3 garlic cloves, peeled
15ml/1 tbsp ground coriander
30ml/2 tbsp ground cumin
5ml/1 tsp ground cinnamon
grated rind of 1 lemon
30ml/2 tbsp sunflower oil

1 To make the harissa, whizz everything in a food processor to a smooth paste.

2 Put the fish in a wide bowl and add 30ml/2 tbsp of the harissa. Toss to coat, cover and chill for at least 1 hour.

3 Heat half the oil in a shallow pan. Cook the onions for about 10 minutes. Stir in the remaining harissa; cook for 5 minutes, stirring occasionally.

4 Heat the remaining olive oil in a separate pan. Add the aubergine cubes and fry for 10 minutes, or until they are golden brown. Add the cubed courgettes and fry the vegetables for a further 2 minutes, stirring occasionally.

5 Tip the aubergine mixture into the shallow pan and combine with the onions, then stir in the chopped tomatoes, the passata and fish stock. Bring to the boil, then lower the heat and simmer the mixture for about 20 minutes.

6 Stir the fish cubes and preserved lemon into the pan. Add the olives and stir gently. Cover and simmer over a low heat for about 15–20 minutes until the fish is just cooked through. Season to taste. Stir in the chopped coriander. Serve with couscous and garnish with coriander sprigs.

COOK'S TIP
To make the fish go further, you could add 225g/8oz/1¼ cups cooked chickpeas to the tagine.

HAKE AU POIVRE with RED PEPPER RELISH

*Use South African hake rather than hake from European waters, where stocks are low due
to overfishing. Or try line-caught tuna or haddock from Icelandic waters.*

3 Make the relish. Cut the red peppers
in half lengthways, remove the core and
seeds from each and cut the flesh into
1cm/½in wide strips. Heat the olive oil
in a wok or a shallow pan that has a lid.
Add the peppers and stir them for
about 5 minutes, or until they are slightly
softened. Stir in the chopped garlic,
tomatoes and the anchovies, then cover
the pan and simmer the mixture very
gently for about 20 minutes, until the
peppers are very soft.

4 Tip the contents of the pan into a
food processor and whizz to a coarse
purée. Transfer to a bowl and season to
taste. Stir in the capers, balsamic vinegar
and basil. Keep the relish hot.

SERVES FOUR

30–45ml/2–3 tbsp mixed peppercorns
(black, white, pink and green)
4 hake steaks, about 175g/6oz each
30ml/2 tbsp olive oil
sea salt and ground black pepper

For the relish
2 red (bell) peppers
15ml/1 tbsp olive oil
2 garlic cloves, chopped
4 ripe tomatoes, peeled, seeded
and quartered
4 drained canned anchovy fillets,
roughly chopped
5ml/1 tsp capers
15ml/1 tbsp balsamic vinegar,
plus a little extra to serve
12 fresh basil leaves, shredded, plus
a few extra to garnish

1 Put the peppercorns in a mortar
and crush them coarsely with a pestle.
Alternatively, put them in a plastic bag
and crush them with a rolling pin.

2 Season the hake fillets lightly with salt,
then coat them evenly on both sides
with the crushed peppercorns. Set the
coated fish steaks aside while you make
the red pepper relish.

5 Heat the olive oil in a shallow pan,
add the hake steaks and fry them, in
batches if necessary, for 5 minutes on
each side, turning them once or twice,
until they are just cooked through.

6 Place the fish on individual plates and
spoon a little red pepper relish on to
each plate. Garnish with basil leaves and
a little extra balsamic vinegar. Serve the
rest of the relish separately.

WATERMELON GRANITA

Pastel pink flakes of ice, subtly blended with the citrus freshness of lime and the delicate, refreshing flavour of organic watermelon, make this granita a treat for the eye and the tastebuds.

SERVES SIX

1 whole watermelon,
    about 1.8–2kg/4–4½lb
150g/5oz/³/4 cup unrefined caster
    (superfine) sugar or rapadura
150ml/¼ pint/²⁄3 cup water
finely grated rind and juice
    of 2 limes
lime wedges, to decorate

COOK'S TIP

If you are using another melon, such as cantaloupe or Charentais, you may not need as much lime juice. Add half in step 3, then taste the mixture and adjust as necessary.

1 Cut the watermelon into quarters. Discard most of the seeds, scoop the flesh into a food processor and process briefly until smooth. Alternatively, use a blender, and process the watermelon quarters in small batches.

2 Bring the sugar and water to the boil in a small pan, stirring constantly until the sugar has dissolved. Pour the syrup into a bowl. Allow the syrup to cool, then chill until needed.

3 Strain the purée through a sieve into a large plastic container. Discard the melon seeds. Pour in the chilled syrup, lime rind and juice and mix well.

4 Cover and freeze for 2 hours until the granita mixture around the sides of the container is mushy. Mash the ice finely with a fork and return to the freezer.

5 Freeze for a further 2 hours, mashing the mixture every 30 minutes, until the granita has a slushy consistency. Scoop it into individual dishes and serve with the wedges of lime.

VARIATION

To serve this granita cocktail-style, dip the rim of each glass serving dish in a little water, then dip it into unrefined caster (superfine) sugar. Spoon in the granita, pour over a little Tequila and decorate with lime wedges.

FROZEN MELON

Freezing sorbet in hollowed out fruit, which is then cut into icy wedges, is an excellent idea. The refreshing flavour makes this dessert irresistible on a hot summer's day.

SERVES SIX

50g/2oz/¼ cup unrefined caster (superfine) sugar or rapadura
30ml/2 tbsp clear honey
15ml/1 tbsp lemon juice
60ml/4 tbsp water
1 medium cantaloupe melon or Charentais melon, about 1 kg/2¼lb
crushed ice, cucumber slices and borage flowers, to decorate

1 Put the sugar, honey, lemon juice and water in a heavy pan, and heat gently until the sugar dissolves. Bring to the boil, and boil for 1 minute, without stirring, to make a syrup. Leave to cool.

2 Cut the cantaloupe or Charentais melon in half and discard the seeds. Carefully scoop out the flesh using a metal spoon or melon baller and place in a food processor, taking care to keep the halved shells intact.

3 Blend the melon flesh until very smooth, then transfer to a mixing bowl. Stir in the cooled sugar syrup and chill until very cold. Invert the melon shells and leave them to drain on kitchen paper for a few minutes, then transfer them to the freezer while making the sorbet.

4 If making by hand, pour the mixture into a container and freeze for 3–4 hours, beating well twice with a fork, a whisk or in a food processor, to break up the ice crystals and produce a smooth texture. If using an ice cream maker, churn the melon mixture in the ice cream maker until the sorbet holds its shape.

5 Pack the sorbet into the melon shells and level the surface with a knife. Use a dessertspoon to scoop out the centre of each filled melon shell to simulate the seed cavity. Freeze the prepared fruit overnight until firm.

6 To serve, use a large knife to cut each melon half into three wedges. Serve on a bed of ice on a large platter or individual serving plates, and decorate with the cucumber slices and borage flowers.

COOK'S TIP
If the melon sorbet is too firm to cut when taken straight from the freezer, let it soften in the refrigerator for 10–20 minutes. Take care when slicing the frozen melon shell into wedges. A serrated kitchen knife is easier to work with.

CHOCOLATE MERINGUES with MIXED FRUIT COMPOTE

Mini-chocolate meringues are sandwiched with crème fraîche and served with a compote of mixed summer berries to make this impressive dessert.

SERVES SIX

105ml/7 tbsp unsweetened red
   grape juice
105ml/7 tbsp unsweetened apple juice
30ml/2 tbsp clear honey
450g/1lb/4 cups mixed fresh summer
   berries, such as blackcurrants, redcurrants, raspberries and blackberries

For the meringues
3 egg whites
175g/6oz/¾ cup unrefined caster
   (superfine) sugar or rapadura
75g/3oz good-quality plain chocolate,
   finely grated
175g/6oz/scant 1 cup crème fraîche

1 Preheat the oven to 110°C/225°F/
Gas ¼. Grease and line two large baking
sheets with baking parchment, cutting
the paper to fit.

2 To make the meringues, whisk the
egg whites in a large mixing bowl until
stiff. Gradually whisk in half the sugar,
then fold in the remaining sugar, using a
metal spoon. Gently fold in the grated
plain chocolate.

3 Carefully spoon the meringue mixture
into a large piping (pastry) bag fitted
with a large star nozzle. Pipe small round
whirls of the mixture on to the prepared
baking sheets.

4 Bake the meringues for 2½–3 hours
until they are firm and crisp. Remove
from the oven. Carefully peel the
meringues off the paper, then transfer
them to a wire rack to cool.

5 Meanwhile, make the compote. Heat
the fruit juices in a small pan with the
honey until almost boiling.

COOK'S TIP
Organic chocolate has a slightly higher
proportion of cocoa and less sugar than
non-organic equivalents. And, as organic
cocoa is naturally high in tannins and
antioxidant flavonoids as well as B vitamins
and iron, organic chocolate consumed in
moderation is actually good for you. Look
for chocolate that has 70 per cent cocoa
solids for the best flavour and higher
nutritional content.

6 Place the mixed fresh berries in a
large bowl and pour over the hot fruit
juice and honey mixture. Stir gently to
mix, then set aside and leave to cool.
Once cool, cover the bowl with clear
film (plastic wrap) and chill until required.

7 When ready to serve, gently sandwich
the cold meringues together with the
crème fraîche and arrange them on a
serving plate or dish.

8 Serve the meringues immediately on
individual plates with the mixed fruit
compote to accompany.

VARIATION
Packs of frozen mixed berries are
available and can be used in place of
fresh in this recipe. Allow the berries
to defrost thoroughly in a sieve over a
mixing bowl, then use as in step 6.

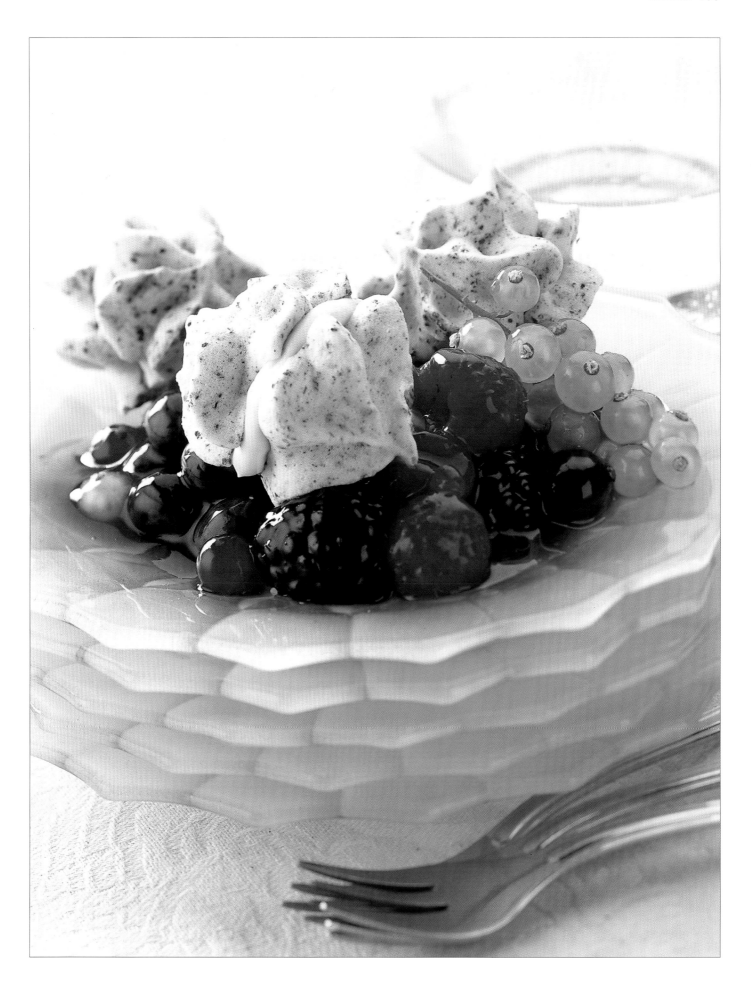

FRAGRANT FRUIT SALAD

Organic summer fruits make a delicious seasonal fruit salad. Any combination of fruits can be used, although this exotic choice is particularly suitable for a dinner party.

SERVES SIX

130g/4½oz/scant ¾ cup unrefined sugar
    or rapadura
thinly pared rind and juice of 1 lime
60ml/4 tbsp brandy
5ml/1 tsp instant coffee granules or powder
    dissolved in 30ml/2 tbsp boiling water
1 small pineapple
1 papaya
2 pomegranates
1 medium mango
2 passion fruits or kiwi fruit
fine strips of lime peel, to decorate

COOK'S TIP

Allow the salad to stand at room temperature for an hour before serving so the flavours can blend.

1 Put the sugar and lime rind in a small pan with 150ml/¼ pint/⅔ cup water. Heat gently until the sugar dissolves, then bring to the boil and simmer for 5 minutes. Leave to cool, then strain into a large serving bowl, discarding the lime rind. Stir in the lime juice, brandy and dissolved coffee.

2 Using a sharp knife, cut the plume and stalk ends from the pineapple. Peel and cut the flesh into bitesize pieces. Add to the bowl. Discard the central core.

3 Halve the papaya and scoop out the seeds. Cut away the skin, then slice the papaya. Halve the pomegranates and scoop out the seeds. Add to the bowl.

4 Cut the mango lengthways into three pieces, along each side of the stone. Peel the skin off the flesh. Cut into chunks and add to the bowl.

5 Halve the passion fruits and scoop out the flesh using a teaspoon or peel and chop the kiwi fruit. Add to the bowl and serve, decorated with lime peel.

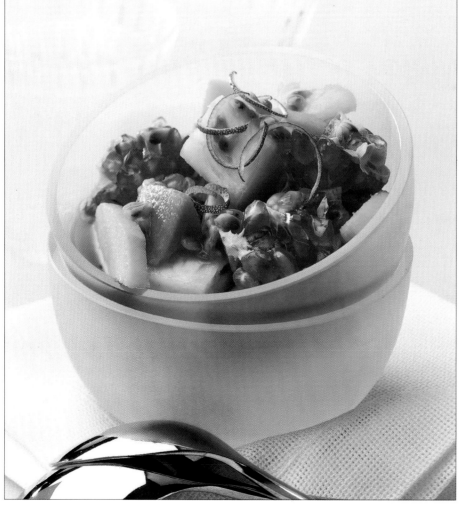

SUMMER BERRIES in WARM SABAYON GLAZE

This luxurious combination of summer berries under a light and fluffy alcoholic sauce is
lightly grilled to form a crisp, caramelized topping.

SERVES FOUR

450g/1lb/4 cups mixed summer berries,
　or soft fruit
4 egg yolks
50g/2oz/¼ cup unrefined caster (superfine)
　sugar or rapadura
120ml/4fl oz/½ cup white dessert wine,
　plus extra to serve (optional)
a little unrefined icing (confectioner's)
　sugar, sifted, and mint leaves,
　to decorate (optional)

COOK'S TIP

If you want to omit the alcohol, use a
pure fruit juice instead, such as grape,
mango or apricot.

1 Arrange the fruit in four flameproof
dishes. Preheat the grill (broiler).

2 Whisk the egg yolks in a large bowl
with the sugar and wine. Place the bowl
over a pan of hot water and whisk
constantly until thick, fluffy and pale.

3 Pour equal quantities of the sabayon
sauce into each dish. Place under the
grill for 1–2 minutes until just turning
brown. Sprinkle the fruit with icing sugar
and scatter with mint leaves just before
serving, if you like. Add an extra splash
of wine to the dishes, if you like.

COFFEE CRÊPES with PEACHES and CREAM

Juicy golden organic peaches and cream conjure up the sweet taste of summer. Here they are delicious as the filling for these light coffee-flavoured buckwheat crêpes.

SERVES SIX

75g/3oz/⅔ cup plain (all-purpose) flour
25g/1oz/¼ cup buckwheat flour
1 egg, beaten
200ml/7fl oz/scant 1 cup milk or
    soya milk
15g/½oz/1 tbsp butter, melted
100ml/3½fl oz/scant ½ cup brewed
    coffee, cooled
sunflower oil, for frying

For the filling
6 ripe peaches
300ml/½ pint/1¼ cups double
    (heavy) cream
15ml/1 tbsp brandy
225g/8oz/1 cup crème fraîche
65g/2½oz/generous ¼ cup unrefined
    caster (superfine) sugar or rapadura
30ml/2 tbsp unrefined icing (confectioner's)
    sugar, for dusting (optional)

1 Sift the flours into a mixing bowl. Make a well in the middle and add the beaten egg, half the milk and the melted butter. Gradually mix in the flour, beating until the mixture is smooth, then beat in the remaining milk and the coffee.

2 Heat a drizzle of sunflower oil in a 15–20cm/6–8in crêpe pan. Pour in just enough batter to cover the base of the pan thinly, swirling the pan to spread the mixture evenly. Cook for 2–3 minutes until the underneath is golden brown, then flip the crêpe over using a metal spatula and cook the other side.

3 Slide the crêpe out of the pan on to a plate. Continue making crêpes until all the mixture is used, stacking and interleaving them with baking parchment.

4 To make the filling, halve the peaches and carefully remove the stones. Cut the peaches into thick slices. Whip the cream and brandy together until soft peaks form. Beat the crème fraîche with the sugar until smooth. Beat 30ml/2 tbsp of the cream into the crème fraîche, then fold in the remainder.

5 Place six of the crêpes on individual serving plates. Spoon a little of the brandy cream on to one half of each crêpe and top with peach slices. Gently fold the crêpe over and dust with a little sifted icing sugar, if you like. Serve immediately.

BLUEBERRY FRANGIPANE FLAN

A tangy lemon pastry case is filled with a nutty sweet almond filling dotted with ripe blueberries. Their wonderful colour and taste are a seasonal favourite.

SERVES SIX

30ml/2 tbsp ground coffee
45ml/3 tbsp milk or soya milk
50g/2oz/¼ cup unsalted (sweet) butter
50g/2oz/¼ cup unrefined caster (superfine)
   sugar or rapadura
1 egg
115g/4oz/1 cup ground almonds
15ml/1 tbsp plain (all-purpose)
   flour, sifted
225g/8oz/2 cups blueberries
30ml/2 tbsp jam
15ml/1 tbsp brandy
crème fraîche or sour cream, to serve

For the pastry
175g/6oz/1½ cups plain (all-purpose) flour
115g/4oz/½ cup unsalted (sweet) butter or
   non-hydrogenated margarine
25g/1oz/2 tbsp unrefined caster sugar
   or rapadura
finely grated rind of ½ lemon
15ml/1 tbsp chilled water

1 Preheat the oven to 190°C/375°F/ Gas 5. To make the pastry, sift the flour into a bowl and rub in the butter. Stir in the sugar and lemon rind, then add the water and mix to a firm dough. Wrap the dough in clear film (plastic wrap) and chill for 20 minutes.

2 Roll out the pastry on a lightly floured work surface and use to line a 23cm/9in loose-based flan tin (quiche pan). Line the pastry with baking parchment and baking beans and bake for 10 minutes. Remove the paper and beans and bake for a further 10 minutes. Remove from the oven.

3 Meanwhile, to make the filling, put the ground coffee in a bowl. Bring the milk almost to the boil, then pour over the coffee and leave to infuse for 4 minutes. Cream the butter and sugar until pale. Beat in the egg, then add the almonds and flour. Strain in the coffee-flavoured milk through a fine sieve and fold in.

4 Spoon the coffee mixture into the pastry case and spread evenly. Scatter the blueberries over the top and push them down slightly into the mixture. Bake for 30 minutes, until firm, covering with foil after 20 minutes.

5 Remove the tart from the oven and allow to cool slightly. Heat the jam and brandy in a small pan until melted. Brush over the flan and remove from the tin. Serve warm with crème fraîche or sour cream.

APRICOT and ALMOND TART

This rich tart relies on a simple but perfect combination of apricots and almond filling.
Fresh apricots are only available during the summer months so make the most of them.

SERVES SIX

115g/4oz/½ cup butter or
   non-hydrogenated margarine
115g/4oz/scant ½ cup unrefined caster
   (superfine) sugar or rapadura
1 egg, beaten
50g/2oz/⅓ cup ground rice
50g/2oz/½ cup ground almonds
few drops of almond essence (extract)
450g/1lb fresh apricots, halved and stoned
sifted unrefined icing (confectioners')
   sugar, for dusting (optional)
apricot slices and fresh mint sprigs,
   to decorate (optional)

For the pastry
115g/4oz/1 cup brown rice flour
115g/4oz/1 cup corn meal
115g/4oz/½ cup butter or
   non-hydrogenated margarine
25g/1oz/2 tbsp unrefined caster (superfine)
   sugar or rapadura
1 egg yolk

1 To make the pastry, place the rice flour and corn meal in a large mixing bowl and stir to mix. Lightly rub in the butter or margarine with your fingertips until the mixture resembles fine breadcrumbs.

VARIATIONS
For a change, use ground hazelnuts and vanilla essence (extract) in place of the ground almonds and almond essence. Pears, peaches or nectarines can be used in this recipe instead of the apricots. Or use a combination of the three fruits to make a mixed fruit tart.

2 Add the sugar, stir in the egg yolk and add enough chilled water to make a smooth, soft but not sticky dough. Wrap the dough in clear film (plastic wrap) and chill for 30 minutes.

3 Preheat the oven to 180°C/350°F/ Gas 4. Line a 24cm/9½in loose-bottomed flan tin (quiche pan) with the pastry by pressing it gently over the base and up the sides of the tin, making sure that there are no holes in the pastry. Trim the edge of the pastry with a sharp knife.

4 To make the almond filling, place the butter or margarine and sugar in a mixing bowl and cream together, using a wooden spoon, until the mixture is light and fluffy.

5 Gradually add the beaten egg to the mixture, beating well after each addition. Fold in the ground rice and almonds and the almond essence and mix well to incorporate them.

6 Spoon the almond mixture into the pastry case, spreading it evenly with the back of a spoon, then arrange the apricot halves cut side down on top.

7 Place the tart on a baking sheet and bake for 40–45 minutes until the filling and pastry are cooked and lightly browned. Serve warm or cold, dusted with icing sugar and decorated with apricots and sprigs of mint, if you like.

COOK'S TIP
Organic apricots are often smaller and are more intensely coloured than non-organic fruit. They have a sweeter, juicier flavour too. Organic apricots, like organic peaches and figs, help regulate the body's digestive system. Try substituting organic peaches and figs in this recipe.

BLUEBERRY MUFFINS

Light and fruity, these well-known American muffins are delicious at any time of day.
Serve them warm for breakfast or brunch, or as a tea-time treat.

MAKES TWELVE

180g/6¼oz/generous 1½ cups plain
    (all-purpose) flour
60g/2¼oz/¼ cup unrefined sugar or rapadura
10ml/2 tsp baking powder
2 eggs
50g/2oz/¼ cup butter or
    non-hydrogenated margarine, melted
175ml/6fl oz/¾ cup milk or soya milk
5ml/1 tsp vanilla essence (extract)
5ml/1 tsp grated lemon rind
175g/6oz/1½ cups fresh blueberries

1 Preheat the oven to 200°C/400°F/
Gas 6. Grease a 12-cup muffin tin or
arrange 12 paper muffin cases on a
baking tray.

2 Sift the plain flour, sugar and baking
powder into a large mixing bowl.

3 In another bowl, whisk the eggs until
blended. Add the melted butter, milk,
vanilla essence and grated lemon rind to
the whisked eggs, and stir thoroughly
to combine.

4 Make a well in the dry ingredients and
pour in the egg mixture. With a large
metal spoon, stir until the flour is just
moistened, but not smooth.

5 Add the blueberries to the muffin
mixture and gently fold in, being careful
not to crush the berries.

6 Spoon the batter into the muffin tin
or paper cases, leaving enough room
for the muffins to rise.

7 Bake for 20–25 minutes until the tops
spring back when touched lightly. Leave
the muffins in the tin, if using, for about
5 minutes before turning out on to a
wire rack to cool a little before serving.

VARIATION
Muffins are delicious with all kinds of
different fruits. Replace the blueberries
with the same weight of bilberries,
blackcurrants, stoned cherries
or raspberries.

COOK'S TIP
If you want to serve these muffins for
breakfast, prepare the dry ingredients
the night before to save time.

STRAWBERRY JAM and SCONES

*There is not much that can beat freshly made scones with good-quality jam. Making your own
is not difficult and their flavour really will be much better than shop-bought varieties.*

MAKES ABOUT 1.3KG/3LB JAM
AND 10–12 SCONES

For the strawberry jam
1kg/2¼lb/9 cups small strawberries
900g/2lb/4½ cups unrefined granulated sugar
juice of 2 lemons

For the scones
225g/8oz/2 cups plain (all-purpose) flour
15ml/1 tbsp baking powder
50g/2oz/¼ cup butter or
    non-hydrogenated margarine, diced
1 egg, beaten, plus extra to glaze
75ml/5 tbsp milk or soya milk
clotted or double (heavy) cream, to serve

1 Layer the strawberries and sugar in a
large bowl. Cover and leave overnight.

2 The next day, tip the strawberries and
their juice into a large heavy pan. Add
the lemon juice. Bring to the boil, stirring
until the sugar has dissolved.

3 Boil steadily for 10–15 minutes. Spoon
a small amount on to a chilled saucer.
Chill for 3 minutes, then push the jam
with your finger; if wrinkles form, it is
ready. Cool for 10 minutes.

4 Pour the strawberry jam into warm,
sterilized jars, filling them right to the
top. Cover the jam with a disc of waxed
paper, waxed side down, and seal the
jar with a damp cellophane round and
secure with an elastic band while the
jam is still hot. Label when the jars are
cold. The jam can be stored in a cool
dark place, and it should keep for up
to 1 year.

5 To make the scones, preheat the oven
to 220°C/425°F/Gas 7. Butter a baking
sheet. Sift the flour and baking powder
together, then rub in the butter or
margarine. Make a well in the centre of
the flour mixture, add the egg and milk
and mix to a soft dough using a fork or
a round-bladed knife.

6 Turn out the scone dough on to a
floured surface, and knead very lightly
until smooth. Roll out the dough to
about a 2cm/¾in thickness and cut into
10 or 12 rounds using a 5cm/2in plain
or fluted cutter dipped in flour.

7 Transfer to the baking sheet, brush
the tops with egg, then bake for about
8 minutes, until risen and golden. Cool
slightly on a wire rack then serve with
the jam and clotted or double cream.

AUTUMN

As the nights start to draw in, warming dishes become popular —
make the most of hearty organic vegetables such as parsnips,
squashes and sweet potatoes. Try Roasted Garlic Squash Soup
with roasted tomato salsa, Orange Candied Sweet Potatoes,
or Potatoes and Parsnips Baked with Garlic and Cream.
Delicious fish dishes to try now include Sole with Wild Mushrooms or
Potato-topped Fish Pie — served simply with roasted root vegetables.
Autumn orchards and hedgerows provide a wonderful array of fresh
fruits — organic apples, plums and pears are full of flavour and are
popular in both sweet and savoury dishes. Try Duck Sausages with
Spicy Plum Sauce, or Spicy Venison Casserole with cranberries and
orange. Sticky Pear Pudding is a delicious sweet treat, while
individual Hot Blackberry and Apple Soufflés are just right for
a dinner party.
Freshly baked cakes are especially satisfying at this time of year —
try Parsnip Cake with Orange Icing. And if you have a glut of
apples, then there is no better way to use them than in
Country Apple Cake — served warm straight from the oven
for a real taste of autumn.

  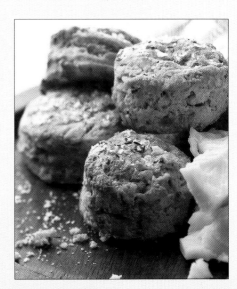

CLAM, MUSHROOM and POTATO CHOWDER

Members of the same family as mussels, scallops and oysters, clams have a sweet flavour and firm texture, which combine beautifully with wild mushrooms in this filling soup.

SERVES 4

48 clams, scrubbed
50g/2oz/¼ cup unsalted (sweet) butter
    or non-hydrogenated margarine
1 large onion, chopped
1 celery stick, sliced
1 carrot, sliced
225g/8oz/3¾ cups assorted wild and
    cultivated mushrooms
225g/8oz floury potatoes (such as
    Maris Piper or King Edward),
    thickly sliced
1.2 litres/2 pints/5 cups boiling light
    chicken or vegetable stock
1 thyme sprig
4 parsley stalks
sea salt and ground black pepper
thyme sprigs, to garnish

1 Place the clams in a large, heavy pan, discarding any that are open. Add 1cm/½in of water to the pan, then cover and bring to the boil. Cook the clams over a medium heat for 6–8 minutes, shaking the pan occasionally, until the clams open (discard any clams that do not open).

2 Drain the clams over a bowl and remove most of the shells, leaving some in the shells as a garnish. Strain the cooking juices into the bowl, add all the clams and set aside.

3 Add the butter, onion, celery and carrot to the pan and cook gently until just softened but not coloured. Add the wild and cultivated mushrooms and cook for 3–4 minutes until their juices begin to appear. Add the potato slices, the clams and their juices, the stock, thyme and parsley stalks.

4 Bring to the boil, then reduce the heat, cover and simmer for 25 minutes. Season to taste, ladle into soup bowls, and garnish with thyme sprigs.

ROASTED GARLIC and SQUASH SOUP

This is a wonderful, richly flavoured dish. A spoonful of hot and spicy tomato salsa gives bite to this sweet-tasting butternut squash and garlic soup.

SERVES FOUR TO FIVE

2 garlic bulbs, outer papery
    skin removed
75ml/5 tbsp olive oil
a few fresh thyme sprigs
1 large butternut squash, halved
    and seeded
2 onions, chopped
5ml/1 tsp ground coriander
1.2 litres/2 pints/5 cups vegetable or
    chicken stock
30–45ml/2–3 tbsp chopped fresh oregano
    or marjoram
sea salt and ground black pepper

For the salsa
4 large ripe tomatoes, halved and seeded
1 red (bell) pepper, halved and seeded
1 large fresh red chilli, halved and seeded
30–45ml/2–3 tbsp extra virgin olive oil
15ml/1 tbsp balsamic vinegar

1 Preheat the oven to 220°C/425°F/ Gas 7. Place the garlic bulbs on a piece of foil and pour over half the olive oil. Add the thyme sprigs, then fold the foil around the garlic bulbs to enclose them completely. Place the foil parcel on a baking sheet with the butternut squash and brush the squash with 15ml/1 tbsp of the remaining olive oil. Add the halved and seeded tomatoes, red pepper and fresh chilli for the salsa.

2 Roast the vegetables for 25 minutes, then remove the tomatoes, pepper and chilli. Reduce the temperature to 190°C/ 375°F/Gas 5 and cook the squash and garlic for 20–25 minutes more, or until the squash is tender.

3 Heat the remaining oil in a large, heavy pan and cook the onions and ground coriander gently for about 10 minutes, or until softened.

4 Skin the pepper and chilli and process in a food processor or blender with the tomatoes and 30ml/2 tbsp olive oil. Stir in the vinegar and seasoning to taste. Add the remaining oil if you think the salsa needs it.

5 Squeeze the roasted garlic out of its papery skin into the onions. Scoop the squash out of its skin and add it to the pan. Add the vegetable or chicken stock, 2.5ml/½ tsp salt and plenty of black pepper. Bring to the boil and simmer for 10 minutes.

6 Stir in half the chopped fresh oregano or marjoram and allow the soup to cool slightly, then process it in batches if necessary, in a food processor or blender until smooth. Alternatively, press the soup through a fine sieve.

7 Reheat the soup in a clean pan without allowing it to boil, then taste for seasoning before ladling it into individual warmed bowls. Top each with a spoonful of the tomato salsa and sprinkle over the remaining chopped fresh oregano or marjoram. Serve immediately.

ROAST GARLIC with GOAT'S CHEESE PÂTÉ

The combination of sweet, mellow roasted garlic and goat's cheese is a classic one. The pâté is flavoured with walnuts and herbs and is particularly good made with the new season's walnuts, sometimes known as "wet" walnuts, which are available in the early autumn.

SERVES FOUR

4 large garlic bulbs
4 fresh rosemary sprigs
8 fresh thyme sprigs
60ml/4 tbsp olive oil
sea salt and ground black pepper
thyme sprigs, to garnish
4–8 slices sourdough bread and
    walnuts, to serve

For the pâté
200g/7oz/scant 1 cup soft goat's cheese
5ml/1 tsp finely chopped fresh thyme
15ml/1 tbsp chopped fresh parsley
50g/2oz/⅓ cup walnuts, chopped
15ml/1 tbsp walnut oil (optional)
fresh thyme, to garnish

1 Preheat the oven to 180°C/350°F/Gas 4. Strip the papery skin from the garlic bulbs. Place them in an ovenproof dish large enough to hold them snugly. Tuck in the fresh rosemary sprigs and fresh thyme sprigs, drizzle the olive oil over and season with a little sea salt and plenty of ground black pepper.

2 Cover the garlic tightly with foil and bake in the oven for 50–60 minutes, opening the parcel and basting once halfway through the cooking time. Set aside and leave to cool.

3 Preheat the grill (broiler). To make the pâté, cream the cheese with the thyme, parsley and chopped walnuts. Beat in 15ml/1 tbsp of the cooking oil from the garlic and season to taste with plenty of ground black pepper. Transfer the pâté to a serving bowl and chill until ready to serve.

4 Brush the sourdough bread slices on one side with the remaining cooking oil from the garlic bulbs, then grill (broil) until lightly toasted.

5 Divide the pâté among four individual plates. Drizzle the walnut oil, if using, over the goat's cheese pâté and grind some black pepper over it. Place some garlic on each plate and serve with the pâté and some toasted bread. Garnish the pâté with a little fresh thyme and serve a few freshly shelled walnuts with each portion.

SLOW-COOKED SHIITAKE with SHOYU

Shiitake mushrooms cooked slowly are so rich and filling, that some people call them "vegetarian steak". This Japanese dish, known as Fukumé-ni, can last a few weeks in the refrigerator, and is a useful and flavourful addition to other dishes.

SERVES FOUR

20 dried shiitake mushrooms
45ml/3 tbsp sunflower or safflower oil
30ml/2 tbsp shoyu
15ml/1 tbsp toasted sesame oil

VARIATION
You can make a delicious rice dish using the slow-cooked shiitake to serve with grilled fish or chicken. Cut the slow-cooked shiitake into thin strips. Mix with 600g/1lb 5oz/5¼ cups cooked brown rice and 15ml/1 tbsp finely chopped chives. Serve in individual rice bowls and sprinkle with toasted sesame seeds.

1 Start soaking the dried shiitake the day before. Put them in a large bowl almost full of water. Cover the shiitake with a plate or lid to stop them floating to the surface of the water. Leave to soak overnight.

2 Measure 120ml/4fl oz/½ cup liquid from the bowl. Drain the shiitake into a sieve. Remove and discard the stalks.

3 Heat the oil in a wok or a large frying pan. Stir-fry the shiitake over a high heat for 5 minutes, stirring continuously.

4 Reduce the heat to the lowest setting, then add the measured liquid and the shoyu. Cook the mushrooms until there is almost no moisture left, stirring frequently. Add the toasted sesame oil and remove from the heat.

5 Leave to cool, then slice and arrange the shiitake on a large plate.

RED ONION and MUSHROOM TARTLETS with GOAT'S CHEESE

Crisp and savoury, these attractive little tarts are delicious served with a few mixed salad leaves drizzled with a garlic-infused French dressing.

SERVES SIX

60ml/4 tbsp olive oil
25g/1oz/2 tbsp butter or
   non-hydrogenated margarine
4 red onions, thinly sliced
5ml/1 tsp unrefined soft light brown sugar
15ml/1 tbsp balsamic vinegar
15ml/1 tbsp soy sauce
200g/7oz/3 cups button (white)
   mushrooms, sliced
1 garlic clove, finely chopped
2.5ml/½ tsp chopped fresh tarragon
30ml/2 tbsp chopped fresh parsley
250g/9oz goat's cheese log (chèvre)
sea salt and ground black pepper
mixed salad leaves, to serve

For the pastry
200g/7oz/1¾ cups plain (all-purpose) flour
pinch of cayenne pepper
90g/3½oz/scant ½ cup butter or
   non-hydrogenated margarine
40g/1½oz/½ cup freshly grated Parmesan
   cheese or premium vegetarian cheese
45–60ml/3–4 tbsp iced water

1 To make the pastry, sift the flour and cayenne into a bowl, add the butter, and rub in with the fingertips.

2 Stir in the grated cheese, then bind the pastry with the iced water. Press the pastry into a ball, then wrap it in clear film (plastic wrap) and chill.

3 Heat 15ml/1 tbsp of the oil and half the butter in a heavy frying pan, then add the onions. Cover and cook gently for 15 minutes, stirring occasionally.

4 Uncover the pan, increase the heat slightly and sprinkle in the sugar. Cook, stirring frequently, until the onions begin to caramelize and brown. Add the balsamic vinegar and soy sauce and cook briskly until the liquid evaporates. Season to taste then set aside.

5 Heat another 30ml/2 tbsp of the oil and the remaining butter or margarine in a pan, then add the sliced mushrooms and chopped garlic and cook fairly briskly for 5–6 minutes, or until the mushrooms are browned and cooked.

6 Set a few cooked mushrooms and onion rings aside, then stir the rest of the mushrooms into the onions with the fresh tarragon and parsley. Adjust the seasoning to taste. Preheat the oven to 190°C/375°F/Gas 5.

COOK'S TIP
Shortcrust pastry is traditionally made with all plain (all-purpose) flour. For a healthier, higher fibre pastry use half plain and half wholemeal (whole-wheat) flour. This gives a nutty, slightly textured result.

7 Roll out the pastry and use to line six 10cm/4in tartlet tins (quiche pans). Prick the pastry bases with a fork and line the sides with strips of foil. Bake for 10 minutes, remove the foil and bake for another 5–7 minutes, or until the pastry is lightly browned and cooked. Remove the tartlets from the oven and increase the temperature to 200°C/400°F/Gas 6.

8 Remove the pastry shells from the tins and arrange them on a baking sheet. Divide the onion mixture equally among the pastry shells. Cut the goat's cheese into six equal slices and place one slice on each tartlet. Distribute the reserved mushrooms and onion rings, drizzle with the remaining oil and season with pepper.

9 Return the tartlets to the oven and bake for 5–8 minutes, or until the goat's cheese is just beginning to turn brown. Serve with mixed salad leaves.

VARIATION
For a milder flavour sliced buffalo mozzarella cheese can be used to top the tartlets instead of the goat's cheese.

FLORETS POLONAISE

Simple steamed organic vegetables become something very special with this pretty egg topping. They make a perfect dinner party side dish or are great with a weekday supper.

SERVES SIX

500g/1¼lb mixed vegetables,
   such as cauliflower, broccoli,
   romanesco and calabrese
50g/2oz/¼ cup butter or 60ml/4 tbsp extra
   virgin olive oil
finely grated rind of ½ lemon
1 large garlic clove, crushed
25g/1oz/½ cup fresh breadcrumbs, lightly
   baked or grilled (broiled) until crisp
2 eggs, hard-boiled
sea salt and ground black pepper

VARIATION
Use wholemeal (whole-wheat) breadcrumbs
instead of the white crumbs. They will give
a nuttier flavour and crunchier texture.

1 Trim the vegetables and break into equal-size florets. Place the florets in a steamer over a pan of boiling water and steam for 5–7 minutes, until just tender.

2 Toss the steamed vegetables in butter or oil and transfer to a serving dish.

3 While the vegetables are cooking, mix together the lemon rind, garlic, seasoning and baked or grilled breadcrumbs. Finely chop the eggs and mix together with the remaining ingredients. Sprinkle the chopped egg mixture over the cooked vegetables and serve at once.

ORANGE CANDIED SWEET POTATOES

Organic sweet potatoes are free of the fungicides sprayed on non-organic tubers and are an excellent source of vitamins, including cancer-preventing betacarotene.

SERVES EIGHT

900g/2lb sweet potatoes
250ml/8fl oz/1 cup orange juice
50ml/2fl oz/¼ cup maple syrup
5ml/1 tsp freshly grated root ginger
7.5ml/1½ tsp ground cinnamon
6.5ml/1¼ tsp ground cardamom
2.5ml/½ tsp salt
ground black pepper
ground cinnamon and orange segments,
     to garnish

COOK'S TIP
This popular American dish is traditionally served with roast turkey at Thanksgiving and Christmas. Serve with extra orange segments to make it really special.

1 Preheat the oven to 180°C/350°F/ Gas 4. Peel and dice the potatoes and then steam them for 5 minutes.

2 Meanwhile, stir the remaining ingredients together. Spread out on to a non-stick shallow baking tin (pan).

3 Scatter the potatoes over the baking tin. Cook for 1 hour, stirring every 15 minutes, until they are tender and well coated in the spicy syrup.

4 Serve garnished with orange segments and ground cinnamon.

GARLIC CHIVE RICE with MUSHROOMS

A wide range of organic mushrooms is readily available. They combine well with rice and garlic chives to make a tasty accompaniment to vegetarian dishes, fish or chicken.

SERVES FOUR

350g/12oz/generous 1¾ cups
    long grain rice
60ml/4 tbsp groundnut (peanut) oil
1 small onion, finely chopped
2 green chillies, seeded and finely chopped
25g/1oz garlic chives, chopped
15g/½oz fresh coriander (cilantro)
600ml/1 pint/2½ cups vegetable or
    mushroom stock
2.5ml/½ tsp sea salt
250g/9oz mixed mushrooms, thickly sliced
50g/2oz cashew nuts, fried in 15ml/1 tbsp
    olive oil until golden brown
ground black pepper

1 Wash and drain the rice. Heat half the oil in a pan and cook the onion and chillies over a gentle heat, stirring occasionally, for 10–12 minutes until soft.

2 Set half the garlic chives aside. Cut the stalks off the coriander and set the leaves aside. Purée the remaining chives and the coriander stalks with the stock in a food processor or blender.

VARIATION

For a higher-fibre alternative make this dish with brown rice. Increase the cooking time in step 3 to 25–30 minutes or follow the packet instructions.

3 Add the rice to the onions and fry over a low heat, stirring frequently, for 4–5 minutes. Pour in the stock mixture, then stir in the salt and a good grinding of black pepper. Bring to the boil, then stir and reduce the heat to very low. Cover tightly with a lid and cook for 15–20 minutes, or until the rice has absorbed all the liquid.

4 Remove the pan from the heat and lay a clean, folded dishtowel over the pan, under the lid, and press on the lid to wedge it firmly in place. Leave the rice to stand for a further 10 minutes, allowing the towel to absorb the steam while the rice becomes completely tender.

5 Meanwhile, heat the remaining oil in a frying pan and cook the mushrooms for 5–6 minutes until tender and browned. Add the remaining garlic chives and cook for another 1–2 minutes.

6 Stir the cooked mushroom and chive mixture and chopped coriander leaves into the rice. Adjust the seasoning to taste, then transfer to a warmed serving dish and serve immediately, scattered with the fried cashew nuts.

ROASTED SHALLOT and SQUASH SALAD

This is especially good served with a grain or starchy salad, based on rice or couscous, for example. Serve with plenty of hand-made organic bread to mop up the juices.

SERVES FOUR TO SIX

75ml/5 tbsp olive oil
15ml/1 tbsp balsamic vinegar, plus a little
   extra, if you like
15ml/1 tbsp sweet soy sauce
350g/12oz shallots, peeled but left whole
3 fresh red chillies
1 butternut squash, peeled, seeded
   and cut into chunks
5ml/1 tsp finely chopped fresh thyme
15g/½oz flat leaf parsley
1 small garlic clove, finely chopped
75g/3oz/¾ cup walnuts, chopped
150g/5oz feta cheese
sea salt and ground black pepper

1 Preheat the oven to 200°C/400°F/ Gas 6. Beat the olive oil, balsamic vinegar and soy sauce together in a large bowl, then season with a little salt and plenty of freshly ground black pepper.

2 Toss the shallots and two of the chillies in the oil mixture and tip into a large roasting pan or ovenproof dish. Roast for 15 minutes, stirring once or twice.

3 Add the butternut squash chunks and roast for a further 30–35 minutes, stirring once, until the squash is tender and browned. Remove from the oven, stir in the chopped fresh thyme and set the vegetables aside to cool.

4 Chop the parsley and garlic together and mix with the walnuts. Seed and finely chop the remaining chilli.

5 Stir the parsley, garlic and walnut mixture into the vegetables. Add chopped chilli to taste and adjust the seasoning, adding a little extra balsamic vinegar, if you like. Crumble the feta and add to the salad. Transfer to a serving dish and serve immediately.

POTATOES and PARSNIPS BAKED with GARLIC and CREAM

As the potatoes and parsnips cook, they gradually absorb the garlic-flavoured cream, while the cheese browns to a crispy finish.

SERVES FOUR TO SIX

3 large potatoes, total weight
    about 675g/1½lb
350g/12oz small–medium parsnips
200ml/7fl oz/scant 1 cup single (light)
    cream or soya cream
105ml/7 tbsp milk or soya milk
2 garlic cloves, crushed
butter or olive oil, for greasing
about 5ml/1 tsp freshly grated
    nutmeg
75g/3oz/¾ cup coarsely grated
    Cheddar cheese
sea salt and ground black pepper

3 Lightly grease a 25cm/10in long, shallow rectangular earthenware baking dish with butter or oil. Preheat the oven to 180°C/350°F/Gas 4.

5 Pour the garlic-flavoured cream and milk mixture into the dish and then press the sliced potatoes and parsnips down into the liquid. The liquid should come to just underneath the top layer of vegetables. Cover the dish with a piece of lightly buttered foil or baking parchment and bake for 45 minutes.

1 Peel the potatoes and parsnips and cut them into thin slices using a sharp knife. Place them in a steamer and cook for 5 minutes. Leave to cool slightly.

4 Arrange the thinly sliced potatoes and parsnips in layers in the greased earthenware dish, sprinkling each layer of vegetables with a little freshly grated nutmeg and a little salt and plenty of ground black pepper.

6 Remove the dish from the oven and remove the foil or paper from the dish. Sprinkle the grated Cheddar cheese over the vegetables in an even layer.

7 Return the dish to the oven and bake uncovered for a further 20–30 minutes, or until the potatoes and parsnips are tender and the topping is golden brown.

2 Meanwhile, pour the cream and milk into a heavy pan, add the crushed garlic and bring to the boil over a medium heat. Remove the pan from the heat and leave to stand at room temperature for about 10 minutes to allow the flavour of the garlic to infuse into the cream and milk mixture.

VARIATIONS

• Use sweet potatoes in place of some or all of the ordinary potatoes – choose orange-fleshed ones for a pretty colour contrast with the parsnips. Other root vegetables such as Jerusalem artichokes, carrots, swede (rutabaga) or turnips would also work well.
• Other hard cheeses would be equally good in this recipe – try Red Leicester or Gruyère, or go for the even more strongly flavoured Parmesan, premium Italian-style vegetarian cheese or Pecorino.

COOK'S TIPS

• If you have one, use a mandolin or a food processor fitted with a slicing blade to slice the potatoes and parsnips thinly and evenly for this gratin.
• At the end of the cooking time, to test if the vegetables are tender, insert a sharp knife through the middle of the potatoes and parsnips. The knife should slide in easily and the vegetables feel soft.

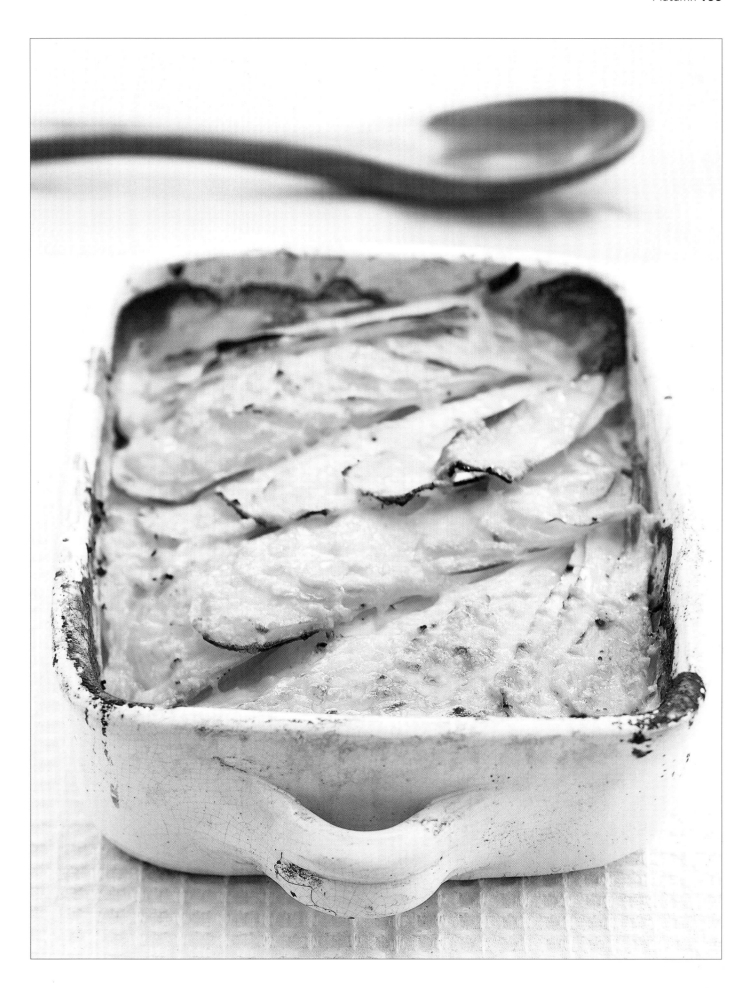

TOFU and VEGETABLE THAI CURRY

Non-organic soya products, including tofu, are often made from genetically modified beans that are resistant to pesticides. By using organic tofu in this fragrant curry you benefit from its great texture and superior nutritional value whilst helping to protect the Earth.

SERVES FOUR

175g/6oz tofu, drained
45ml/3 tbsp dark soy sauce
15ml/1 tbsp sesame oil
5ml/1 tsp chilli sauce
2.5cm/1in piece fresh root ginger,
   finely grated
225g/8oz cauliflower
225g/8oz broccoli
30ml/2 tbsp sunflower oil
1 onion, sliced
400ml/14fl oz/1⅔ cups coconut milk
150ml/¼ pint/⅔ cup water
1 red (bell) pepper, seeded and chopped
175g/6oz green beans, halved
115g/4oz/1½ cups shiitake or button
   (white) mushrooms, halved
shredded spring onions (scallions),
   to garnish
boiled brown rice or noodles, to serve

For the curry paste
2 chillies, seeded and chopped
1 lemon grass stalk, chopped
2.5cm/1in piece fresh galangal or
   fresh root ginger, chopped
2 kaffir lime leaves
10ml/2 tsp ground coriander
a few sprigs fresh coriander (cilantro),
   including the stalks

1 Cut the drained tofu into 2.5cm/1in cubes and place in an ovenproof dish. Mix together the soy sauce, sesame oil, chilli sauce and ginger and pour over the tofu. Toss gently to coat all the cubes evenly, then leave to marinate for at least 2 hours or overnight if possible, turning and basting the tofu occasionally.

2 To make the curry paste, place the chopped chillies, lemon grass, galangal, kaffir lime leaves, ground coriander and fresh coriander in a food processor, and process for a few seconds until well blended. Add 45ml/3 tbsp water and process to a thick paste.

3 Preheat the oven to 190°C/375°F/ Gas 5. Using a large sharp knife, cut the cauliflower and broccoli into small florets and cut any stalks into thin slices.

4 Heat the sunflower oil in a frying pan, add the sliced onion and gently fry for about 8 minutes, or until soft and lightly browned. Stir in the prepared curry paste and the coconut milk.

5 Add the water and bring to the boil, then stir in the red pepper, green beans, cauliflower and broccoli. Transfer to an earthenware casserole or Chinese sand pot. Cover and place in the oven.

6 Stir the tofu and marinade, then place the dish in the top of the oven and cook for 30 minutes. After 30 minutes, stir the tofu and marinade into the curry with the mushrooms.

7 Reduce the oven temperature to 180°C/350°F/Gas 4 and cook for about 15 minutes more, or until the vegetables are tender. Garnish with spring onions and serve with boiled rice or noodles.

COOK'S TIP
Organic tofu or beancurd is made from organic soya beans and is sold in blocks. It is a creamy white colour and has a solid gel-like texture. Tofu has a bland flavour and its absorbent nature means that it takes on the flavours of marinades or any other food that it is cooked with.

SPAGHETTI with EGGS and BACON

Organic ingredients really enhance the flavours of simple, classic dishes such as this Italian favourite, which makes a great last-minute supper.

SERVES FOUR

30ml/2 tbsp olive oil
1 small onion, finely chopped
1 large garlic clove, crushed
8 pancetta or rindless smoked streaky
  (fatty) bacon rashers (strips), cut into
  1cm/½in strips
350g/12oz fresh or dried spaghetti
4 eggs
90–120ml/6–8 tbsp reduced-fat
  crème fraîche
60ml/4 tbsp freshly grated Parmesan
  cheese or premium Italian-style
  vegetarian cheese, plus extra
  to serve
sea salt and ground black pepper

1 Heat the oil in a large pan, add the onion and garlic and fry gently for about 5 minutes until softened.

2 Add the pancetta or bacon to the pan and cook for 10 minutes, stirring.

3 Meanwhile, cook the spaghetti in a large pan of salted boiling water for 10 minutes or according to the instructions on the packet until *al dente*.

4 Put the eggs, crème fraîche and grated Parmesan in a bowl. Stir in plenty of black pepper, then beat together well.

5 Drain the pasta thoroughly, tip it into the pan with the pancetta or bacon and toss well to mix.

6 Turn off the heat under the pan, then immediately add the egg mixture and toss thoroughly so that it cooks lightly and coats the pasta.

7 Season to taste, then divide the spaghetti among four warmed bowls and sprinkle with freshly ground black pepper. Serve immediately, with extra grated cheese handed separately.

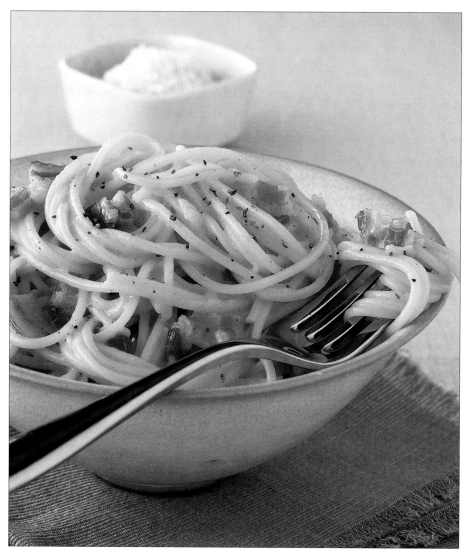

COOK'S TIP
You can replace the crème fraîche with double (heavy) cream, sour cream or soya cream, if you prefer.

CHICKEN with CASHEW NUTS

This popular Chinese dish is quick and easy to make and can be enjoyed to the full by using good-quality organic products that are full of flavour.

SERVES FOUR

350g/12oz skinless chicken
   breast fillets
pinch of ground white pepper
15ml/1 tbsp dry sherry
300ml/½ pint/1¼ cups chicken stock
15ml/1 tbsp sunflower oil
1 garlic clove, finely chopped
1 small carrot, cut into cubes
½ cucumber, about 75g/3oz, cut into
   1cm/½in cubes
50g/2oz/½ cup drained canned bamboo
   shoots, cut into 1cm/½in cubes
   (optional)
5ml/1 tsp cornflour (cornstarch)
15ml/1 tbsp soy sauce
25g/1oz/¼ cup dry-roasted cashew nuts
2.5ml/½ tsp sesame oil
noodles, to serve

1 Cut the chicken into 2cm/¾in cubes. Place the cubes in a bowl, stir in the white pepper and sherry, cover and marinate for 15 minutes.

2 Bring the stock to the boil in a large pan. Add the chicken and cook, stirring, for 3 minutes. Drain, reserving 90ml/6 tbsp of the stock, and set aside.

3 Heat the sunflower oil in a large non-stick frying pan until it is very hot, add the finely chopped garlic and stir-fry for a few seconds. Add the cubed carrot, cucumber and bamboo shoots, if using, and continue to stir-fry the vegetables over a medium heat for 2 minutes.

4 Stir in the chicken and reserved stock. Mix the cornflour with the soy sauce and add the mixture to the pan. Cook, stirring, until the sauce thickens slightly. Finally, add the cashew nuts and sesame oil. Toss to mix thoroughly, then serve with noodles.

MOUSSAKA

This is a traditional eastern Mediterranean dish, popular in both Greece and Turkey. Layers of minced mutton, aubergines, tomatoes and onions are topped with a creamy yogurt and cheese sauce in this delicious, authentic recipe.

SERVES FOUR

450g/1lb aubergines (eggplant)
150ml/¼ pint/⅔ cup olive oil
1 large onion, chopped
2–3 garlic cloves, finely chopped
675g/1½lb lean minced (ground) mutton
15ml/1 tbsp plain (all-purpose) flour
400g/14oz can chopped tomatoes
30ml/2 tbsp chopped mixed fresh herbs,
    such as parsley, marjoram and oregano
sea salt and ground black pepper

For the topping
300ml/½ pint/1¼ cups natural
    (plain) yogurt
2 eggs
25g/1oz feta cheese, crumbled
25g/1oz/⅓ cup freshly grated Parmesan
    cheese or premium Italian-style
    vegetarian cheese

1 Slice the aubergines and layer them in a colander, sprinkling with salt. Cover the aubergines with a plate and a weight, then leave to drain for about 30 minutes.

2 Drain the aubergines, rinse well, then pat dry with kitchen paper.

3 Heat 45ml/3 tbsp of the oil in a large, heavy pan. Fry the onion and garlic until softened, but not coloured. Add the mutton and cook over a high heat, stirring often, until browned.

4 Stir in the flour until mixed, then stir in the tomatoes, herbs and seasoning. Bring to the boil, reduce the heat and simmer gently for 20 minutes.

5 Meanwhile, heat a little of the remaining olive oil in a large frying pan. Add as many aubergine slices as can be laid in the pan in a single layer. Cook until golden on both sides then remove from the pan. Heat more oil and continue frying the aubergines in batches, adding olive oil as necessary.

COOK'S TIP
Many kinds of organic aubergines do not taste bitter; therefore it is not usually necessary to salt them before cooking. However, if they are to be fried, as in this recipe, salting and drying them reduces the amount of fat that they absorb and helps them to brown during cooking.

6 Preheat the oven to 180°C/350°F/ Gas 4. Arrange half the aubergine slices in a large, shallow ovenproof dish.

7 Top the aubergine slices with about half of the meat and tomato mixture, then add the remaining aubergine slices. Spread the remaining meat mixture over the aubergines.

8 To make the topping, beat together the yogurt and eggs, then mix in the feta and Parmesan or Italian-style cheeses. Pour the mixture over the meat and spread it evenly.

9 Transfer the moussaka to the oven and bake for 35–40 minutes, or until golden and bubbling.

VARIATION
Use large courgettes (zucchini) in place of the aubergines, if you like, and cut them diagonally into fairly thick slices. There is no need to salt the courgettes before frying them.

DUCK SAUSAGES with SPICY PLUM SAUCE

A variety of organic sausages is available direct from farmers and small butchers, and any pork or game sausages would work in this dish. Rich duck sausages are best baked in their own juices.

SERVES FOUR

8–12 duck sausages

For the sweet potato mash
1.5kg/3¼lb sweet potatoes, cut
    into chunks
25g/1oz/2 tbsp butter or
    30ml/2 tbsp olive oil
60ml/4 tbsp milk
sea salt and ground black pepper

For the plum sauce
30ml/2 tbsp olive oil
1 small onion, chopped
1 small red chilli, seeded and chopped
450g/1lb plums, stoned and chopped
30ml/2 tbsp red wine vinegar
45ml/3 tbsp clear honey

1 Preheat the oven to 190°C/375°F/ Gas 5. Arrange the duck sausages in a single layer in a large, shallow ovenproof dish. Bake the sausages, uncovered, in the oven for 25–30 minutes, turning the sausages two or three times during cooking, to ensure that they brown and cook evenly.

2 Meanwhile, put the sweet potatoes in a pan and add water to cover. Bring to the boil, then reduce the heat and simmer for 20 minutes, or until tender.

3 Drain and mash the potatoes, then place the pan over a low heat. Stir frequently for about 5 minutes to dry out the mashed potato. Beat in the butter or oil and milk, season to taste.

4 Make the plum sauce. Heat the oil in a small pan and fry the onion and chilli gently for 5 minutes. Stir in the plums, vinegar and honey, then simmer gently for 10 minutes.

5 Serve the freshly cooked sausages with the sweet potato mash and plum sauce.

SPICY VENISON CASSEROLE

Being high in flavour but low in saturated fat, organic venison is a good choice for healthy, yet rich, casseroles. Cranberries and orange bring a delicious fruitiness to this spicy recipe.

SERVES FOUR

15ml/1 tbsp olive oil
1 onion, chopped
2 celery sticks, sliced
10ml/2 tsp ground allspice
15ml/1 tbsp plain (all-purpose) or
    wholemeal (whole-wheat) flour
675g/1½lb stewing venison, cubed
225g/8oz fresh or frozen cranberries
grated rind and juice of 1 orange
900ml/1½ pints/3¾ cups beef or
    venison stock
sea salt and ground black pepper

1 Heat the oil in a flameproof casserole. Add the onion and celery and fry for about 5 minutes, or until softened.

2 Meanwhile, mix the ground allspice with the flour and either spread the mixture out on a large plate or place in a large plastic bag. Toss a few pieces of venison at a time (to prevent them becoming soggy) in the flour mixture until they are all lightly coated. Spread the floured venison out on a large plate until ready to cook.

3 When the onion and celery are just softened, remove them from the casserole using a slotted spoon and set aside. Add the venison pieces to the casserole in batches and cook until well browned and sealed on all sides.

COOK'S TIP

Freshly made home-made stock is always best, but if you are short of time, look for cartons or tubs of fresh stock in the chilled food cabinets of organic stores.

4 Add the cranberries and the orange rind and juice to the casserole along with the stock and stir well. Return the vegetables and the browned venison to the casserole and heat until simmering. Cover tightly and reduce the heat.

5 Simmer for about 45 minutes, or until the venison is tender, stirring occasionally. Season the venison casserole to taste with a little salt and plenty of ground black pepper before serving.

VARIATIONS

Farmed organic venison is increasingly easy to find and is available from many good butchers and organic meat delivery companies. It makes a rich and flavourful stew, but lean pork or braising steak could be used in place of the venison, if you prefer. You could also replace the cranberries with pitted and halved prunes and, for extra flavour, use either ale or stout instead of about half the stock.

STUFFED ROAST LOIN of PORK with APPLE SAUCE

The secret of a good roast with apple sauce is simple, good-quality ingredients, such as organic pork and traditionally made cider.

SERVES SIX

15ml/1 tbsp light olive oil
2 leeks, chopped
150g/5oz/⅔ cup ready-to-eat dried
   apricots, chopped
150g/5oz/scant 1 cup dried dates, stoned
   and chopped
75g/3oz/1½ cups fresh white or wholemeal
   (whole-wheat) breadcrumbs
2 eggs, beaten
15ml/1 tbsp fresh thyme leaves
1.5kg/3¼lb boned loin of pork
sea salt and ground black pepper

For the apple sauce
450g/1lb cooking apples
30ml/2 tbsp cider or water
25g/1oz/2 tbsp butter or 30ml/2 tbsp
   olive oil

1 Preheat the oven to 220°C/425°F/ Gas 7. Heat the oil in a large pan and cook the leeks until softened. Stir in the apricots, dates, breadcrumbs, eggs and thyme, and season with salt and pepper.

2 Lay the pork skin side up, and use a sharp knife to score the rind crossways.

3 Turn the meat over and cut down the centre of the joint to within 1cm/½in of the rind and fat, then work from the middle outwards towards one side, cutting most of the meat off the rind but keeping a 1cm/½in layer of meat on top of the rind. Cut to within 2.5cm/1in of the side of the joint. Repeat on the other side of the joint.

4 Spoon half the stuffing over the joint, then fold the meat over it.

5 Tie the joint back into its original shape, then place in a roasting pan and rub the skin with salt. Roast the pork for 40 minutes, then reduce the oven temperature to 190°C/375°F/Gas 5 and cook for a further 1½ hours, or until the meat is tender and cooked through.

6 Meanwhile, shape the remaining stuffing into walnut-size balls. Arrange on a tray, cover with clear film (plastic wrap) and chill until 20 minutes before the pork is cooked. Then add the stuffing balls to the roasting pan and baste them with the cooking juices from the meat.

7 When cooked, cover the meat closely with foil and leave to stand in a warm place for 10 minutes before carving.

8 To make the apple sauce, peel, core and chop the apples, then place in a small pan with the cider or water and cook for 5–10 minutes, stirring occasionally, or until very soft. Beat well or process in a food processor or blender to make smooth apple sauce. Beat in the butter or oil. Reheat the apple sauce just before serving, if necessary.

9 Carve the joint into thick slices. If the crackling is very hard, you may find that it is easier to slice the crackling off the joint first, before carving the meat, then cut the crackling into serving pieces using poultry shears or a heavy, sharp chef's knife or cleaver. Serve the stuffed loin of pork with the crackling, stuffing balls, apple sauce and a selection of seasonal autumn vegetables.

COOK'S TIP
The resting time before carving is very important, so don't be tempted to skip it.

SALMON and RICE GRATIN

This all-in-one supper dish is ideal for informal autumn entertaining as it can be made in advance and reheated for about half an hour before being served with a tossed salad.

4 Remove the pan from the heat and, without lifting the lid, allow the rice to stand, undisturbed, for 5 minutes.

5 Meanwhile, make the sauce. Mix the milk, flour and butter or margarine in a pan. Bring to the boil over a low heat, whisking constantly until the sauce is smooth and thick. Stir in the curry paste with salt and pepper to taste. Simmer for 2 minutes.

6 Preheat the grill (broiler). Remove the sauce from the heat and stir in the chopped parsley and rice, with half the cheese. Using a large metal spoon, fold in the flaked fish and eggs. Spoon into a shallow gratin dish and sprinkle with the rest of the cheese. Cook under the grill until the topping is golden brown and bubbling. Serve in individual dishes, garnished with chopped parsley.

SERVES SIX

675g/1½lb fresh salmon fillet, skinned
1 bay leaf
a few parsley stalks
1 litre/1¾ pints/4 cups water
400g/14oz/2 cups basmati rice, soaked and drained
30–45ml/2–3 tbsp chopped fresh parsley, plus extra to garnish
175g/6oz/1½ cups grated Cheddar cheese
3 hard-boiled eggs, chopped
sea salt and ground black pepper

For the sauce
1 litre/1¾ pints/4 cups milk or soya milk
40g/1½oz/⅓ cup plain (all-purpose) flour
40g/1½oz/3 tbsp butter or non-hydrogenated margarine
5ml/1 tsp mild curry paste

1 Put the salmon fillet in a wide, shallow pan. Add the bay leaf and parsley stalks, with a little salt and plenty of black pepper. Pour in the water and bring to simmering point. Poach the fish for about 12 minutes until just tender.

2 Lift the salmon fillet out of the pan using a slotted spoon, then strain the cooking liquid into a large pan. Leave the fish to cool, then remove any visible bones and flake the flesh gently into bitesize pieces with a fork.

3 Add the soaked and drained rice to the pan containing the fish-poaching liquid. Bring the liquid to the boil, then lower the heat, cover tightly with a lid and simmer gently for 10 minutes without lifting the lid.

VARIATIONS
Organically farmed prawns (shrimp) could be substituted for the salmon, and other hard cheeses, such as Gruyère or Red Leicester, could be used instead of the Cheddar cheese.

POTATO-TOPPED FISH PIE

This traditional Scottish dish should be prepared from wild fish such as hoki, caught sustainably. Always ensure you buy wild fish bearing the MSC logo.

SERVES FOUR

675g/1½lb hoki fillets (or other sustainably caught white fish)
300ml/½ pint/1¼ cups milk or soya milk
½ lemon, sliced
1 bay leaf
1 fresh thyme sprig
4–5 black peppercorns
50g/2oz/¼ cup butter or non-hydrogenated margarine
25g/1oz/¼ cup plain (all-purpose) flour
30ml/2 tbsp chopped fresh parsley
5ml/1 tsp anchovy essence
150g/5oz/2 cups shiitake or chestnut mushrooms, sliced
sea salt, ground black pepper and cayenne pepper

For the topping
450g/1lb potatoes, cooked and mashed with milk or soya milk
50g/2oz/¼ cup butter or non-hydrogenated margarine
2 tomatoes, sliced
25g/1oz/¼ cup grated Cheddar cheese

1 Put the fish skin side down in a shallow pan. Add the milk, lemon slices, bay leaf, thyme and peppercorns. Bring to the boil, then lower the heat and poach gently for about 5 minutes until just cooked. Strain off and reserve the milk. Remove the fish skin and flake the flesh, discarding any bones.

2 Melt half the butter in a small pan, stir in the flour and cook gently for 1 minute. Add the reserved milk and boil, whisking, until smooth and creamy. Stir in the parsley and anchovy essence and season to taste.

3 Heat the remaining butter in a frying pan, add the sliced mushrooms and sauté until tender. Season and add to the flaked fish. Mix the sauce into the fish and stir gently to combine. Transfer the mixture to an ovenproof casserole.

4 Preheat the oven to 200°C/400°F/ Gas 6. Beat the mashed potato with the butter until very creamy. Season, then spread the topping evenly over the fish. Fork up the surface and arrange the sliced tomatoes around the edge. Sprinkle the exposed topping with the grated cheese.

5 Bake for 20–25 minutes until the topping is browned. If you prefer, finish the browning under a hot grill (broiler).

VARIATION
Instead of using plain mashed potatoes, try a mixture of mashed potato and mashed swede (rutabaga) or sweet potato.

GRILLED MACKEREL with SPICY DHAL

Oily fish such as mackerel are nutritious and great for your nervous system. They are complemented by a tart or sour accompaniment, like these delicious tamarind-flavoured lentils or split peas. Serve with chopped fresh tomatoes, onion salad and flat bread.

SERVES FOUR

250g/9oz/generous 1 cup red lentils, or
    yellow split peas (soaked overnight)
1 litre/1¾ pints/4 cups water
30ml/2 tbsp sunflower oil
2.5ml/½ tsp each mustard seeds,
    cumin seeds, fennel seeds and
    fenugreek or cardamom seeds
5ml/1 tsp ground turmeric
3–4 dried red chillies, crumbled
30ml/2 tbsp tamarind paste
30ml/2 tbsp chopped fresh coriander
    (cilantro)
4 mackerels
ground black pepper
fresh red chilli slices and finely chopped
    coriander, to garnish
flat bread and tomatoes, to serve

1 Rinse the lentils or split peas, drain them thoroughly and put them in a pan. Pour in the water and bring to the boil. Lower the heat, partially cover the pan and simmer the lentils or split peas for 30–40 minutes, stirring occasionally, until they are tender and mushy.

2 Heat the oil in a wok or shallow pan. Add the mustard seeds, then cover and cook for a few seconds until they pop. Remove the lid, add the rest of the seeds, with the turmeric and chillies and fry for a few more seconds.

3 Stir in the lentils or split peas and the tamarind paste and mix well. Bring to the boil, then simmer for 10 minutes until thick. Stir in the coriander.

4 Clean the fish then heat a ridged griddle or the grill (broiler) until very hot. Make six diagonal slashes on either side of each fish and remove the head. Season, then grill for 5–7 minutes on each side. Serve, garnished with red chilli and chopped coriander, accompanied by the dhal, flat bread and tomatoes.

SOLE with WILD MUSHROOMS

If possible, use organic chanterelles for this dish; their glowing orange colour combines really wonderfully with the intensely golden sauce. Otherwise, use any pale-coloured or oyster mushrooms that you can find instead.

SERVES FOUR

4 Dover sole fillets, about 115g/4oz
    each, skinned
50g/2oz/¼ cup butter or
    non-hydrogenated margarine
500ml/17fl oz/generous 2 cups fish stock
150g/5oz/2 cups chanterelles or
    oyster mushrooms
a large pinch of saffron threads
150ml/¼ pint/⅔ cup double (heavy) cream
    or soya cream
1 egg yolk
sea salt and ground white pepper
flat leaf parsley sprigs, to garnish
boiled new potatoes and steamed broccoli
    florets, to serve

1 Preheat the oven to 200°C/400°F/ Gas 6. Cut the sole fillets in half lengthways and place them on a board with the skinned side uppermost. Season, then roll them up. Use a little of the butter to grease a baking dish just large enough to hold all the sole fillets in a single layer. Arrange the rolls in it, then pour over the fish stock. Cover tightly with foil and bake for 12–15 minutes until cooked through.

2 Meanwhile, pick off any bits of fern or twig from the chanterelles and wipe the mushrooms with a damp cloth. Halve or quarter any large ones. Heat the remaining butter in a frying pan until foaming and sauté the mushrooms for 3–4 minutes until just tender. Season with salt and pepper and keep hot.

3 Lift the cooked sole fillets out of the cooking liquid and place them on a heated serving dish. Keep hot. Strain the liquid into a small pan, add the saffron, set over a very high heat and boil until reduced to about 250ml/8fl oz/1 cup. Stir in the cream and let the sauce bubble gently for a few seconds.

4 Lightly beat the egg yolk in a small bowl, pour on a little of the hot sauce and stir well. Stir the mixture into the remaining sauce in the pan and cook over a very low heat for 1–2 minutes until slightly thickened. Season to taste. Stir the chanterelles into the sauce and pour it over the sole fillets. Garnish with parsley sprigs and serve at once. Boiled new potatoes and steamed broccoli florets make the perfect accompaniment.

HONEY BAKED FIGS with HAZELNUT ICE CREAM

Organic figs have a deliciously intense flavour. They are smaller than non-organic fruit as they are not forced to absorb water during growing, so you may need three per person.

SERVES FOUR

1 lemon grass stalk, finely chopped
1 cinnamon stick, roughly broken
60ml/4 tbsp clear honey
200ml/7fl oz/scant 1 cup water
8 large or 12 small figs

For the hazelnut ice cream
450ml/¾ pint/scant 2 cups double (heavy)
   cream or soya cream
50g/2oz/¼ cup unrefined caster (superfine)
   sugar or rapadura
3 egg yolks
1.5ml/¼ tsp vanilla essence (extract)
75g/3oz/¾ cup hazelnuts

1 To make the ice cream, place the cream in a pan and heat slowly until almost boiling. Place the sugar and egg yolks in a bowl and whisk until creamy.

2 Pour a little cream on to the egg yolk mixture and stir. Pour into the pan and mix with the rest of the cream. Cook over a low heat, stirring constantly, until the mixture lightly coats the back of the spoon – do not allow it to boil. Pour into a bowl, stir in the vanilla and leave to cool.

3 Preheat the oven to 180°C/350°F/ Gas 4. Place the hazelnuts on a baking sheet and roast for 10–12 minutes, or until they are golden brown. Leave the nuts to cool, then place them in a food processor or blender and process until they are coarsely ground.

4 Transfer the ice cream mixture to a metal or plastic freezer container and freeze for 2 hours, or until the mixture feels firm around the edge. Remove the container from the freezer and whisk the ice cream to break down the ice crystals. Stir in the ground hazelnuts and freeze the mixture again until half-frozen. Whisk again, then freeze until firm.

COOK'S TIPS
• If you prefer, rather than whisking the semi-frozen ice cream, tip it into a food processor and process until smooth.
• There are several different types of organic figs available and they can all be used in this recipe. Choose from green-skinned figs that have an amber-coloured flesh, dark purple-skinned fruit with a deep red flesh or green/yellow-skinned figs with a pinky-coloured flesh.

5 Place the lemon grass, cinnamon stick, honey and water in a small pan and heat slowly until boiling. Simmer the mixture for 5 minutes, then leave the syrup to stand for 15 minutes.

6 Preheat the oven to 200°C/400°F/ Gas 6. Meanwhile, carefully cut the figs into quarters, leaving them intact at the bases. Place the figs in an ovenproof baking dish and pour over the honey-flavoured syrup.

7 Cover the dish tightly with foil and bake the figs for about 15 minutes, or until tender.

8 Take the ice cream from the freezer about 10 minutes before serving, to soften slightly. Transfer the figs to serving plates. Strain a little of the cooking liquid over the figs and then serve them with a scoop or two of hazelnut ice cream.

VARIATION
This recipe also works well with halved, stoned organic nectarines or peaches – cook as from step 6 and serve with the home-made ice cream.

STICKY PEAR PUDDING

Pears are at their best in autumn and, combined with other organic ingredients such as cloves, coffee and maple syrup, they form the basis of this indulgent dessert.

SERVES SIX

30ml/2 tbsp ground coffee
15ml/1 tbsp near-boiling water
4 ripe pears
juice of ½ orange
50g/2oz/½ cup toasted hazelnuts
115g/4oz/½ cup butter or
   non-hydrogenated margarine, softened
115g/4oz/generous ½ cup unrefined caster
   (superfine) sugar or rapadura, plus an
   extra 15ml/1 tbsp for baking
2 eggs, beaten
50g/2oz/½ cup self-raising (self-rising)
   flour, sifted
pinch of ground cloves
8 whole cloves (optional)
45ml/3 tbsp maple syrup
fine strips of orange rind, to decorate

For the orange cream
300ml/½ pint/1¼ cups whipping cream
15ml/1 tbsp unrefined icing
   (confectioners') sugar, sifted
finely grated rind of ½ orange

1 Preheat the oven to 180°C/350°F/ Gas 4. Lightly grease a 20cm/8in loose-based sandwich tin (shallow cake pan). Put the ground coffee in a small bowl and pour the water over. Leave to infuse for 4 minutes, then strain through a fine sieve.

VARIATION
Apple and cinnamon could be used in this pudding instead of pears and cloves, with a lemon cream in place of orange cream.

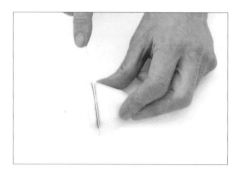

2 Peel, halve and core the pears. Thinly slice across the pear halves part of the way through. Brush the pears with orange juice. Grind the hazelnuts in a coffee grinder until fine.

3 Beat the butter and the caster sugar together until very light and fluffy. Gradually beat in the eggs, then fold in the flour, ground cloves, hazelnuts and coffee.

4 Spoon the mixture into the prepared sandwich tin and level the surface with a spatula.

5 Pat the pears dry on kitchen paper, then arrange them carefully in the sponge mixture, flat side down.

6 Lightly press two whole cloves, if using, into each pear half. Brush the pears with 15ml/1 tbsp maple syrup.

7 Sprinkle 15ml/1 tbsp caster sugar over the pears. Bake for 45–50 minutes, or until firm and well-risen.

8 While the sponge is cooking, make the orange cream. Whip the cream, icing sugar and orange rind until soft peaks form. Spoon into a serving dish and chill until needed.

9 Allow the sponge to cool for about 10 minutes in the tin, then remove and place on a serving plate. Lightly brush with the remaining maple syrup before decorating with orange rind and serving warm with the orange cream.

COOK'S TIP
Organic pears are a good source of soluble fibre and are great at lowering cholesterol and easing constipation. Buy slightly underripe fruit and leave them to ripen on a sunny windowsill for a few days – overripe pears go off quickly.

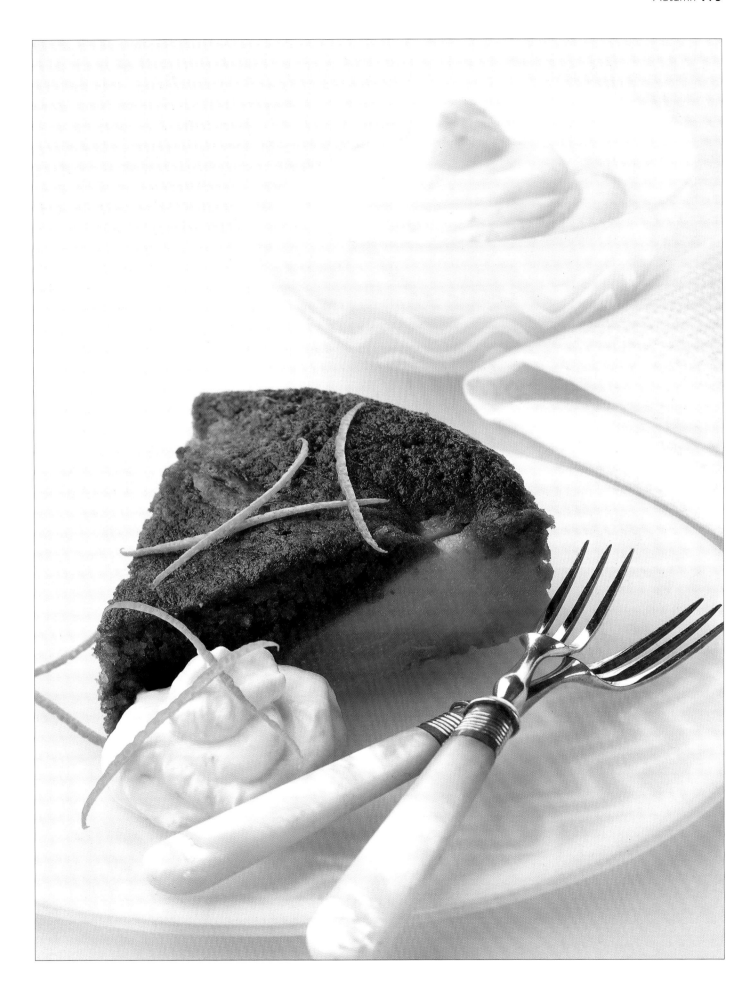

CUSTARD TART with PLUMS

When this tart is made with really ripe, organic sweet plums, it makes a wonderful
hot or cold weekend dessert. Serve it with thick cream, ice cream or Greek yogurt.

2 Flour a deep 18cm/7in square or 20cm/8in round loose-bottomed flan tin (tart pan). Roll out the pastry and use to line the tin. This pastry is soft at this stage, so don't worry if you have to push it into shape. Chill for another 10–20 minutes.

3 Preheat the oven to 200°C/400°F/ Gas 6. Line the pastry case with baking parchment and fill with baking beans, then bake for 15 minutes. Remove the paper and baking beans, reduce the oven temperature to 180°C/350°F/Gas 4 and bake for a further 5–10 minutes until the base is dry.

4 Halve and stone the plums, and arrange them neatly in the pastry case. Whisk together the remaining egg and egg yolks with the sugar, the milk and vanilla essence and pour over the fruit.

5 Return the tart to the oven and bake for 25–30 minutes, or until the custard is just firm to the touch. Remove the tart from the oven and allow to cool. Sprinkle with flaked almonds and dredge with icing sugar before serving with cream, ice cream or Greek yogurt.

SERVES FOUR TO SIX

175g/6oz/1½ cups plain (all-purpose)
  flour, sifted
pinch of salt
45ml/3 tbsp unrefined caster (superfine)
  sugar or rapadura
115g/4oz/½ cup unsalted (sweet) butter
  or non-hydrogenated margarine
2 eggs, plus 2 egg yolks
350g/12oz ripe plums
300ml/½ pint/1¼ cups milk or soya milk
few drops of vanilla essence (extract)
toasted flaked (sliced) almonds and sifted
  unrefined icing (confectioners') sugar,
  to decorate

1 Place the flour, salt, 15ml/1 tbsp of the sugar, the butter and one of the eggs in a food processor or blender and process until thoroughly combined. Tip out the mixture on to a clean, lightly floured surface and bring it together into a ball. Wrap the pastry in clear film (plastic wrap) and chill for 10 minutes to rest.

VARIATIONS
• This tart is equally delicious made with organic apricots, peaches or nectarines.
• Make a nutty pastry by replacing 15ml/ 1 tbsp of the flour with ground almonds.

BUTTERNUT SQUASH and MAPLE PIE

This American-style pie has a rich shortcrust pastry case and a creamy filling, sweetened
with maple syrup and flavoured with fresh organic ginger and a dash of brandy.

SERVES TEN

1 small butternut squash
60ml/4 tbsp water
2.5cm/1in piece of fresh root ginger,
    peeled and grated
beaten egg, to glaze
120ml/4fl oz/½ cup double (heavy) cream
    or soya cream, plus extra to serve
90ml/6 tbsp maple syrup
45ml/3 tbsp unrefined light muscovado
    (brown) sugar or rapadura
3 eggs, lightly beaten
30ml/2 tbsp brandy
1.5ml/¼ tsp grated nutmeg

For the pastry
175g/6oz/1½ cups plain (all-purpose) flour
115g/4oz/½ cup butter or
    non-hydrogenated margarine, diced
10ml/2 tsp unrefined caster (superfine)
    sugar or rapadura
1 egg, lightly beaten

1 To make the pastry, sift the flour into
a mixing bowl. Rub in the butter or
margarine until the mixture resembles
fine breadcrumbs. Add the sugar and the
egg. Mix to a dough. Wrap in clear film
(plastic wrap). Chill for 30 minutes.

2 Cut the butternut squash in half, then
peel and scoop out the seeds. Cut the
flesh into cubes and put in a pan with
the water. Cover and cook gently for
15 minutes. Remove the lid, stir in the
ginger and cook for a further 5 minutes
until all the liquid has evaporated and
the squash is tender. Cool slightly, then
purée in a food processor until smooth.

3 Roll out the pastry and use to line a
23cm/9in flan tin (tart pan). Gather up
the trimmings, re-roll them thinly, then
cut them into maple-leaf shapes. Brush
the edge of the pastry case with beaten
egg and attach the maple leaf shapes at
regular intervals to make a decorative
rim. Cover with clear film and chill for
30 minutes.

4 Put a heavy baking sheet in the oven
and preheat to 200°C/400°F/Gas 6.
Prick the pastry base with a fork, line
with foil and fill with baking beans. Bake
on the hot baking sheet for 12 minutes.

5 Remove the foil and beans and bake
the pastry case for a further 5 minutes.
Brush the base of the pastry case with
beaten egg and return to the oven for
about 3 minutes. Reduce the oven
temperature to 180°C/350°F/Gas 4.

6 Mix 200g/7oz/scant 1 cup of the
butternut purée with the cream, syrup,
sugar, eggs, brandy and grated nutmeg.
(Discard any remaining purée.) Pour
into the pastry case. Bake for about
30 minutes, or until the filling is lightly
set. Cool slightly, then serve with cream.

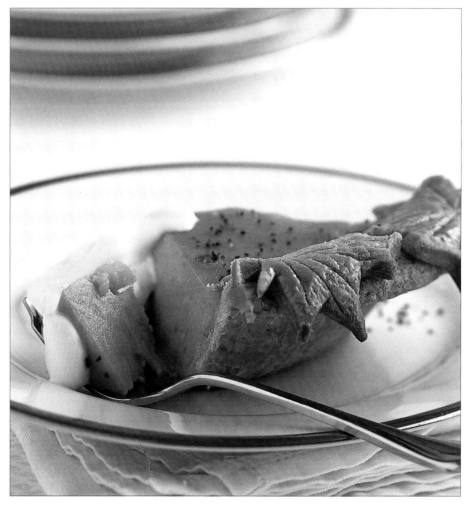

BAKED APPLE DUMPLINGS

A wonderful way to make the most of apples in season. The sharpness of the fruit contrasts perfectly with the maple syrup drizzled over this delightful pastry parcel.

SERVES EIGHT

8 firm cooking apples, peeled
1 egg white
130g/4½oz/⅔ cup unrefined caster
    (superfine) sugar or rapadura
45ml/3 tbsp double (heavy) cream or
    soya cream, plus extra whipped cream,
    to serve
2.5ml/½ tsp vanilla essence (extract)
250ml/8fl oz/1 cup maple syrup

For the pastry
475g/1lb 2oz/4½ cups plain
    (all-purpose) flour
350g/12oz/1½ cups butter or
    non-hydrogenated margarine, diced

1 To make the pastry, sift the flour into a large bowl. Rub in the butter until the mixture resembles fine breadcrumbs.

2 Sprinkle over 175ml/6fl oz/¾ cup water and mix until the dough holds together, adding more water if necessary. Gather into a ball. Wrap in clear film (plastic wrap) and chill for 10 minutes. Preheat the oven to 220°C/425°F/Gas 7.

3 Cutting from the stem end, core the apples without cutting through the base. Roll out the pastry thinly. Cut squares almost large enough to enclose the apples; brush with egg white and set an apple in the centre of each.

4 Cut pastry rounds to cover the tops of the cored apples. Reserve the pastry trimmings. Combine the unrefined sugar, cream and vanilla essence in a small bowl. Spoon one-eighth of the mixture into the hollow of each apple.

5 Place a pastry round on top of each apple, then bring up the sides of the pastry square to enclose it, pleating the larger piece of pastry to make a snug fit around the apple. Moisten the joins with cold water where they overlap and press down so they stick in place.

6 Make apple stalks and leaves from the pastry trimmings and use to decorate the dumplings. Set them in a large greased baking dish, at least 2cm/¾in apart. Bake for 30 minutes, then reduce the oven temperature to 180°C/350°F/Gas 4 and continue baking for 20 minutes more, or until the pastry is golden brown and the apples are tender.

7 Transfer the dumplings to a serving dish. Mix the maple syrup with the juices in the baking dish and drizzle over the dumplings. Serve the dumplings hot with whipped cream.

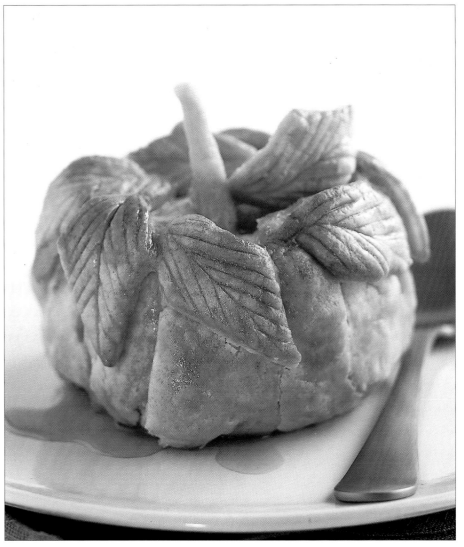

HOT BLACKBERRY and APPLE SOUFFLÉS

The deliciously tart autumn flavours of blackberry and apple complement each other perfectly to make a light, mouthwatering hot pudding.

MAKES SIX

butter or non-hydrogenated margarine,
    for greasing
150g/5oz/¾ cup unrefined caster (superfine)
    sugar or rapadura, plus extra for dusting
350g/12oz/3 cups blackberries
1 large cooking apple, peeled and finely diced
grated rind and juice of 1 orange
3 egg whites
unrefined icing (confectioner's) sugar,
    for dusting

1 Preheat the oven to 200°C/400°F/
Gas 6. Generously grease six 150ml/
¼ pint/⅔ cup individual soufflé dishes
with butter and dust with caster sugar,
shaking out the excess sugar.

2 Put a baking sheet in the oven to heat.
Cook the blackberries, diced apple and
orange rind and juice in a pan for about
10 minutes or until the apple has pulped
down well. Press through a sieve into a
bowl. Stir in 50g/2oz/¼ cup of the caster
sugar. Set aside to cool.

3 Put a spoonful of the fruit purée into
each prepared soufflé dish and spread
evenly. Set the dishes aside.

4 Place the egg whites in a grease-free
bowl and whisk until they form stiff
peaks. Very gradually whisk in the
remaining caster sugar to make a stiff,
glossy meringue mixture.

5 Fold in the remaining fruit purée and
spoon the flavoured meringue into the
prepared dishes. Level the tops with a
palette knife, and run a table knife
around the edge of each dish.

6 Place the dishes on the hot baking
sheet and bake for 10–15 minutes until
the soufflés have risen well and are
lightly browned. Dust the tops with
icing sugar and serve immediately.

COOK'S TIP
Running a table knife around the inside
edge of the soufflé dishes before baking
helps the soufflés to rise evenly without
sticking to the rim of the dish.

PLUM CHARLOTTES with FOAMY CALVADOS SAUCE

A variety of different types of organic plums are available at this time of year — from tangy yellow greengages to sweet and juicy Victorias.

SERVES FOUR

115g/4oz/½ cup butter or
    non-hydrogenated margarine, melted
50g/2oz/¼ cup demerara (raw) sugar
    or rapadura
450g/1lb ripe plums, stoned (pitted) and
    thickly sliced
25g/1oz/2 tbsp unrefined caster (superfine)
    sugar or rapadura
30ml/2 tbsp water
1.5ml/¼ tsp ground cinnamon
25g/1oz/¼ cup ground almonds
8–10 large slices of white or wholemeal
    (whole-wheat) bread

For the Calvados sauce
3 egg yolks
40g/1½oz/3 tbsp unrefined caster
    (superfine) sugar or rapadura
30ml/2 tbsp Calvados

1 Preheat the oven to 190°C/375°F/ Gas 5. Line the base of four individual 10cm/4in-diameter deep, earthenware ramekin dishes with baking parchment. Brush evenly and thoroughly with a little of the melted butter or margarine, then sprinkle each dish with a little of the demerara sugar, rotating the dish in your hands to coat each dish evenly.

VARIATIONS
• Slices of peeled pear or eating apples can be used in this recipe instead of the stoned, sliced plums.
• If you cannot find organic Calvados any organic fruit-based spirit will work in this dish.

2 Place the stoned plum slices in a pan with the caster sugar, water and ground cinnamon and cook gently for 5 minutes, or until the plums have softened slightly. Leave the plums to cool, then stir in the ground almonds.

3 Cut the crusts off the bread and then use a plain pastry cutter to cut out four rounds to fit the bases of the ramekins. Dip the bread rounds into the melted butter and fit them into the dishes. Cut four more rounds to fit the tops of the dishes and set aside.

4 Cut the remaining bread into strips, dip into the melted butter and use to line the sides of the ramekins completely.

5 Divide the plum mixture among the lined dishes and level the tops with the back of a spoon. Place the bread rounds on top and brush with the remaining butter. Place the ramekins on a baking sheet and bake for 25 minutes.

6 Make the sauce just before the charlottes are ready. Place the egg yolks and caster sugar in a large bowl, and whisk them together until pale. Place the bowl over a pan of simmering water and whisk in the Calvados. Continue whisking until the mixture is very light and frothy.

7 Remove the charlottes from the oven and turn out on to warm serving plates. Pour a little sauce over and around the charlottes and serve immediately.

COOK'S TIP
For an extra creamy dessert, serve the puddings with Greek (US strained plain) yogurt or crème fraîche.

PARSNIP CAKE with ORANGE ICING

This fabulous vegan cake is similar to the ever-popular carrot cake, but uses non-dairy alternatives to margarine and cream cheese.

SERVES TEN

250g/9oz/2¼ cups wholemeal (whole-wheat) self-raising (self-rising) flour
15ml/1 tbsp baking powder
5ml/1 tsp ground cinnamon
5ml/1 tsp freshly ground nutmeg
130g/4½oz/9 tbsp vegan margarine
130g/4½oz/scant ½ cup unrefined soft light brown sugar or rapadura
250g/9oz parsnips, coarsely grated
1 banana, mashed
finely grated rind and juice of 1 orange

For the topping
225g/8oz/1 cup organic soya cream cheese
45ml/3 tbsp unrefined icing (confectioner's) sugar
juice of 1 small orange
fine strips of orange peel

1 Preheat the oven to 180°C/350°F/Gas 4. Lightly grease and line the base of a 900g/2lb loaf tin (pan).

2 Sift the flour, baking powder and spices into a large bowl. Add any bran remaining in the sieve.

COOK'S TIP
If you can't find self-raising wholemeal flour, use ordinary wholemeal flour and add an extra 15ml/1 tbsp baking powder.

VARIATION
Serve the cake as a dessert with a generous spoonful of organic natural (plain) yogurt, crème fraîche or soya cream, flavoured with grated orange rind or a little Calvados.

3 Melt the margarine in a pan, add the sugar and stir until dissolved. Make a well in the flour mixture, then add the melted margarine and sugar. Mix in the parsnips, banana and orange rind and juice. Spoon the mixture into the prepared tin and level the top with the back of a spoon.

4 Bake for 45–50 minutes until a skewer inserted into the centre of the cake comes out clean. Allow the cake to cool slightly before removing from the tin, then transfer to a wire rack to cool completely.

5 To make the topping, beat together the cream cheese, icing sugar, orange juice and strips of orange peel until smooth. Spread the topping evenly over the cake.

COUNTRY APPLE CAKE

This perennial favourite is a great way to take advantage of the season's apple harvest. There are any number of organic apples available nowadays, including heirloom and almost-lost local varieties, which makes cooking and eating this cake a real treat.

MAKES ONE 18CM/7IN CAKE

115g/4oz/½ cup soft non-hydrogenated margarine
115g/4oz/½ cup unrefined soft light brown sugar or rapadura
2 eggs, beaten
115g/4oz/1 cup self-raising (self-rising) flour, sifted
50g/2oz/½ cup rice flour
5ml/1 tsp baking powder
10ml/2 tsp mixed (apple-pie) spice
1 cooking apple, cored and chopped
115g/4oz/scant 1 cup raisins
about 60ml/4 tbsp milk or soya milk
15g/½oz/2 tbsp flaked (sliced) almonds

1 Preheat the oven to 160°C/325°F/ Gas 3. Lightly grease and line a deep 18cm/ 7in round, loose-bottomed cake tin (pan).

2 Cream the margarine and sugar in a mixing bowl. Gradually add the eggs, then fold in the flours, baking powder and spice.

3 Stir in the chopped apple, raisins and enough of the milk to make a soft, dropping consistency.

4 Turn the mixture into the prepared tin and level the surface. Sprinkle the flaked almonds over the top. Bake the cake for 1–1¼ hours until risen, firm to the touch and golden brown.

5 Cool the apple cake in the tin for about 10 minutes, then turn out on to a wire rack to cool. Cut into slices when cold. Alternatively, serve the cake warm, in slices, with custard or ice cream. Store the cold cake in an airtight container or wrapped in foil.

VARIATIONS
• Use sultanas (golden raisins) or chopped dried apricots or pears instead of the raisins.
• A wide variety of organic ice creams is available from independent dairies and supermarkets – vanilla goes particularly well with this cake.

OAT and RAISIN DROP SCONES

Serve these easy-to-make organic scones at tea time or as a dessert – or even a special breakfast or brunch – with real maple syrup or clear honey.

MAKES ABOUT SIXTEEN

75g/3oz/⅔ cup self-raising (self-rising) flour
2.5ml/½ tsp baking powder
50g/2oz/scant ½ cup raisins
25g/1oz/¼ cup fine oatmeal
25g/1oz/2 tbsp unrefined caster (superfine) sugar or rapadura
grated rind of 1 orange
2 egg yolks
10g/¼oz/½ tbsp unsalted (sweet) butter or non-hydrogenated margarine, melted
200ml/7fl oz/scant 1 cup single (light) cream or soya cream
200ml/7fl oz/scant 1 cup water
sunflower oil, for greasing
icing (confectioner's) sugar, for dusting

1 Sift the self-raising flour and baking powder together into a large mixing bowl.

COOK'S TIP
Wrap the cooked scones in a clean dishtowel to keep them soft.

2 Add the raisins, oatmeal, sugar and orange rind. Gradually beat in the egg yolks, butter, cream and water to make a creamy batter.

3 Lightly grease and heat a large heavy frying pan or griddle and drop about 30ml/2 tbsp of batter at a time on to the pan or griddle to make six or seven small pancakes.

4 Cook over a moderate heat until bubbles show on the scones' surface, then turn them over and cook for a further 2 minutes until golden.

5 Transfer to a plate and dust with icing sugar. Keep warm while cooking the remaining mixture. Serve warm.

CARAMELIZED ONION and WALNUT SCONES

These scones are very good buttered and served with mature Cheddar cheese. Make small scones to use as a base for cocktail savouries, served topped with a little soft goat's cheese.

4 Add the cooked onion and cumin mixture, chopped walnuts and chopped fresh thyme, then bind to make a soft, but not sticky, dough with the buttermilk.

5 Roll or pat out the mixture to an even thickness of just over 1cm/½in. Stamp out 10–12 scones using a 5–6cm/ 2–2½in plain round cutter.

6 Place the scones on a floured baking tray, glaze with the milk or soya milk and scatter with a little salt and the remaining cumin seeds. Bake the scones for 12–15 minutes until well-risen and golden brown. Allow to cool for a few minutes on a wire rack and serve warm spread with butter, non-hydrogenated margarine or goat's cheese.

MAKES TEN TO TWELVE

90g/3½oz/7 tbsp butter or
   non-hydrogenated margarine
15ml/1 tbsp olive oil
1 Spanish onion, chopped
5ml/1 tsp cumin seeds, lightly crushed
200g/7oz/1¾ cups self-raising
   (self-rising) flour
5ml/1 tsp baking powder
25g/1oz/¼ cup fine oatmeal
5ml/1 tsp light unrefined muscovado
   (brown) sugar
90g/3½oz/scant 1 cup chopped walnuts
5ml/1 tsp chopped fresh thyme
120–150ml/4–5fl oz/½–⅔ cup buttermilk
a little milk or soya milk
sea salt and ground black pepper

1 Melt 15g/½oz/1 tbsp of the butter with the oil in a small pan and cook the onion gently, covered, for 10–12 minutes. Uncover, then continue to cook gently until it begins to brown.

2 Add half the cumin seeds and increase the heat slightly. Continue to cook, stirring occasionally, until the onion begins to caramelize. Cool. Preheat the oven to 200°C/400°F/Gas 6.

3 Sift the flour and baking powder into a large bowl and add the oatmeal, sugar, 2.5ml/½ tsp salt and black pepper. Add the remaining butter or margarine and rub in until the mixture resembles fine breadcrumbs.

FRUIT, NUT AND SEED TEABREAD

*Cut into slices and spread with a little butter or non-hydrogenated margarine,
jam or honey, this teabread makes an ideal breakfast bread. The dried fruit,
nuts and seeds mean it is a fine source of fibre.*

MAKES ONE 900G/2LB LOAF

115g/4oz/⅔ cup dried dates, chopped
115g/4oz/½ cup dried apricots, chopped
115g/4oz/1 cup sultanas (golden raisins)
115g/4oz/½ cup unrefined soft light brown
    sugar or rapadura
225g/8oz/2 cups self-raising (self-rising)
    flour
5ml/1 tsp baking powder
10ml/2 tsp mixed (apple pie) spice
75g/3oz/¾ cup chopped mixed nuts
75g/3oz/¾ cup mixed seeds, such as
    linseed, sunflower and sesame seeds
2 eggs, beaten
150ml/¼ pint/⅔ cup semi-skimmed
    (low-fat) milk or soya milk

1 Preheat the oven to 180°C/350°F/
Gas 4. Lightly grease a 900g/2lb loaf tin
(pan). Place the chopped dates and
apricots and sultanas in a large mixing
bowl and stir in the sugar.

COOK'S TIPS
• Use wholemeal (whole-wheat) self-
raising (self-rising) flour for an unbeatable
nutty flavour.
• Organic dates have an extremely sweet
taste, which makes them wonderful to
bake with.
• Try adding hemp seeds to the seed
mixture for a really nutritious touch.

2 Place the flour, baking powder, mixed
spice, mixed nuts and seeds in a
separate bowl and mix well.

3 Stir the eggs and milk into the fruit
mixture, then add the flour mixture and
beat together until well mixed.

4 Spoon the mixture into the prepared
tin and level the surface. Bake for about
1 hour until the teabread is firm to the
touch and lightly browned.

5 Allow to cool in the tin for a few
minutes, then turn out on to a wire rack
to cool completely. Serve warm or cold,
cut into slices. Wrap the teabread in foil
to store.

HUNGARIAN FRUIT BREAD

When dried, many of the nutrients and sugars in fruit are concentrated but so, unfortunately, are any pesticide residues. So, to ensure a clear conscience as you tuck into a slice of this delightful light bread, always use organic dried fruits – a much healthier choice.

SERVES EIGHT TO TEN

sunflower oil, for greasing
7 egg whites
175g/6oz/scant 1 cup unrefined caster
  (superfine) sugar or rapadura
115g/4oz/1 cup flaked (sliced)
  almonds, toasted
115g/4oz/¾ cup sultanas (golden raisins)
grated rind of 1 lemon
165g/5½oz/1⅓ cups plain (all-purpose)
  flour, sifted, plus extra for flouring
75g/3oz/6 tbsp butter or
  non-hydrogenated margarine, melted

1 Preheat the oven to 180°C/350°F/ Gas 4 and grease and flour a 1kg/2¼lb loaf tin (pan). Whisk the egg whites until they are very stiff, but not crumbly. Fold in the sugar gradually, then the flaked, toasted almonds, sultanas and lemon rind.

2 Fold the flour and butter into the mixture and tip it into the prepared tin. Bake for about 45 minutes until well risen and pale golden brown. Cool for a few minutes in the tin, then turn out and serve warm or cold, in slices.

WINTER

Warming comfort food is the order of the day in cold weather to help
keep out winter chills. Root vegetables such as swede (rutabaga),
carrots, turnips and parsnips are readily available and can be included
in winter soups, stews and casseroles such as Chicken Casserole with
Winter Vegetables, or Braised Shoulder of Mutton with
Pearl Barley and Baby Vegetables.

For vegetarians, substantial main courses include warming
ingredients such as pulses and spices – try Parsnips and Chickpeas
in Garlic, Onion, Chilli and Ginger Paste, or Barley Risotto with
Roasted Squash and Leeks.

Rich, meaty dishes to enjoy during the coldest months of the year
include Chilli Con Carne and Boeuf Bourguignonne – delicious
served with mashed root vegetables and organic red wine.

Fish dishes for the winter season are best served with the addition
of well-flavoured ingredients: try Fillets of Brill in Red Wine Sauce
or Smoked Haddock with Mustard Cabbage.

Sweet winter treats to enjoy include Baked Maple and Pecan
Croissant Pudding, Orange Marmalade Chocolate Loaf and
a fragrant Dried Fruit Compote.

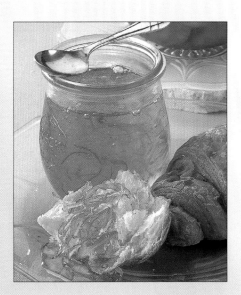

WINTER FARMHOUSE SOUP

Root vegetables form the base of this chunky, minestrone-style main meal soup.
Always choose organic vegetables and vary according to what you have to hand.

SERVES FOUR

30ml/2 tbsp olive oil
1 onion, roughly chopped
3 carrots, cut into large chunks
175–200g/6–7oz turnips, cut into
large chunks
about 175g/6oz swede (rutabaga), cut into
large chunks
400g/14oz can chopped Italian tomatoes
15ml/1 tbsp tomato purée (paste)
5ml/1 tsp dried mixed herbs
5ml/1 tsp dried oregano
50g/2oz dried (bell) peppers, washed and
thinly sliced (optional)
1.5 litres/2½ pints/6¼ cups vegetable
stock or water
50g/2oz/½ cup dried macaroni
400g/14oz can red kidney beans, rinsed
and drained
30ml/2 tbsp chopped fresh flat leaf parsley
sea salt and ground black pepper
freshly grated Parmesan cheese or premium
Italian-style vegetarian cheese, to serve

1 Heat the olive oil in a large pan, add the onion and cook over a low heat for about 5 minutes until softened. Add the carrot, turnip and swede chunks, canned chopped tomatoes, tomato purée, dried mixed herbs, dried oregano and dried peppers, if using. Stir in a little salt and plenty of pepper to taste.

2 Pour in the vegetable stock or water and bring to the boil. Stir well, cover the pan, then lower the heat and simmer for 30 minutes, stirring occasionally.

3 Add the pasta to the pan and bring quickly to the boil, stirring. Lower the heat and simmer, uncovered, for about 8 minutes until the pasta is only just tender, or according to the instructions on the packet. Stir frequently.

4 Stir in the kidney beans. Heat through for 2–3 minutes, then remove the pan from the heat and stir in the parsley. Taste the soup for seasoning. Serve hot in warmed soup bowls, with grated cheese handed separately.

MOROCCAN SPICED MUTTON SOUP

Classic north African spices – ginger, turmeric and cinnamon – are combined with chickpeas and mutton to make this hearty, warming main-course soup.

SERVES SIX

75g/3oz/½ cup chickpeas, soaked overnight
15g/½oz/1 tbsp butter or 15ml/1 tbsp
   olive oil
225g/8oz mutton, cut into cubes
1 onion, chopped
450g/1lb tomatoes, peeled and chopped
a few celery leaves, chopped
30ml/2 tbsp chopped fresh parsley
15ml/1 tbsp chopped fresh coriander
   (cilantro)
2.5ml/½ tsp ground ginger
2.5ml/½ tsp ground turmeric
5ml/1 tsp ground cinnamon
1.75 litres/3 pints/7½ cups water
75g/3oz/scant ½ cup green lentils
75g/3oz/¾ cup vermicelli or soup pasta
2 egg yolks
juice of ½–1 lemon, to taste
sea salt and ground black pepper
fresh coriander (cilantro), to garnish
lemon wedges, to serve

1 Drain the chickpeas and set aside. Heat the butter or oil in a large pan and fry the mutton and onion for 2–3 minutes, stirring, until the mutton is just browned.

2 Add the chopped tomatoes, celery leaves, herbs and spices and season well with ground black pepper. Cook for about 1 minute, then stir in the water and add the green lentils and the soaked, drained and rinsed chickpeas.

3 Slowly bring to the boil and skim the surface to remove the froth. Boil rapidly for 10 minutes, then reduce the heat and simmer very gently for 2 hours, or until the chickpeas are very tender.

4 Season with salt and pepper, then add the vermicelli or soup pasta to the pan and cook for 5–6 minutes until it is just tender. If the soup is very thick at this stage, add a little more water.

5 Beat the egg yolks with the lemon juice and stir into the simmering soup. Immediately remove the soup from the heat and stir until thickened. Pour into warmed serving bowls and garnish with plenty of fresh coriander. Serve the soup with lemon wedges.

COOK'S TIP
If you have forgotten to soak the chickpeas overnight, place them in a pan with about four times their volume of cold water. Bring very slowly to the boil, then cover the pan, remove it from the heat and leave to stand for 45 minutes before using as described in the recipe.

CHICKEN, LEEK and CELERY SOUP

This makes a substantial main course soup with fresh crusty bread. You will need nothing more than a mixed green salad or fresh winter fruit to follow, such as satsumas, tangerines or apricots.

SERVES FOUR TO SIX

1.3kg/3lb chicken
1 small head of celery, trimmed
1 onion, coarsely chopped
1 fresh bay leaf
a few fresh parsley stalks
a few fresh tarragon sprigs
2.5 litres/4 pints/10 cups cold water
3 large leeks
65g/2½oz/5 tbsp butter or 75ml/5 tbsp
   olive oil
2 potatoes, cut into chunks
150ml/¼ pint/⅔ cup dry white wine
30–45ml/2–3 tbsp single (light) or soya
   cream (optional)
sea salt and ground black pepper
90g/3½oz pancetta, grilled until crisp,
   to garnish

1 Cut the breasts off the chicken and set aside. Chop the rest of the chicken carcass into 8–10 pieces and place in a large pan or stockpot.

2 Chop 4–5 of the outer sticks of the head of celery and add them to the pan with the coarsely chopped onion. Tie the bay leaf, parsley stalks and tarragon sprigs together to make a bouquet garni and add to the pan. Pour in the cold water to cover the ingredients and bring to the boil. Reduce the heat and cover the pan with a lid, then simmer for 1½ hours.

3 Remove the chicken from the pan using a slotted spoon and cut off and reserve the meat. Strain the stock through a sieve, then return it to the cleaned pan and boil rapidly until it has reduced in volume to about 1.5 litres/2½ pints/6¼ cups.

4 Meanwhile, set about 150g/5oz of the leeks aside. Slice the remaining leeks and the remaining celery, reserving any celery leaves. Chop the celery leaves and set them aside to garnish the soup or reserve a few of the leek pieces.

5 Heat half the butter or oil in a large, heavy pan. Add the sliced leeks and celery, cover and cook over a low heat for about 10 minutes, or until the vegetables are softened but not browned. Add the potatoes, wine and 1.2 litres/2 pints/5 cups of the stock.

6 Season with a little salt and plenty of black pepper, bring to the boil and reduce the heat. Part-cover the pan and simmer the soup for 15–20 minutes, or until the potatoes are cooked.

COOK'S TIP
There are a vast number of different varieties of organic potatoes but all fall into two main types: floury and waxy. Floury potatoes such as Maris Piper and Estima are ideal for soups, mashing or baking. Waxy potatoes such as Charlotte or Pink Fir Apple are delicious simply boiled and served with butter.

7 Meanwhile, skin the reserved chicken breasts and cut the flesh into small pieces. Melt the remaining butter or oil in a frying pan, add the chicken and fry for 5–7 minutes until cooked.

8 Thickly slice the reserved leeks, add to the frying pan and cook, stirring occasionally, for a further 3–4 minutes until they are just cooked.

9 Process the soup with the cooked chicken from the stock in a food processor or blender. Taste and adjust the seasoning, and add more stock if the soup is very thick.

10 Stir in the cream, if using, and the chicken and leek mixture. Reheat the soup gently. Serve in warmed bowls. Crumble the pancetta over the soup and sprinkle with the chopped celery leaves or reserved leek slices.

VARIATIONS
• If you prefer, use ready-cut chicken portions instead of jointing a whole chicken.
• Streaky (fatty) bacon can be used instead of pancetta to add a delicious flavour to the soup.

SPICED ONION KOFTAS

These delicious Indian onion fritters are made with chickpea flour, otherwise known as gram flour or besan, which has a distinctive nutty flavour. Serve with chutney or a yogurt dip.

3 Add the chickpea flour and baking powder to the onion mixture in the bowl, then use your hand to mix all the ingredients thoroughly.

4 Shape the mixture by hand into 12–15 koftas about the size of golf balls.

5 Heat the sunflower oil for deep-frying to 180–190°C/350–375°F, or until a cube of day-old bread browns in about 30–45 seconds. Fry the koftas, four to five at a time, until deep golden brown all over. Remove with a slotted spoon and drain each batch on kitchen paper and keep warm until all the koftas are cooked. Serve the koftas warm with lemon wedges (if using), coriander sprigs and a yogurt and herb dip.

MAKES TWELVE TO FIFTEEN

675g/1½lb onions, halved and thinly sliced
5ml/1 tsp sea salt
5ml/1 tsp ground coriander
5ml/1 tsp ground cumin
2.5ml/½ tsp ground turmeric
1–2 green chillies, seeded and
   finely chopped
45ml/3 tbsp chopped fresh coriander
   (cilantro)
90g/3½oz/¾ cup chickpea flour
2.5ml/½ tsp baking powder
sunflower oil, for deep-frying

To serve
lemon wedges (optional)
fresh coriander sprigs
yogurt and herb dip (see Cook's Tip)

1 Place the onions in a colander, add the salt and toss. Place on a plate and leave to stand for 45 minutes, tossing once or twice. Rinse the onions, then squeeze out any excess moisture.

2 Place the onions in a bowl. Add the ground coriander, cumin, turmeric, finely chopped chillies and chopped fresh coriander. Mix well.

COOK'S TIP
To make a yogurt and herb dip to serve with the koftas, stir 30ml/2 tbsp each of chopped fresh coriander (cilantro) and mint into about 225g/8oz/1 cup set natural (plain) yogurt. Season with salt, ground toasted cumin seeds and a pinch of muscovado (brown) sugar

LENTIL DHAL with ROASTED GARLIC

This spicy lentil dhal makes a sustaining and comforting meal when served with brown rice or Indian breads and any dry-spiced dish, particularly a cauliflower or potato dish.

SERVES FOUR TO SIX

40g/1½oz/3 tbsp butter or ghee
1 onion, chopped
2 green chillies, seeded and chopped
15ml/1 tbsp chopped fresh root ginger
225g/8oz/1 cup yellow or red lentils
900ml/1½ pints/3¾ cups water
45ml/3 tbsp roasted garlic purée (paste)
5ml/1 tsp ground cumin
5ml/1 tsp ground coriander
200g/7oz tomatoes, peeled and diced
a little lemon juice
sea salt and ground black pepper
30–45ml/2–3 tbsp coriander (cilantro)
    sprigs, to garnish

For the spicy garnish
30ml/2 tbsp sunflower oil
4–5 shallots, sliced
2 garlic cloves, thinly sliced
15g/½oz/1 tbsp butter or ghee
5ml/1 tsp cumin seeds
5ml/1 tsp mustard seeds
3–4 small dried red chillies
8–10 fresh curry leaves

1 First begin the spicy garnish. Heat the oil in a large, heavy pan. Add the shallots and fry them over a medium heat for 5–10 minutes, stirring occasionally, until they are crisp and browned. Add the garlic and cook, stirring frequently, for a moment or two until the garlic colours slightly. Remove the pan from the heat and use a slotted spoon to remove the shallots and garlic from the pan and set aside.

COOK'S TIP
Ghee is clarified butter that has had all the milk solids removed by heating – it was originally made to extend the keeping qualities of butter in India. It is the main cooking fat used in Indian cooking. Because the milk solids have been removed, ghee has a high smoking point and can therefore be cooked at higher temperatures than ordinary butter. Look for organic ghee in whole food stores.

2 Melt the 40g/½oz/3 tbsp butter or ghee for the dhal in the pan, add the onion, chillies and ginger, and cook for 10 minutes until golden.

3 Stir in the yellow or red lentils and water, then bring to the boil, reduce the heat and part-cover the pan. Simmer, stirring occasionally, for 50–60 minutes until it is the same consistency as a very thick soup.

4 Stir in the roasted garlic purée, cumin and ground coriander, then season with salt and pepper to taste. Cook the dhal for a further 10–15 minutes, uncovered, stirring frequently.

5 Stir in the tomatoes and then adjust the seasoning, adding a little lemon juice to taste if necessary.

6 To finish the spicy garnish: melt the butter or ghee in a frying pan. Add the cumin and mustard seeds and fry until the mustard seeds begin to pop. Stir in the small dried red chillies and fresh curry leaves, then immediately swirl the mixture into the cooked dhal. Garnish with coriander and the spicy fried shallots and garlic and serve.

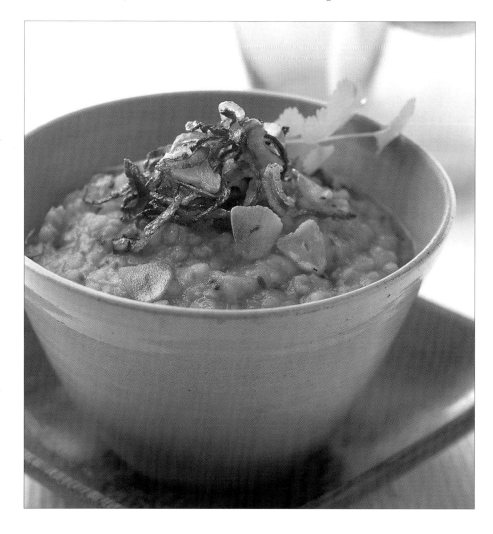

JERUSALEM ARTICHOKES with GARLIC

The slightly smoky and earthy flavour of Jerusalem artichokes is excellent with garlic, shallots and smoked bacon. These are good with chicken, pork or a classic nut roast.

SERVES FOUR

50g/2oz/¼ cup butter or 50ml/3½ tbsp
   olive oil
115g/4oz smoked bacon, chopped
800g/1¾lb Jerusalem artichokes
8–12 garlic cloves, peeled
115g/4oz shallots, chopped
75ml/5 tbsp water
30ml/2 tbsp olive oil
25g/1oz/½ cup fresh white or wholemeal
   (whole-wheat) breadcrumbs
30–45ml/2–3 tbsp chopped fresh parsley
sea salt and ground black pepper

1 Melt half the butter or heat half the olive oil in a heavy frying pan, add the chopped bacon and cook until it is brown and just beginning to crisp. Remove half the bacon from the frying pan and set aside.

COOK'S TIP
If you are unable to find organic shallots, try using another mild and sweet allium instead, such as red onions. Their dark colour also complements the creamy artichokes in this dish.

2 Add the artichokes, garlic and shallots to the pan, and cook, stirring frequently, until the artichokes and garlic begin to brown slightly.

3 Season with salt and black pepper to taste and stir in the water. Cover and cook for a further 8–10 minutes, shaking the pan occasionally.

4 Uncover the pan, increase the heat and cook for 5 minutes, or until all the moisture has evaporated and the artichokes are tender.

5 In another frying pan, heat the remaining butter or oil with the 30ml/ 2 tbsp olive oil. Add the white or wholemeal breadcrumbs and fry over a moderate heat, stirring frequently with a wooden spoon, until crisp and golden. Stir in the chopped parsley and the reserved cooked bacon.

6 Combine the artichokes with the crispy breadcrumb and bacon mixture, mixing well. Season to taste with a little salt and plenty of ground black pepper, if necessary. Transfer to a warmed serving dish and serve immediately.

BRAISED RED CABBAGE with BEETROOT

Cook this vibrantly coloured dish in the oven at the same time as a pork casserole
or joint of meat for a simple, easy-to-prepare meal.

SERVES SIX TO EIGHT

675g/1½lb red cabbage
1 Spanish onion, thinly sliced
30ml/2 tbsp olive oil
2 tart eating apples, peeled,
    cored and sliced
300ml/½ pint/1¼ cups vegetable stock
60ml/4 tbsp red wine vinegar
375g/13oz raw beetroot (beet), peeled
    and coarsely grated
sea salt and ground black pepper

COOK'S TIP
When buying any type of cabbage, choose
one that is firm and heavy for its size.
The leaves should look healthy – avoid
any with curling leaves or blemishes.

1 Cut the red cabbage into fine shreds,
discarding any tough outer leaves and
the core, and place in an ovenproof dish.

2 Place the thinly sliced onion and the
olive oil in a frying pan and sauté until
the onion is soft and golden.

3 Preheat the oven to 190°C/375°F/
Gas 5. Stir the apple slices, vegetable
stock and wine vinegar into the onions,
then transfer to the dish. Season with
salt and pepper, and cover.

4 Cook the cabbage for 1 hour. Stir in
the beetroot, re-cover the dish and cook
for a further 20–30 minutes, or until the
cabbage and beetroot are tender.

PARSNIPS and CHICKPEAS in GARLIC, ONION, CHILLI and GINGER PASTE

Organic root vegetables, such as parsnips, often have a knobbly appearance that makes them interesting and individual, and their flavours are sweeter and more intense.

SERVES FOUR

200g/7oz/1 cup dried chickpeas, soaked
    overnight in cold water, then drained
7 garlic cloves, finely chopped
1 small onion, chopped
5cm/2in piece fresh root ginger, chopped
2 green chillies, seeded and finely chopped
450ml/¾ pint/scant 2 cups plus
    75ml/5 tbsp water
60ml/4 tbsp sunflower oil
5ml/1 tsp cumin seeds
10ml/2 tsp ground coriander seeds
5ml/1 tsp ground turmeric
2.5–5ml/½–1 tsp chilli powder
    or mild paprika
50g/2oz/½ cup cashew nuts, toasted
    and ground
250g/9oz tomatoes, peeled and chopped
900g/2lb parsnips, cut into chunks
5ml/1 tsp ground roasted cumin seeds
juice of 1 lime, to taste
sea salt and ground black pepper

To serve
fresh coriander (cilantro) leaves
a few cashew nuts, toasted
natural (plain) yogurt
naan bread or chapatis

1 Put the soaked chickpeas in a pan, cover with cold water and bring to the boil. Boil vigorously for 10 minutes, then reduce the heat so that the water boils steadily. Cook for 1–1½ hours, or until the chickpeas are tender. (The cooking time depends on how long the chickpeas have been stored.) Drain and set aside.

2 Set 10ml/2 tsp of the finely chopped garlic aside, then place the remainder in a food processor or blender with the onion, ginger and half the chopped chillies. Add the 75ml/5 tbsp water and process to make a smooth paste.

COOK'S TIP
Do not add salt to the water when cooking dried chickpeas, as this will toughen them.

3 Heat the oil in a frying pan and cook the cumin seeds for 30 seconds. Stir in the coriander seeds, turmeric, chilli powder or paprika and the ground cashew nuts. Add the ginger paste and cook, stirring frequently, until the water begins to evaporate. Add the tomatoes and stir-fry for 2–3 minutes.

4 Mix in the cooked chickpeas and parsnip chunks with the 450ml/¾ pint/scant 2 cups water, a little salt and plenty of black pepper. Bring to the boil, stir, then simmer, uncovered, for 15–20 minutes until the parsnips are completely tender.

5 Reduce the liquid, if necessary, by bringing the sauce to the boil and then boiling fiercely until the sauce is thick. Add the ground roasted cumin with more salt and/or lime juice to taste. Stir in the reserved garlic and green chilli, and cook for a further 1–2 minutes. Scatter the fresh coriander leaves and toasted cashew nuts over and serve straight away with yogurt and warmed naan bread or chapatis.

BARLEY RISOTTO with ROASTED SQUASH and LEEKS

This is more like a pilaff made with slightly chewy, nutty-flavoured pearl barley than a classic risotto. Sweet organic leeks and roasted squash are superb with this earthy grain.

SERVES FOUR TO FIVE

200g/7oz/1 cup pearl barley
1 butternut squash, peeled, seeded and
    cut into chunks
10ml/2 tsp chopped fresh thyme
60ml/4 tbsp olive oil
25g/1oz/2 tbsp butter
4 leeks, cut into fairly thick diagonal slices
2 garlic cloves, finely chopped
175g/6oz/2½ cups chestnut mushrooms, sliced
2 carrots, coarsely grated
about 120ml/4fl oz/½ cup vegetable stock
30ml/2 tbsp chopped fresh flat leaf parsley
50g/2oz/⅔ cup Parmesan cheese or
    premium Italian-style vegetarian cheese,
    grated or shaved
45ml/3 tbsp pumpkin seeds, toasted, or
    chopped walnuts
sea salt and ground black pepper

1 Rinse the barley, then cook it in simmering water, keeping the pan part-covered, for 35–45 minutes, or until tender. Drain. Preheat the oven to 200°C/400°F/Gas 6.

2 Place the squash in a roasting pan with half the thyme. Season with pepper and toss with half the oil. Roast, stirring once, for 30–35 minutes, until the squash is tender and beginning to brown.

3 Heat half the butter with the remaining olive oil in a large frying pan. Cook the leeks and garlic gently for 5 minutes. Add the mushrooms and remaining thyme, then cook until the liquid from the mushrooms evaporates and they begin to fry.

4 Stir in the carrots and cook for about 2 minutes, then add the barley and most of the vegetable stock. Season well and part-cover the pan. Cook for a further 5 minutes. Pour in the remaining stock if the mixture seems dry.

5 Stir in the parsley, the remaining butter and half the cheese, then stir in the squash. Add seasoning to taste and serve immediately, sprinkled with the toasted pumpkin seeds or walnuts and the remaining cheese.

VARIATIONS
• Make the risotto with organic brown rice instead of the barley – cook following the packet instructions and continue from step 2.
• Any type of organic mushrooms can be used in this recipe – try sliced field (portabello) mushrooms for a hearty flavour.

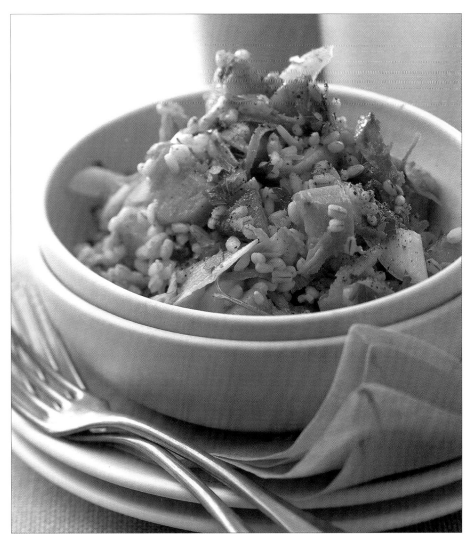

PEPPERS FILLED with SPICED VEGETABLES

Indian spices season the potato and aubergine stuffing in these colourful baked peppers.
They are good with brown rice and a lentil dhal. Alternatively, serve them with a salad,
Indian breads and a cucumber or mint and yogurt raita.

SERVES SIX

6 large evenly shaped red (bell) or
    yellow (bell) peppers
500g/1¼lb waxy potatoes
1 small onion, chopped
4–5 garlic cloves, chopped
5cm/2in piece fresh root ginger, chopped
1–2 fresh green chillies, seeded
    and chopped
105ml/7 tbsp water
90–105ml/6–7 tbsp sunflower oil
1 aubergine (eggplant), diced
10ml/2 tsp cumin seeds
5ml/1 tsp kalonji seeds
2.5ml/½ tsp ground turmeric
5ml/1 tsp ground coriander
5ml/1 tsp ground toasted cumin seeds
pinch of cayenne pepper
about 30ml/2 tbsp lemon juice
sea salt and ground black pepper
30ml/2 tbsp chopped fresh coriander
    (cilantro), to garnish

1 Cut the tops off the red or yellow peppers, then remove and discard the seeds. Cut a thin slice off the base of the peppers, if necessary, to make them stand upright.

2 Bring a large pan of lightly salted water to the boil. Add the peppers and cook for 5–6 minutes. Drain and leave them upside down in a colander.

COOK'S TIP
The hottest part of a chilli is the white membrane that connects the seeds to the flesh. Removing the seeds and membrane before cooking gives a milder flavour.

3 Cook the potatoes in lightly salted, boiling water for 10–12 minutes until just tender. Drain, cool and peel, then cut into 1cm/½in dice.

4 Put the onion, garlic, ginger and green chillies in a food processor or blender with 60ml/4 tbsp of the water and process to a purée.

5 Heat 45ml/3 tbsp of the sunflower oil in a large, deep frying pan and cook the diced aubergine, stirring occasionally, until it is evenly browned on all sides. Remove from the pan and set aside. Add another 30ml/2 tbsp of the sunflower oil to the pan, add the diced potatoes and cook until lightly browned on all sides. Remove the potatoes from the pan and set aside.

6 If necessary, add another 15ml/1 tbsp sunflower oil to the pan, then add the cumin and kalonji seeds. Fry briefly until the seeds darken, then add the turmeric, coriander and ground cumin. Cook for 15 seconds. Stir in the onion and garlic purée and fry, scraping the pan with a spatula, until the onions begin to brown.

7 Return the potatoes and aubergine to the pan, season with salt, pepper and 1–2 pinches of cayenne. Add the remaining water and 15ml/1 tbsp lemon juice and then cook, stirring, until the liquid evaporates. Preheat the oven to 190°C/375°F/Gas 5.

8 Fill the peppers with the spiced vegetable mixture and place on a lightly greased baking tray. Brush the peppers with a little oil and bake for 30–35 minutes until they are cooked. Allow to cool a little, then sprinkle with a little more lemon juice, garnish with the coriander and serve.

COOK'S TIP
Kalonji, or nigella as it is also known, is a tiny black seed. It is widely used in Indian cookery, especially sprinkled over breads or in potato dishes. It has a mild, slightly nutty flavour and is best toasted for a few seconds in a dry or lightly oiled frying pan over a medium heat before using in a recipe. This helps to bring out its flavour, as with most spices.

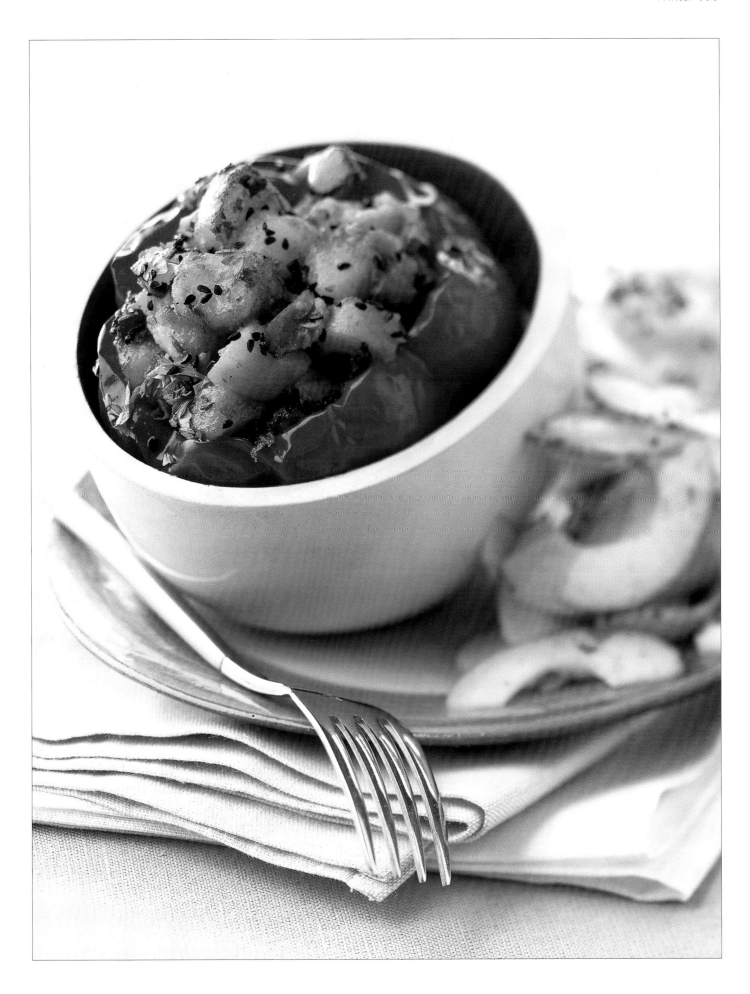

MARMALADE-GLAZED GOOSE

Succulent roast goose is the classic centrepiece for a traditional British winter family lunch. Red cabbage cooked with leeks, and braised fennel are tasty accompaniments.

SERVES EIGHT

4.5kg/10lb goose
1 cooking apple, peeled, cored and
    cut into eighths
1 large onion, cut into eighths
bunch of fresh sage, plus extra to garnish
30ml/2 tbsp ginger marmalade, melted
sea salt and ground black pepper

For the stuffing
25g/1oz/2 tbsp butter or 30ml/2 tbsp
    olive oil
1 onion, finely chopped
15ml/1 tbsp ginger marmalade
450g/1lb/2 cups ready-to-eat
    prunes, chopped
45ml/3 tbsp Madeira
225g/8oz/4 cups fresh white or wholemeal
    (whole-wheat) breadcrumbs
30ml/2 tbsp chopped fresh sage

For the gravy
1 onion, chopped
15ml/1 tbsp plain (all-purpose) or
    wholemeal (whole-wheat) flour
150ml/¼ pint/⅔ cup Madeira
600ml/1 pint/2½ cups chicken stock

1 Preheat the oven to 200°C/400°F/ Gas 6. Prick the skin of the goose all over and season it inside and out.

COOK'S TIP
Red cabbage goes well with goose. Cook 1 small leek, sliced, in 75g/3oz/6 tbsp butter or 90ml/6 tbsp olive oil, add 1kg/ 2¼lb/9 cups shredded red cabbage, with the grated rind of 1 orange, and cook for 15 minutes.

2 Mix the apple, onion and sage leaves together and spoon the mixture into the parson's nose end of the goose.

3 To make the stuffing, melt the butter or oil in a large pan and cook the onion for about 5 minutes, or until softened but not coloured. Remove the pan from the heat and stir in the marmalade, chopped prunes, Madeira, breadcrumbs and chopped sage.

4 Stuff the neck end of the goose with some of the stuffing, and then set the remaining stuffing aside in the refrigerator. Sew up the bird or secure it with skewers to prevent the stuffing from escaping during cooking.

5 Place the goose in a large roasting pan. Butter a piece of foil and use to cover the goose loosely, then roast in the preheated oven for 2 hours.

6 Baste the goose frequently during cooking and remove any excess fat from the pan as necessary, using a small ladle or serving spoon. (Strain, cool and chill the fat in a covered container: it is excellent for roasting potatoes.)

7 Remove the foil from the goose and brush the melted ginger marmalade over the goose, then roast for 30–40 minutes more, or until cooked through. To check if the goose is cooked, pierce the thick part of the thigh with a metal skewer; the juices will run clear when the bird is cooked. Remove from the oven and cover with foil, then leave to stand for 15 minutes before carving.

8 While the goose is cooking, shape the remaining stuffing into walnut-size balls and place them in an ovenproof dish. Spoon 30ml/2 tbsp of the goose fat over the stuffing balls and bake for about 15 minutes before the goose is cooked.

9 To make the gravy, pour off all but 15ml/1 tbsp of fat from the roasting pan, leaving the meat juices behind. Add the onion and cook for 3–5 minutes, or until softened but not coloured. Sprinkle in the flour and then gradually stir in the Madeira and stock. Bring to the boil, stirring continuously, then simmer for 3 minutes, or until thickened and glossy. Strain the gravy and serve it with the carved goose and stuffing. Garnish with fresh sage leaves.

CHICKEN CASSEROLE with WINTER VEGETABLES

A casserole of wonderfully tender organic chicken, winter root vegetables and lentils,
finished with crème fraîche, mustard and tarragon.

SERVES FOUR

350g/12oz onions
350g/12oz leeks
225g/8oz carrots
450g/1lb swede (rutabaga)
30ml/2 tbsp olive oil
4 chicken portions, about 900g/2lb
    total weight
115g/4oz/½ cup green lentils
475ml/16fl oz/2 cups chicken stock
300ml/½ pint/1¼ cups apple juice
10ml/2 tsp cornflour (cornstarch)
45ml/3 tbsp crème fraîche
10ml/2 tsp wholegrain mustard
30ml/2 tbsp chopped fresh tarragon
sea salt and ground black pepper
fresh tarragon sprigs, to garnish

1 Preheat the oven to 190°C/375°F/ Gas 5. Prepare and chop the vegetables.

2 Heat the oil in a large flameproof casserole. Season the chicken portions and brown them in the hot oil until golden. Remove the chicken from the pan.

3 Add the onions to the casserole and cook for 5 minutes, stirring, until they begin to soften and colour. Add the leeks, carrots, swede and lentils to the casserole and stir over a medium heat for 2 minutes.

4 Return the chicken to the pan, then add the stock, apple juice and seasoning. Bring to the boil and cover tightly. Cook in the oven for 50–60 minutes, or until the chicken and lentils are tender.

5 Place the casserole on the hob (stovetop) over a medium heat. In a small bowl, blend the cornflour with about 30ml/2 tbsp water to make a smooth paste and add to the casserole with the crème fraîche, wholegrain mustard and chopped tarragon. Adjust the seasoning, then simmer gently for about 2 minutes, stirring, until thickened slightly, before serving, garnished with tarragon sprigs.

COOK'S TIP
Chop the vegetables into similarly sized pieces so that they cook evenly. Organic vegetables do not need to be peeled.

BRAISED SHOULDER of MUTTON with PEARL BARLEY and BABY VEGETABLES

A wonderful variety of organic grains is readily available. In this tasty winter stew, pearl barley absorbs all the juices to become full-flavoured with a nutty texture when cooked.

SERVES FOUR

60ml/4 tbsp olive oil
1 large onion, chopped
2 garlic cloves, chopped
2 celery sticks, sliced
a little plain (all-purpose) or wholemeal (whole-wheat) flour
675g/1½lb boned shoulder of mutton, cut into cubes
900ml–1 litre/1½–1¾ pints/3¾–4 cups mutton stock
115g/4oz/½ cup pearl barley
225g/8oz baby carrots
225g/8oz baby turnips
sea salt and ground black pepper
30ml/2 tbsp chopped fresh marjoram, to garnish
warm, crusty bread, to serve

1 Heat 45ml/3 tbsp of the oil in a flameproof casserole. Cook the onion and garlic until softened, add the celery, then cook until the vegetables brown.

2 Season the flour and toss the mutton in it. Use a draining spoon to remove the vegetables from the casserole. Add the remaining oil to the juices in the casserole and heat. Brown the mutton in batches until golden.

3 When all the meat is browned, return it to the casserole with the vegetables. Stir in 900ml/1½ pints/3¾ cups of the stock and the pearl barley. Cover, then bring to the boil, reduce the heat and simmer for 1 hour, or until the pearl barley and mutton are tender.

4 Add the baby carrots and turnips to the casserole for the final 15 minutes of cooking. Stir the meat occasionally during cooking and add the remaining stock, if necessary. Stir in seasoning to taste, and serve piping hot, garnished with marjoram, with warm, crusty bread as an accompaniment.

MUTTON SHANKS with BEANS and HERBS

In this hearty winter dish, full-flavoured organic mutton shanks are slowly cooked in the oven until tender on a bed of tasty cannellini beans and mixed vegetables.

SERVES FOUR

175g/6oz/1 cup dried cannellini, butter (lima) or haricot (navy) beans, soaked overnight in cold water
150ml/¼ pint/⅔ cup water
45ml/3 tbsp olive oil
4 large mutton shanks, 225g/8oz each
1 large onion, chopped
450g/1lb carrots or swede (rutabaga), cut into thick chunks
2 celery sticks, cut into thick chunks
450g/1lb tomatoes, quartered
250ml/8fl oz/1 cup vegetable or mutton stock
4 fresh rosemary sprigs
2 bay leaves
sea salt and ground black pepper

1 Drain and rinse the soaked cannellini beans and place them in a large pan of unsalted boiling water. Bring back to the boil and boil rapidly for 10 minutes, then drain again.

2 Place the 150ml/¼ pint/⅔ cup water in a large casserole and then add the drained cannellini beans. Preheat the oven to 220°C/425°F/Gas 7.

3 Heat 30ml/2 tbsp of the olive oil in a large frying pan, add the mutton shanks and cook over a high heat, turning them occasionally until brown on all sides. Remove the mutton shanks from the pan and set aside.

4 Add the remaining oil to the pan, then add the onion, and sauté for 5 minutes until soft and translucent.

5 Add the carrots or swede and celery to the pan and cook for 2–3 minutes. Stir in the quartered tomatoes and the vegetable or mutton stock and mix well. Transfer the vegetable mixture to the casserole and season well with salt and pepper. Add the fresh rosemary and bay leaves and stir again to combine.

6 Place the mutton shanks on top of the beans and vegetables. Cover the casserole and cook in the preheated oven for about 30 minutes, or until the liquid is bubbling.

7 Reduce the oven temperature to 160°C/325°F/Gas 3 and continue cooking for about 1½ hours, or until the meat is tender. Check the seasoning and serve on deep, warmed plates, placing each mutton shank on a bed of beans and vegetables.

COOK'S TIP
Mutton shanks are small joints cut from the lower end of the leg. One shank is an ideal-size portion for one. Until recently you would have had to order them from the butcher, but they are now becoming increasingly available, especially from good farmers' markets and home delivery services. To obtain a tender result, shanks should be cooked for a long time at a low temperature.

VARIATIONS
• If you prefer, two 400g/14oz cans cannellini beans can be used in this dish – simply place the drained beans in the casserole with the water and continue from step 3.
• A variety of other organic root vegetables would work well in this recipe – try sweet potatoes, butternut squash, parsnips or celeriac instead of the carrots or swede. In spring, replace the mutton with spring lamb and add a mixture of baby turnips and baby carrots.

CHILLI CON CARNE and RICE

Originally made with finely chopped beef, chillies and kidney beans by hungry labourers working on the Texan railroad, this famous Tex-Mex stew has become an international favourite. Be authentic by using organic ingredients.

SERVES EIGHT

1.2kg/2½lb lean braising steak
30ml/2 tbsp sunflower oil
1 large onion, chopped
2 garlic cloves, finely chopped
15ml/1 tbsp plain (all-purpose) or
    wholemeal (whole-wheat) flour
300ml/½ pint/1¼ cups red wine
300ml/½ pint/1¼ cups beef stock
30ml/2 tbsp tomato purée (paste)
sea salt and ground black pepper
fresh coriander (cilantro) leaves, to garnish
boiled white or brown rice, to serve

For the beans
30ml/2 tbsp olive oil
1 onion, chopped
1 red chilli, seeded and chopped
2 × 400g/14oz cans red kidney beans,
    drained and rinsed
400g/14oz can chopped tomatoes

For the topping
6 tomatoes, peeled and chopped
1 green chilli, seeded and chopped
30ml/2 tbsp chopped fresh chives
30ml/2 tbsp chopped fresh coriander
150ml/¼ pint/⅔ cup sour cream

1 Cut the meat into thick strips and then cut it crossways into small cubes. Heat the oil in a large, flameproof casserole. Add the chopped onion and garlic, and cook, stirring occasionally, for 5–8 minutes until softened but not coloured. Meanwhile, season the flour with a little salt and plenty of pepper and place it on a plate, then toss a batch of meat in it.

2 Use a draining spoon to remove the onion from the pan, then add the floured beef and cook over a high heat, stirring occasionally with a wooden spoon until browned on all sides. Remove from the pan and set aside, then flour and brown another batch of meat.

3 When the last batch of meat is browned, return the first batches with the onion to the pan. Stir in the wine, stock and tomato purée. Bring to the boil, reduce the heat and simmer for 45 minutes, or until the beef is tender.

4 Meanwhile, to make the beans, heat the olive oil in a frying pan and cook the onion and chilli until softened. Add the kidney beans and tomatoes and simmer gently for 20–25 minutes.

5 Mix the tomatoes, chilli, chives and coriander for the topping. Ladle the meat on to plates, then add the beans and the tomato topping. Top with sour cream and coriander leaves and serve with rice.

BOEUF BOURGUIGNONNE

The classic French dish of beef cooked in Burgundy style, with red wine, small pieces of bacon, baby onions and mushrooms, is traditionally cooked for several hours at a low temperature. Using organic top rump or braising steak reduces the cooking time.

SERVES SIX

175g/6oz rindless streaky (fatty) bacon
    rashers (strips), chopped
900g/2lb lean braising steak, such as top
    rump of beef or braising steak
30ml/2 tbsp plain (all-purpose) or
    wholemeal (whole-wheat) flour
45ml/3 tbsp sunflower oil
25g/1oz/2 tbsp butter or 30ml/2 tbsp
    olive oil
12 shallots
2 garlic cloves, crushed
175g/6oz/2½ cups mushrooms, sliced
450ml/¾ pint/scant 2 cups robust red wine
150ml/¼ pint/⅔ cup beef stock
    or consommé
1 bay leaf
2 sprigs each of fresh thyme, parsley
    and marjoram
sea salt and ground black pepper
mashed root vegetables, such as celeriac
    and potatoes, to serve

1 Preheat the oven to 160°C/325°F/ Gas 3. Heat a large flameproof casserole, then add the bacon and cook, stirring occasionally, until the pieces are crisp and golden brown.

2 Meanwhile, cut the meat into 2.5cm/1in cubes. Season the flour and use to coat the meat. Use a draining spoon to remove the bacon from the casserole and set aside. Add and heat the sunflower oil, then brown the beef in batches and set aside with the bacon.

COOK'S TIP
Boeuf Bourguignonne freezes very well. Freeze for up to 2 months. Thaw overnight in the refrigerator, then transfer to a flameproof casserole and add 150ml/ ¼ pint/⅔ cup water. Stir well, bring to the boil, stirring occasionally, and simmer steadily for at least 10 minutes, or until the meat is piping hot.

3 Add the butter or olive oil to the casserole. Cook the shallots and garlic until just starting to colour, then add the mushrooms and cook for 5 minutes. Replace the bacon and meat, and stir in the wine and stock or consommé. Tie the herbs together and add to the casserole.

4 Cover and cook for 1½ hours, or until the meat is tender, stirring once or twice. Season to taste before serving with mashed root vegetables.

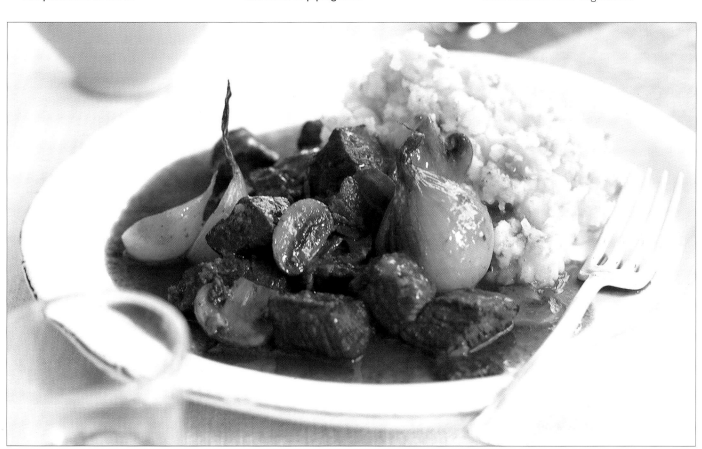

STEAK, MUSHROOM and ALE PIE

*Organic steak has a great quality and fine texture and flavour – it is delicious in this
Anglo-Irish dish. Creamy mashed potatoes or parsley-dressed boiled potatoes and slightly
crunchy carrots and green beans or cabbage are perfect accompaniments. For a bar-style
meal, French fries and a side salad can be served with the pie.*

SERVES FOUR

30ml/2 tbsp olive oil
1 large onion, finely chopped
115g/4oz/1½ cups chestnut or button
  (white) mushrooms, halved
900g/2lb lean beef in one piece, such as
  rump or braising steak
30ml/2 tbsp plain (all-purpose) wholemeal
  (whole-wheat) flour
45ml/3 tbsp sunflower oil
300ml/½ pint/1¼ cups stout or brown ale
300ml/½ pint/1¼ cups beef stock
  or consommé
500g/1¼lb puff pastry, thawed if frozen
beaten egg, to glaze
sea salt and ground black pepper
steamed organic vegetables, to serve

1 Heat the olive oil in a large,
flameproof casserole, add the onion
and cook gently, stirring occasionally, for
about 5 minutes, or until it is softened
but not coloured. Add the halved
mushrooms and continue cooking for a
further 5 minutes, stirring occasionally.

2 Meanwhile, trim the meat and cut it
into 2.5cm/1in cubes. Season the flour
and toss the meat in it.

COOK'S TIP
To make individual pies, divide the filling
among four individual pie dishes. Cut the
pastry into quarters and cover as above.
If the dishes do not have rims, press a
narrow strip of pastry around the edge of
each dish to seal the lid in place. Cook as
above, reducing the cooking time slightly.

3 Use a draining spoon to remove the
onion mixture from the casserole and
set aside. Add and heat the oil, then
brown the steak in batches over a high
heat to seal in the juices.

4 Replace the vegetables, then stir in the
stout or ale and stock or consommé.
Bring to the boil, reduce the heat and
simmer for about 1 hour, stirring
occasionally, or until the meat is tender.
Season to taste and transfer to a 1.5 litre/
2½ pint/6¼ cup pie dish. Cover and
leave to cool. If you have time, chill the
meat filling overnight as this allows the
flavour to develop. Preheat the oven
to 230°C/450°F/Gas 8.

5 Roll out the pastry in the shape of
the dish and about 4cm/1½in larger
all around. Cut a 2.5cm/1in strip from
around the edge of the pastry. Brush the
rim of the pie dish with water and press
the pastry strip onto it. Brush the pastry
rim with beaten egg and cover the pie
with the pastry lid. Press the lid firmly in
place and then trim the excess pastry
from around the edge of the dish.

6 Use the blunt edge of a knife to tap
the outside edge of the pastry rim,
pressing it down with your finger as you
seal the steak and mushroom filling into
the dish. (This sealing technique is
known as knocking up.)

7 Pinch the outside edge of the pastry
between your fingers to flute the edge.
Roll out any remaining pastry trimmings
and cut out five or six leaf shapes to
garnish the centre of the pie. Brush the
shapes with a little beaten egg before
pressing them lightly in place.

8 Make a hole in the middle of the pie
using the point of a sharp knife to allow
the steam to escape during cooking.
Brush the top carefully with beaten
egg and chill for 10 minutes in the
refrigerator to rest the pastry.

9 Bake the pie for 15 minutes, then
reduce the oven temperature to 200°C/
400°F/Gas 6 and bake for a further
15–20 minutes, or until the pastry is
risen and golden brown. Serve the pie
hot with steamed organic vegetables.

FILLETS of BRILL in RED WINE SAUCE

Forget the old maxim that red wine and fish do not go well together. The robust sauce adds colour and richness to this excellent dish.

SERVES FOUR

4 fillets of brill, about 175–200g/6–7oz
    each, skinned
150g/5oz/10 tbsp chilled butter or
    non-hydrogenated margarine, diced,
    plus extra for greasing
115g/4oz shallots, thinly sliced
200ml/7fl oz/scant 1 cup robust
    red wine
200ml/7fl oz/scant 1 cup fish stock
salt and ground white pepper
fresh chervil or flat leaf parsley leaves,
    to garnish

COOK'S TIP
If your baking dish is not flameproof,
then tip the liquid into a pan to cook
on the stove.

1 Preheat the oven to 180°C/350°F/
Gas 4. Season the fish on both sides
with a little salt and plenty of pepper.
Generously butter a flameproof dish,
which is large enough to take all the
brill fillets in a single layer without
overlapping. Spread the shallots over the
base and lay the fish fillets on top. Season.

2 Pour in the red wine and fish stock,
cover the dish and bring the liquid to
just below boiling point. Transfer the dish
to the oven and bake for 6–8 minutes,
or until the brill is just cooked.

3 Using a fish slice, carefully lift the fish
and shallots on to a serving dish, cover
with foil and keep hot.

4 Transfer the dish to the hob and bring
the cooking liquid to the boil over a high
heat. Cook it until it has reduced by half.
Lower the heat and whisk in the chilled
butter or margarine, one piece at a time,
to make a smooth, shiny sauce. Season
with salt and ground white pepper, set
aside and keep hot.

5 Divide the shallots among four
warmed plates and lay the brill fillets on
top. Pour the sauce over and around the
fish and garnish with the chervil or flat
leaf parsley.

VARIATION
Turbot, halibut or John Dory fillets can
also be cooked in this way. Make sure
that your fish is caught sustainably.

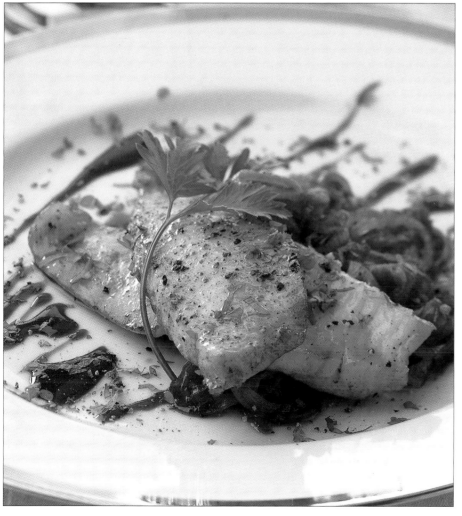

SMOKED HADDOCK with MUSTARD CABBAGE

A wide range of organic mustards are available – wholegrain is used in this warming winter dish, but any type can be used instead.

2 Meanwhile put the smoked haddock fillet in a large shallow pan with the milk, onion rings and bay leaves. Add the lemon slices and white peppercorns. Bring to simmering point, cover and poach until the fish flakes easily when tested with the tip of a sharp knife. This will take 8–10 minutes, depending on the thickness of the fillets. Take the pan off the heat and set aside until needed. Preheat the grill (broiler).

3 Cut the tomatoes in half horizontally, season them with a little salt and plenty of pepper and grill (broil) until lightly browned. Drain the cabbage, refresh under cold water and drain again.

4 Heat the butter or oil in a shallow pan or wok, add the cabbage and toss over the heat for 2 minutes. Mix in the mustard and season to taste, then tip the cabbage into a warmed serving dish.

SERVES FOUR

1 Savoy or pointu cabbage
675g/1½lb undyed smoked haddock fillet
300ml/½ pint/1¼ cups milk or
    soya milk
½ onion, peeled and sliced into rings
2 bay leaves
½ lemon, sliced
4 white peppercorns
4 ripe tomatoes
50g/2oz/¼ cup butter or 50ml/3½ tbsp
    olive oil
30ml/2 tbsp wholegrain mustard
juice of 1 lemon
sea salt and ground black pepper
30ml/2 tbsp chopped fresh parsley,
    to garnish

1 Cut the Savoy or pointu cabbage in half, remove the central core and thick ribs, then shred the cabbage. Cook in a pan of lightly salted boiling water, or steam over boiling water for about 10 minutes until just tender. Leave in the pan or steamer until required.

5 Drain the haddock. Skin and cut the fish into four pieces. Place on top of the cabbage with some of the cooked onion rings and grilled tomato halves. Pour on the lemon juice, then sprinkle with chopped fresh parsley and serve.

SEAFOOD LASAGNE

This dish can be as simple or as elegant as you like. For an elegant dinner party, you can dress it up with scallops, mussels or prawns; for a casual family supper, you can use simple fish such as haddock and hoki. Whatever fish or shellfish you choose, ensure it comes from a sustainable source.

SERVES EIGHT

350g/12oz haddock
350g/12oz salmon fillet
350g/12oz undyed smoked haddock
1 litre/1¾ pints/4 cups milk or
    soya milk
500ml/17fl oz/2¼ cups fish stock
2 bay leaves
1 small onion, peeled and halved
75g/3oz/6 tbsp butter or
    non-hydrogenated margarine,
    plus extra for greasing
45ml/3 tbsp plain (all-purpose) or
    wholemeal (whole-wheat) flour
150g/5oz/2 cups mushrooms, sliced
225–300g/8–11oz fresh lasagne
60ml/4 tbsp freshly grated Parmesan
    cheese or premium Italian-style
    vegetarian cheese
sea salt, ground black pepper, freshly
    grated nutmeg and paprika
rocket (arugula) leaves, to garnish

For the tomato sauce
30ml/2 tbsp olive oil
1 red onion, finely chopped
1 garlic clove, finely chopped
400g/14oz can chopped tomatoes
15ml/1 tbsp tomato purée (paste)
15ml/1 tbsp torn fresh basil leaves

1 Make the tomato sauce. Heat the oil in a pan and fry the onion and garlic over a low heat for 5 minutes, until softened and golden. Stir in the tomatoes and tomato purée and simmer for 20–30 minutes, stirring occasionally. Season with a little salt and plenty of black pepper and stir in the basil.

VARIATION
A good selection of organic pastas are available, including a variety of types of lasagne. Choose from classic lasagne, lasagne all'uovo (rich egg pasta sheets) or lasagne verdi (spinach lasagne), which is an attractive dark green colour.

2 Put all the fish in a shallow flameproof dish or pan with the milk, stock, bay leaves and onion. Bring to the boil over a moderate heat; poach for 5 minutes, until almost cooked. Leave to cool.

3 When the fish is almost cold, strain it, reserving the liquid. Remove the skin and any bones, and flake the fish.

4 Preheat the oven to 180°C/350°F/ Gas 4. Melt the butter in a pan, stir in the flour; cook for 2 minutes, stirring. Gradually add the poaching liquid and bring to the boil, stirring. Add the mushrooms and cook for 2–3 minutes. Season with salt, pepper and nutmeg.

5 Lightly grease a shallow rectangular ovenproof dish. Spoon a thin layer of the mushroom sauce over the base of the dish and spread it out evenly with a spatula. Stir the flaked fish into the remaining mushroom sauce in the pan.

6 Add a layer of lasagne, then a layer of fish and sauce. Add another layer of lasagne, then spread over all the tomato sauce. Continue to layer the lasagne and fish, finishing with a layer of fish.

7 Sprinkle over the grated cheese, then bake for 30–45 minutes until golden. Before serving, sprinkle with paprika and garnish with rocket leaves.

SPICY PUMPKIN and ORANGE BOMBE

In this fabulous ice cream dessert, the subtle flavour of organic pumpkin is transformed with the addition of citrus fruits and spices. The delicious ice cream mixture is then encased in syrupy sponge and served with an orange and whole-spice syrup.

SERVES EIGHT

115g/4oz/½ cup unsalted (sweet) butter or
   non-hydrogenated margarine, softened
115g/4oz/generous ½ cup unrefined caster
   (superfine) sugar or rapadura
115g/4oz/1 cup self-raising
   (self-rising) flour
2.5ml/½ tsp baking powder
2 eggs

For the ice cream
450g/1lb fresh pumpkin, seeded and cubed
1 orange
300g/11oz/scant 1½ cups unrefined
   granulated sugar or rapadura
300ml/½ pint/1¼ cups water
2 cinnamon sticks, halved
10ml/2 tsp whole cloves
30ml/2 tbsp orange flower water
300ml/½ pint/1¼ cups extra thick double
   (heavy) cream or soya cream
2 pieces preserved stem ginger, grated
unrefined icing (confectioners') sugar,
   for dusting

1 Preheat the oven to 180°C/350°F/
Gas 4. Grease and base-line a 450g/1lb
loaf tin (pan).

2 To make the sponge, beat the butter
or margarine, caster sugar, flour, baking
powder and eggs in a bowl until creamy.

3 Spoon the mixture into the prepared
tin, then level the surface and bake in
the preheated oven for 30–35 minutes
until firm in the centre. Leave in the tin
for a few minutes then turn out on to a
wire rack to cool.

4 Make the ice cream. Steam the cubes
of pumpkin for about 15 minutes, or
until tender. Drain and blend in a food
processor to form a smooth purée.
Leave to cool.

5 Pare thin strips of rind from the
orange, scrape off any white pith, then
cut the strips into very fine shreds.
Squeeze the orange and set the juice
aside. Heat the unrefined sugar and water
in a small, heavy pan until the sugar
dissolves. Bring the syrup to the boil and
boil rapidly without stirring for 3 minutes.

6 Stir in the orange shreds, orange juice,
cinnamon and cloves and heat gently for
5 minutes. Strain the syrup, reserving
the orange shreds and spices. Measure
300ml/½ pint/1¼ cups of the syrup
and reserve. Return the spices to the
remaining syrup and stir in the orange
flower water. Pour into a jug (pitcher)
and set aside to cool.

COOK'S TIP
If you prefer a smooth syrup, strain to
remove the cinnamon sticks and cloves
before spooning it over the bombe.

7 Beat the pumpkin purée with 175ml/
6fl oz/¾ cup of the measured strained
syrup until evenly combined. Stir in the
cream and ginger. Cut the cake into 1cm/
½in slices. Dampen a 1.5 litre/2½ pint/
6¼ cup deep bowl and line it with clear
film (plastic wrap). Pour the remaining
strained syrup into a shallow dish.

8 Dip the cake slices one at a time
briefly in the syrup and use to line the
prepared bowl, placing the syrupy
coated sides against the bowl.

9 To freeze the ice cream by hand, pour
the pumpkin mixture into a shallow
container and freeze until firm. Scrape
the ice cream into the sponge-lined bowl,
level the surface and freeze until firm,
preferably overnight. If using an ice cream
maker, churn the pumpkin mixture until
very thick, then spoon it into the
sponge-lined bowl. Level the surface and
freeze until firm, preferably overnight.

10 To serve, invert the bombe on to a
plate. Lift off the bowl and clear film.
Dust with the icing sugar and serve
with the spiced syrup spooned over.

CHOCOLATE MOUSSE with GLAZED KUMQUATS

Bright orange kumquats balance this rich, dark mousse perfectly. There are some excellent organic chocolates available. It is worth spending a little more on them because they have such a luxurious taste and texture, and good fair trade values.

SERVES SIX

225g/8oz dark (bittersweet) chocolate, broken into squares
4 eggs, separated
30ml/2 tbsp brandy
90ml/6 tbsp double (heavy) cream or soya cream

For the glazed kumquats
275g/10oz kumquats
115g/4oz/generous ½ cup unrefined granulated sugar or rapadura
150ml/¼ pint/⅔ cup water
15ml/1 tbsp brandy

1 Make the glazed kumquats. Slice the fruit lengthways and place cut side up in a shallow serving dish.

2 Place the sugar in a pan with the water. Heat gently, stirring constantly, until the sugar has dissolved, then bring to the boil and boil rapidly, without stirring, until a golden-brown caramel forms.

VARIATION
If you can't find kumquats, then use peeled and sliced small, seedless organic oranges, pink-fleshed grapefruit or satsumas instead.

3 Remove the pan from the heat and very carefully stir in 60ml/4 tbsp boiling water to dissolve the caramel. Stir in the brandy, then pour the caramel over the kumquats and leave to cool. Once completely cold, cover and chill.

4 Line a shallow 20cm/8in round cake tin (pan) with clear film (plastic wrap). Melt the chocolate in a bowl over a pan of barely simmering water, then remove the bowl from the heat.

5 Add the egg yolks and brandy to the chocolate and beat well, then fold in the cream, mixing well. In a separate clean bowl, whisk the egg whites until stiff, then gently fold them into the chocolate mixture.

6 Pour the mixture into the prepared tin and level the surface with a spatula. Chill for several hours until set.

7 To serve, turn the mousse out on to a plate and cut into slices or wedges. Serve the chocolate mousse on serving plates and spoon some of the glazed kumquats and syrup alongside.

CHRISTMAS ICE CREAM TORTE

*This fruity ice cream cake makes an exciting alternative to traditional Christmas pudding,
but don't feel that you have to limit it to the festive season. Packed with dried organic
fruit and nuts, it is perfect for any special occasion and tastes sensational.*

SERVES EIGHT TO TEN

75g/3oz/¾ cup dried cranberries
75g/3oz/scant ½ cup pitted prunes
50g/2oz/⅓ cup sultanas (golden raisins)
175ml/6fl oz/¾ cup port
2 pieces preserved stem ginger, chopped
25g/1oz/2 tbsp unsalted (sweet) butter or
    non-hydrogenated margarine
45ml/3 tbsp light muscovado (brown) sugar
90g/3½oz/scant 2 cups fresh white or
    wholemeal (whole-wheat) breadcrumbs
600ml/1 pint/2½ cups double (heavy)
    cream or soya cream
30ml/2 tbsp unrefined icing
    (confectioners') sugar
5ml/1 tsp mixed (apple pie) spice
75g/3oz/¾ cup brazil nuts, finely chopped
2–3 bay leaf sprigs, egg white, caster
    (superfine) sugar or rapadura and
    fresh cherries, to decorate

1 Put the dried fruit in a food processor
and process briefly to chop roughly. Tip
the fruit into a bowl and add the port
and ginger. Leave to marinate for 2 hours.

2 Melt the butter in a frying pan. Add the
muscovado sugar and heat gently until
dissolved. Tip in the breadcrumbs and
fry gently for 5 minutes. Leave to cool.

3 Tip the breadcrumbs into a food
processor and process to finer crumbs.
Sprinkle a third into an 18cm/7in loose-
based springform tin (pan) and freeze.

4 Whip the cream with the icing sugar
and mixed spice to soft peaks. Fold in
the nuts and dried fruit mixture.

5 To make sugared bay leaves for
decoration, wash and dry the sprigs,
then paint both sides with beaten egg
white. Dust evenly with sugar. Leave to
dry for 2–3 hours.

6 Spread a third of the spiced fruit
cream mixture over the frozen
breadcrumb base in the tin, taking care
not to dislodge any of the crumbs.
Sprinkle the cream mixture with another
layer of the fine, crispy breadcrumbs.
Repeat the layering, finishing with a layer
of the spiced fruit cream mixture. Cover
the torte with clear film (plastic wrap)
and freeze it overnight.

7 Remove the torte from the freezer
and place in the refrigerator for about
1 hour before serving, decorated with
sugared bay leaves and fresh cherries.

DRIED FRUIT COMPOTE

Compotes made with dried fruit are just as wonderful as those made with fresh fruits,
especially in winter when fewer organic fresh fruit varieties are in season.

SERVES FOUR

225g/8oz/1⅓ cups mixed dried fruit
75g/3oz/⅔ cup dried cherries
75g/3oz/⅔ cup sultanas (golden raisins)
10 dried prunes
10 dried apricots
hot, freshly brewed fragrant tea, such as
   Earl Grey or jasmine, to cover
15–30ml/1–2 tbsp unrefined caster
   (superfine) sugar or rapadura
¼ lemon, sliced
60ml/4 tbsp brandy

1 Put the dried fruits in a bowl and pour over the hot tea. Add sugar to taste and the lemon slices. Cover with a plate, set aside and leave to cool to room temperature.

2 When the fruits are cool, cover the bowl with clear film (plastic wrap) and chill in the refrigerator for at least 2 hours and preferably overnight. Just before serving, pour in the brandy and stir well.

MOROCCAN RICE PUDDING

A simple and delicious alternative to a traditional British rice pudding. The rice is cooked in almond-flavoured milk and delicately flavoured with cinnamon and orange flower water.

SERVES SIX

25g/1oz/¼ cup almonds, chopped
450g/1lb/2¼ cups pudding rice
25g/1oz/¼ cup unrefined icing
    (confectioners') sugar or rapadura
1 cinnamon stick
50g/2oz/¼ cup butter or
    non-hydrogenated margarine
1.5ml/¼ tsp almond essence (extract)
175ml/6fl oz/¾ cup milk or soya milk
175ml/6fl oz/¾ cup single (light) cream or
    soya cream
30ml/2 tbsp orange flower water
toasted flaked (sliced) almonds and ground
    cinnamon, to decorate

1 Put the almonds in a food processor or blender with 60ml/4 tbsp of very hot water. Process until the almonds are finely chopped, then push through a sieve into a bowl. Return the almond mixture to the food processor or blender, add a further 60ml/4 tbsp very hot water, and process again. Push the almond mixture through the sieve into a pan.

2 Add 300ml/½ pint/1¼ cups water and bring the mixture to the boil. Add the rice, icing sugar or rapadura, cinnamon stick, half the butter, the almond essence, half the milk and half the cream.

3 Bring to the boil, then simmer, covered, for about 30 minutes, adding more milk and cream as the rice mixture thickens. Continue to cook the rice, stirring, and adding the remaining milk and cream, until the pudding becomes thick and creamy. Stir in the orange flower water, then taste the rice pudding for sweetness, adding a little extra sugar, if necessary.

4 Pour the rice pudding into a serving bowl and sprinkle with the toasted flaked almonds. Dot with the remaining butter and dust with a little ground cinnamon. Serve the pudding hot.

BAKED MAPLE and PECAN CROISSANT PUDDING

This variation of the classic English bread and butter pudding uses rich, flaky croissants, topped with a delicious mixture of organic fruit and nuts. Maple-syrup-flavoured custard completes this mouthwatering dessert.

SERVES FOUR

75g/3oz/scant ½ cup sultanas
    (golden raisins)
45ml/3 tbsp brandy
4 large croissants
50g/2oz/¼ cup butter or non-hydrogenated
    margarine, plus extra for greasing
40g/1½oz/⅓ cup pecan nuts,
    roughly chopped
3 eggs, lightly beaten
300ml/½ pint/1¼ cups milk or soya milk
150ml/¼ pint/⅔ cup single (light) cream
    or soya cream
120ml/4fl oz/½ cup maple syrup
25g/1oz/2 tbsp demerara (raw) sugar
maple syrup and pouring (half-and-half)
    cream or soya cream, to serve (optional)

1 Lightly grease the base and sides of a small, shallow ovenproof dish. Place the sultanas and brandy in a small pan and heat gently, until warm. Leave to stand for 1 hour.

2 Cut the croissants into thick slices and then spread with butter on one side.

3 Arrange the croissant slices butter side uppermost and slightly overlapping in the greased dish. Scatter the brandy-soaked sultanas and the roughly chopped pecan nuts evenly over the buttered croissant slices.

4 In a large bowl, beat the eggs and milk together, then gradually beat in the single or soya cream and maple syrup.

COOK'S TIPS
• The main sweetener in this recipe is maple syrup. It is made by tapping the sap of the maple tree. Organic maple syrup is not overprocessed so it retains its natural richness.
• Pecan nuts are an elongated nut in a glossy red oval-shaped shell, but are usually sold shelled. They are native to the USA and have a sweet, mild flavour. Pecans are most commonly used in pecan pie but are also popular in ice creams and cakes. Walnuts can be substituted for pecans in most recipes, and they would be perfect in this one if you don't have any pecan nuts.

5 Pour the egg custard through a sieve, over the croissants, fruit and nuts in the dish. Leave the pudding to stand for 30 minutes so that some of the custard is absorbed by the croissants. Preheat the oven to 180°F/350°C/Gas 4.

6 Sprinkle the demerara sugar evenly over the top, then cover the dish with foil. Bake the pudding for 30 minutes, then remove the foil and continue to cook for about 20 minutes, or until the custard is set and the top is golden brown.

7 Leave the pudding to cool for about 15 minutes before serving warm with extra maple syrup and a little pouring cream or soya cream, if you like.

VARIATION
Thickly sliced one-day-old bread, large slices of brioche or fruit bread could be used instead of the croissants. Slightly stale one-day-old croissants are easier to slice and butter; they also soak up the custard more easily.

ORANGE MARMALADE CHOCOLATE LOAF

Do not be alarmed at the amount of cream in this recipe – it's naughty but necessary, and replaces butter to make a deliciously mouthwatering moist dark chocolate cake, finished with a bitter-sweet sticky marmalade filling and topping.

SERVES EIGHT

115g/4oz dark (bittersweet) chocolate
3 eggs
175g/6oz/scant 1 cup unrefined caster
    (superfine) sugar or rapadura
175ml/6fl oz/¾ cup sour cream
200g/7oz/1¾ cups self-raising
    (self-rising) flour

For the filling and topping

200g/7oz/⅔ cup bitter orange marmalade
115g/4oz dark (bittersweet) chocolate
60ml/4 tbsp sour cream
shredded orange rind, to decorate

1 Preheat the oven to 190°C/375°F/ Gas 5. Grease a 900g/2lb loaf tin (pan) lightly, then line the base with a piece of baking parchment. Break the chocolate into pieces. Melt the chocolate in a heatproof bowl placed over hot water.

2 Combine the eggs and sugar in a separate bowl. Using a hand-held electric mixer, beat the mixture until it is thick and creamy, then stir in the sour cream and melted chocolate. Fold in the flour evenly using a metal spoon.

3 Pour the mixture into the prepared tin and bake for about 1 hour, or until well risen and firm to the touch. Cool for a few minutes in the tin, then turn out onto a wire rack and let the loaf cool completely.

4 Make the filling. Spoon two-thirds of the marmalade into a small pan and melt over a low heat. Break the chocolate into pieces. Melt the chocolate in a heatproof bowl placed over hot water. Stir the chocolate into the marmalade with the sour cream.

5 Slice the cake across into three layers and sandwich back together with about half the marmalade filling. Spread the rest over the top of the cake and leave to set. Spoon the remaining marmalade over the cake and scatter with shredded orange rind, to decorate.

COOK'S TIP

A fantastic variety of different types of organic marmalades are available, including farmhouse and hand-made regional varieties.

SEMOLINA and NUT HALVA

In Eastern Mediterranean cooking semolina is used in many desserts.
Here it provides a spongy base for soaking up a deliciously fragrant spicy syrup.

SERVES TEN

For the halva
115g/4oz/½ cup unsalted (sweet) butter or
    non-hydrogenated margarine, softened
115g/4oz/generous ½ cup unrefined caster
    (superfine) sugar or rapadura
finely grated rind of 1 orange, plus
    30ml/2 tbsp juice
3 eggs
175g/6oz/1 cup semolina
10ml/2 tsp baking powder
115g/4oz/1 cup ground hazelnuts
natural (plain) yogurt, to serve

To finish
350g/12oz/1¾ cups unrefined caster
    (superfine) sugar or rapadura
2 cinnamon sticks, halved
juice of 1 lemon
60ml/4 tbsp orange flower water
50g/2oz/½ cup unblanched hazelnuts,
    toasted and chopped
50g/2oz/½ cup blanched almonds, toasted
    and chopped
shredded rind of 1 orange, to decorate

1 Preheat the oven to 220°C/425°F/
Gas 7. Grease and line the base of a deep
23cm/9in square solid-based cake tin (pan).

2 Lightly cream the butter in a large
bowl. Add the sugar or rapadura, orange
rind and juice, eggs, semolina, baking
powder and hazelnuts and beat the
ingredients together until smooth.

3 Tip into the prepared tin and level the
surface. Bake for 20–25 minutes until
just firm and golden. Leave to cool in
the tin.

4 To make the syrup, put the unrefined
caster sugar in a small heavy pan with
550ml/18fl oz/2½ cups water and the
halved cinnamon sticks. Heat gently,
stirring occasionally with a wooden spoon,
until the sugar has dissolved completely.

5 Bring to the boil and boil fast, without
stirring, for 5 minutes. Measure half the
boiling syrup and add the lemon juice
and orange flower water to it. Pour over
the halva. Reserve the remainder of the
syrup in the pan.

6 Leave the halva in the tin until the
syrup is absorbed, then turn it out on to
a plate and cut diagonally into diamond-
shaped portions. Scatter with the nuts.

7 Boil the remaining syrup until slightly
thickened then pour it over the halva.
Scatter the shredded orange rind over
the cake to decorate and serve with
natural yogurt.

GREEK FRUIT and NUT PASTRIES

These aromatic sweet pastry crescents are packed with walnuts, which are a really rich source of nutrients. Serve with a cup of organic coffee.

3 Meanwhile, to make the filling, mix the honey and coffee. Add the fruit, walnuts and nutmeg. Stir well, cover and leave to soak for at least 20 minutes.

4 Roll out a portion of dough on a lightly floured surface until about 3mm/ ⅛in thick. Stamp out rounds using a 10cm/4in round cutter.

5 Place a heaped teaspoonful of filling on one side of each round. Brush the edges with a little milk, then fold over and press the edges together to seal. Repeat with the remaining pastry until all the filling is used.

6 Put the pastries on lightly greased baking sheets, brush with milk and sprinkle with caster sugar.

7 Make a steam hole in each with a skewer. Bake for 35 minutes, or until lightly browned. Cool on a wire rack.

VARIATIONS
Any dried fruit can be used in this recipe – try a combination of the following: sultanas (golden raisins), raisins, currants, apricots, cherries or prunes.

MAKES SIXTEEN

60ml/4 tbsp clear honey
60ml/4 tbsp strong brewed coffee
75g/3oz/½ cup mixed dried fruit, chopped
175g/6oz/1 cup walnuts, chopped
1.5ml/¼ tsp freshly grated nutmeg
milk, to glaze
caster (superfine) sugar or rapadura,
    for sprinkling

For the pastry
450g/1lb/4 cups plain (all-purpose) flour
2.5ml/½ tsp ground cinnamon
2.5ml/½ tsp baking powder
150g/5oz/10 tbsp unsalted (sweet) butter
    or non-hydrogenated margarine
1 egg
120ml/4fl oz/½ cup chilled milk
    or soya milk

---

1 Preheat the oven to 180°C/350°F/ Gas 4. To make the pastry, sift the flour, ground cinnamon and baking powder into a bowl. Rub in the butter until the mixture resembles fine breadcrumbs. Make a well in the middle.

2 Beat the egg and chilled milk or soya milk together and add to the well in the dry ingredients. Mix to a soft dough. Divide the dough into two equal pieces and wrap each in clear film (plastic wrap). Chill for 30 minutes.

COOK'S TIP
These traditional Greek pastries are known as *moshopoungia* in Greece. Serve them warm with morning coffee or afternoon tea with a dollop of whipped cream or crème fraîche.

ORANGE and CORIANDER BRIOCHES

The warm spicy flavour of coriander combines particularly well with orange.
Serve these little buns with marmalade for a lazy weekend breakfast.

MAKES TWELVE

225g/8oz/2 cups strong white bread flour
15g/½oz fresh yeast
2.5ml/½ tsp salt
15ml/1 tbsp unrefined caster (superfine)
   sugar or rapadura
10ml/2 tsp coriander seeds, coarsely ground
grated rind of 1 orange
2 eggs, beaten
50g/2oz/¼ cup unsalted (sweet) butter or
   non-hydrogenated margarine, melted
1 small egg, beaten, to glaze
shredded orange rind, to decorate (optional)

1 Grease 12 individual brioche tins.
Blend the yeast with 25ml/1½ tbsp tepid
water in a bowl until smooth. Sift the
flour into a mixing bowl and stir in the
yeast, salt, sugar, coriander seeds and
orange rind. Make a well in the centre,
pour in 30ml/2 tbsp hand-hot water, the
eggs and melted butter and beat to
make a soft dough. Turn the dough on
to a lightly floured surface and knead for
5 minutes. Return to the clean, lightly
oiled bowl, cover with clear film (plastic
wrap) and leave in a warm place for
about 1 hour, or until doubled in bulk.

2 Tip the dough out on to a floured
surface, knead briefly and roll into a
sausage shape. Cut into 12 pieces. Break
off a quarter of each piece and set aside.
Shape the larger pieces of dough into
balls and place in the prepared tins.

VARIATION
If you prefer, use 10ml/2 tsp easy-blend
(rapid-rise) dried yeast instead of fresh
yeast, and add to the flour in step 1.

3 With a floured wooden spoon handle,
press a hole in each dough ball. Shape
each small piece of dough into a little
plug and press into the holes.

COOK'S TIP
These little brioches look particularly
attractive if they are made in special
brioche tins. However, they can also be
made in bun or muffin tins.

4 Place the brioche tins on a baking
sheet. Cover with lightly oiled clear film
and leave in a warm place until the
dough rises almost to the top of the tins.
Preheat the oven to 220°C/425°F/Gas 7.
Brush the brioches with beaten egg and
bake for 15 minutes until golden brown.
Scatter over extra shreds of orange rind
to decorate, if you like, and serve the
brioches warm with butter.

SPICED POACHED KUMQUATS

Kumquats are not available throughout the year, but they are undoubtedly at their best just before the Christmas season. These fruits can be bottled and given as presents. Their marvellous spicy-sweet citrus flavour complements both sweet and savoury dishes.

SERVES SIX

450g/1lb/4 cups kumquats
115g/4oz/generous ½ cup unrefined caster (superfine) sugar or rapadura
150ml/¼ pint/⅔ cup water
1 small cinnamon stick
1 star anise
a bay leaf, to decorate (optional)

COOK'S TIP
To prepare jars for home preserves, preheat the oven to 160°C/325°F/Gas 3. Wash the jars in hot soapy water, rinse and dry thoroughly. Place the jars in the oven for 10 minutes, then turn off the oven.

1 Cut the kumquats in half and discard the pips. Place the kumquats in a pan with the sugar, water and spices. Cook over a gentle heat, stirring until the sugar has dissolved.

2 Increase the heat, cover the pan and boil the mixture for 8–10 minutes until the kumquats are tender. To bottle the kumquats, spoon them into warm, sterilized jars, seal and label. Decorate the kumquats with a bay leaf before serving, if you like.

COOK'S TIP
Serve these delectable treats with baked ham, roast turkey or venison steaks. They would also make a perfect accompaniment for moist almond or chocolate cake; or serve with organic vanilla or chocolate ice cream.

THREE-FRUIT MARMALADE

Seville oranges have a fine flavour and are the best variety for marmalade. They are only available for a limited time in winter so make the most of them then.

MAKES 2.25KG/5LB

2 Seville oranges
2 lemons
1 grapefruit
1.75 litres/3 pints/7½ cups water
1.5kg/3¼lb/7½ cups unrefined granulated sugar
croissants, to serve (optional)

1 Wash the fruit, halve and squeeze their juice. Pour into a large heavy pan. Tip the pips and pulp in a square of muslin (cheesecloth), gather into a bag and tie tightly with string. Tie the bag to the pan handle so it dangles in the juice.

2 Cut the citrus skins into thin wedges; scrape off and discard the membranes and pith. Cut the rinds into slivers and add to the pan with the measured water. Bring to a simmer and cook gently for 2 hours until the rinds are very tender and the water has reduced by half. Test the rinds for softness by pressing a cooled piece with a finger.

3 Remove the muslin bag from the pan, squeezing out the juice into the pan. Discard the bag. Stir the unrefined granulated sugar into the pan and heat very gently, stirring occasionally with a wooden spoon, until all the sugar has dissolved.

4 Bring the mixture to the boil and then boil vigorously for 10–15 minutes, or until the marmalade reaches 105°C/220°F.

5 Alternatively, test the marmalade for setting by pouring a small amount on to a chilled saucer. Chill for 2 minutes, then push the marmalade with your finger; if wrinkles form on the surface, it is ready. Cool for 15 minutes.

6 Stir the marmalade and pour it into warm, sterilized jars. Cover with waxed paper discs. Seal and label when cold. Store in a cool dark cupboard. Serve with warm croissants, if you like.

SAUCES, SALSAS, CHUTNEYS AND BREADS

You can buy ready-made organic sauces, salsas and breads from farmers' markets, supermarkets and health food shops. However, home-made varieties are often much better — and by making your own you can make the most of fresh produce when it's in season. Reasonably priced organic fruit and vegetables are easy to find at farmers' markets and farm shops. As they come into season, start making large quantities of such sauces and chutneys as Chilli Sauce and Apple and Tomato Chutney. Delicious accompaniments such as Garlic Mayonnaise or Onion Sauce can transform simply cooked dishes. Take your pick from a wide range of organic flavoured breads, such as Pumpkin and Walnut Bread, Wholemeal Sunflower Bread, or Cheese and Onion Cornbread and serve with organic cheeses and cold meats. Or try making Chapatis to go with your favourite curry, or Pitta Bread to dip in a creamy avocado Guacamole.

  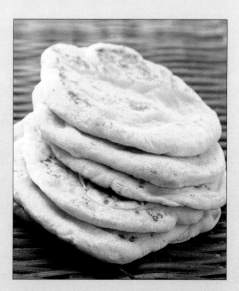

TAHINI SAUCE

Made of sesame seeds, spiced with garlic and lemon juice, this is Israel's most famous sauce. It makes a delicious dip and, when thinned with water, can be spooned over falafel.

SERVES FOUR TO SIX

150–175g/5–6oz/²⁄₃–¾ cup tahini
3 garlic cloves, finely chopped
juice of 1 lemon
1.5ml/¼ tsp ground cumin
small pinch of ground coriander
small pinch of curry powder
50–120ml/2–4fl oz/¼–½ cup water
cayenne pepper
sea salt

For the garnish
15–30ml/1–2 tbsp extra virgin olive oil
chopped fresh coriander (cilantro) or
    flat leaf parsley leaves
handful of olives and/or pickled vegetables
a few chillies or a hot pepper sauce

1 Put the tahini and garlic in a bowl and mix together well. Stir in the lemon juice, cumin, ground coriander and curry powder.

COOK'S TIP
Tahini sauce forms the basis of many of the salads and dips popular in Middle Eastern cuisine.

2 Slowly add the water to the tahini, beating all the time. The mixture will thicken, then become thin. Season with cayenne pepper and salt.

3 To serve, spoon the tahini on to a serving plate, individual plates or into a shallow bowl. Drizzle over the oil and sprinkle with the other garnishes.

CHILLI SAUCE

Hot with chillies, pungent with garlic, and fragrant with exotic cardamom, this spicy sauce can be served with rice, couscous, soup and roast chicken or vegetable dishes.

MAKES ABOUT 475ML/16FL OZ/2 CUPS

5–8 garlic cloves, chopped
2–3 medium-hot chillies, such as jalapeño,
 seeded and chopped
5 tomatoes, diced
1 small bunch coriander (cilantro),
 roughly chopped
1 small bunch flat leaf parsley, chopped
30ml/2 tbsp extra virgin olive oil
10ml/2 tsp ground cumin
2.5ml/½ tsp ground turmeric
2.5ml/½ tsp curry powder
seeds from 3–5 cardamom pods
juice of ½ lemon
sea salt
a few sprigs of parsley or coriander,
 to garnish

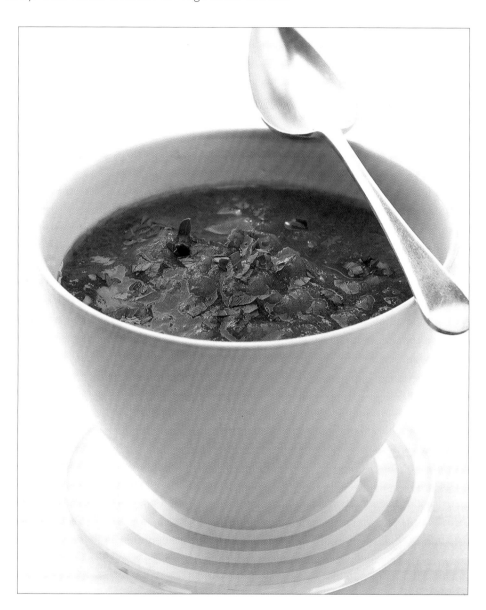

COOK'S TIP
There is simply no comparison between the flavour of a freshly picked organic tomato that has been allowed to ripen naturally and the taste of an artificially ripened tomato. Organic growers select the sweetest, tastiest varieties, and whether you buy tiny cherry tomatoes or big beefsteaks, you will not be disappointed.

VARIATIONS
• To make a spicy dip, put 400g/14oz chopped fresh tomatoes, or a mixture of chopped fresh and canned tomatoes, in a bowl. Stir in 120ml/4fl oz/½ cup of the chilli sauce, or to taste, and season with salt, if necessary. Spread the dip on to wedges of flat bread, such as pitta bread, or serve in a bowl with strips of raw vegetables for dipping.
• To make a spicy tomato relish, soak 30ml/2 tbsp fenugreek seeds in cold water for at least 2 hours and preferably overnight. Drain, then grind the seeds in a spice grinder or pound them in a mortar with a pestle until they form a smooth paste. In a bowl, combine the paste with 15ml/1 tbsp of the chilli sauce and 2 diced tomatoes. Season with salt and black pepper to taste.

1 Put all the sauce ingredients except the salt in a food processor or blender. Process until finely chopped, then season with salt if necessary.

2 Pour the sauce into a bowl, cover and chill. Garnish with chopped herbs before serving. The sauce can be stored in the refrigerator for 3–4 days.

PEANUT SAUCE

Organic peanuts are an especially good source of iron, protein and fibre.
This peanut sauce goes well with Indonesian meat or seafood satay.

SERVES FOUR TO SIX

30ml/2 tbsp groundnut (peanut) oil
75g/3oz/¾ cup unsalted peanuts, blanched
2 shallots, chopped
2 garlic cloves, chopped
15ml/1 tbsp chopped fresh root ginger
1–2 green chillies, seeded and
   thinly sliced
5ml/1 tsp ground coriander
1 lemon grass stalk, tender base only, chopped
5–10ml/1–2 tsp unrefined light muscovado
   (brown) sugar or rapadura
15ml/1 tbsp dark soy sauce
105–120ml/3–4fl oz/scant ½ cup canned
   coconut milk
15–30ml/1–2 tbsp Thai fish sauce
15–30ml/1–2 tbsp tamarind purée (paste)
lime juice
sea salt and ground black pepper

1 Heat the oil in a small, heavy frying pan and gently fry the peanuts, stirring frequently, until they are lightly browned. Use a slotted spoon to remove the nuts from the pan and drain them thoroughly on kitchen paper. Set aside to cool.

2 Add the shallots, garlic, ginger, most of the sliced chillies and the ground coriander to the pan and cook over a low heat, stirring occasionally, for 4–5 minutes, until the shallots are softened but not at all browned.

3 Transfer the spice mixture to a food processor or blender and add the peanuts, lemon grass, 5ml/1 tsp of the sugar, the soy sauce, and 105ml/3fl oz of the coconut milk and the fish sauce. Blend to form a fairly smooth sauce.

4 Taste the mixture and add more fish sauce, tamarind purée, seasoning, lime juice and/or more sugar as necessary.

5 Stir in the extra coconut milk and a little water if the sauce seems very thick, but do not make it too runny.

6 Serve the sauce cool or reheat it gently, stirring all the time to prevent it from spitting. Garnish with the remaining sliced chilli before serving.

COOK'S TIP

To make tamarind purée, soak 25g/1oz tamarind pulp in 120ml/4fl oz/½ cup boiling water in a non-metallic bowl for about 30 minutes, mashing the pulp occasionally with a fork. Then press the pulp through a stainless steel sieve. This purée will keep for several days in a covered container in the refrigerator.

ONION SAUCE

This delicious, dark onion sauce goes really well with organic meat or vegetarian sausages.
It is also good with mashed potatoes, swede or turnip.

SERVES FOUR

45ml/3 tbsp olive oil
450g/1lb onions, halved and thinly sliced
45ml/3 tbsp plain (all-purpose) or
    wholemeal (whole-wheat) flour
400–500ml/14–17fl oz/1²/₃–2 cups
    vegetable stock
1 fresh thyme sprig
10ml/2 tsp dark soy sauce
sea salt and ground black pepper

1 Put the oil in a small, heavy pan and heat gently. Add the sliced onions and fry, stirring occasionally, for 15–20 minutes until the onions are soft and beginning to brown.

2 Increase the heat slightly and cook for another 20–30 minutes, stirring occasionally, until the onions are a dark, golden brown.

3 Stir in the flour, then cook for a few minutes, stirring all the time. Gradually stir in 400ml/14fl oz/1²/₃ cups of the hot stock. Simmer, stirring, for a few minutes until thickened, adding a little more stock if the gravy is too thick.

4 Add the thyme, season with salt and pepper, then cook very slowly, stirring frequently, for 10–15 minutes.

5 Stir in the soy sauce and a little more seasoning, if necessary. Add a little more stock if the gravy is too thick, remove the thyme, and serve immediately.

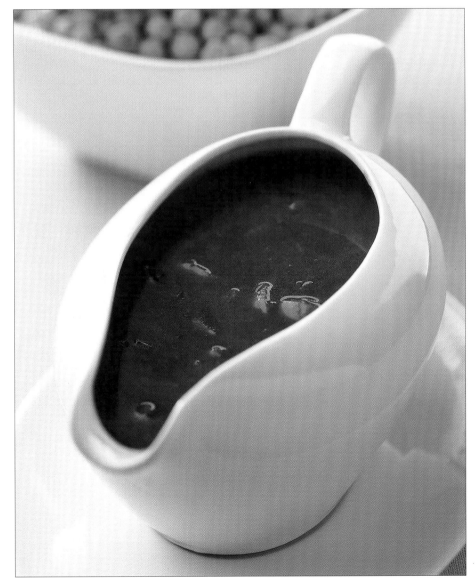

VARIATIONS
• The onions can be browned in the oven instead of on the stove-top. This is best done in sunflower or olive oil rather than butter, which would burn. Place the sliced onions in an ovenproof dish and toss with 45ml/3 tbsp oil. Cook in an oven preheated to 190°C/375°F/Gas 5 for 20 minutes, stirring once or twice, then raise the oven temperature to 220°C/425°F/Gas 7 and cook for a further 15–25 minutes.
• Part of the vegetable stock may be replaced with red wine or dark beer. You may need to add a little extra sugar to balance the acidity of the wine or beer.

GUACAMOLE

Many different types of organic onion are available; this chunky guacamole uses sweet red onion for flavour and colour. Serve as a dip or sauce.

SERVES FOUR

2 large ripe avocados
1 small red onion, very finely chopped
1 red or green chilli, seeded and very
    finely chopped
½–1 garlic clove, crushed with a little
    sea salt
finely shredded rind of ½ lime and juice
    of 1–1½ limes
225g/8oz tomatoes, seeded and
    chopped
30ml/2 tbsp roughly chopped fresh
    coriander (cilantro)
2.5–5ml/½–1 tsp ground toasted
    cumin seeds
15ml/1 tbsp olive oil
15–30ml/1–2 tbsp sour cream (optional)
sea salt and ground black pepper
lime wedges dipped in sea salt (optional),
    and fresh coriander sprigs,
    to garnish

1 Cut one of the avocados in half and lift out and discard the stone (pit). Scrape the flesh from both halves into a bowl and mash it roughly with a fork.

2 Add the onion, chilli, garlic, lime rind, tomatoes and coriander and stir well to mix. Add the ground cumin and seasoning to taste, then stir in the olive oil.

3 Halve and stone (pit) the remaining avocado. Dice the flesh and stir it into the guacamole.

4 Squeeze in fresh lime juice to taste, mix well, then cover and leave to stand for 15 minutes so that the flavour develops. Stir in the sour cream, if using. Serve with lime wedges dipped in sea salt, if you wish, and garnish with fresh coriander sprigs.

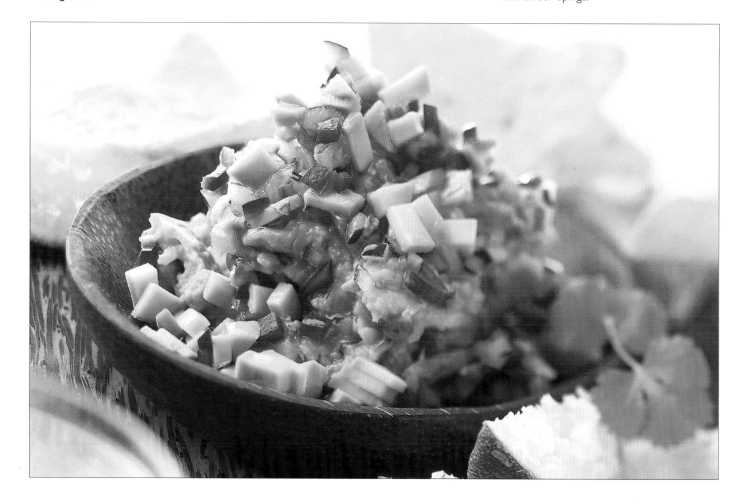

GARLIC MAYONNAISE

Fresh wet organic garlic is available in spring and summer, but try to use dried, cured bulbs as they have a more pungent flavour for this mouthwatering creamy mayonnaise.

SERVES FOUR TO SIX

2 large egg yolks
pinch of dried mustard
about 300ml/½ pint/1¼ cups mild olive oil
15–30ml/1–2 tbsp lemon juice, white wine
    vinegar or warm water
2–4 garlic cloves
sea salt and ground black pepper

1 Make sure the egg yolks and oil have come to room temperature before you start. Place the yolks in a bowl with the mustard and a pinch of salt, and whisk together to mix.

2 Gradually whisk in the oil, one drop at a time. When almost half the oil has been fully incorporated, start to add it in a slow, steady stream, whisking all the time.

3 As the mayonnaise starts to thicken, thin it down with a few drops of lemon juice or vinegar, or a few teaspoons of warm water.

4 When the mayonnaise is as thick as soft butter, stop adding oil. Season the mayonnaise to taste and add more lemon juice or vinegar as required.

WATCHPOINT
The very young, the elderly, pregnant women and those in ill-health or with a compromised immune system are advised against consuming raw eggs or dishes containing them.

5 Crush the garlic with the blade of a knife and stir it into the mayonnaise. For a slightly milder flavour, blanch the garlic twice in plenty of boiling water, then purée the cloves before beating them into the mayonnaise.

VARIATIONS
• To make Provençal aioli, crush 3–5 garlic cloves with a pinch of salt in a bowl, then whisk in the egg yolks. Omit the mustard but continue as above.
• For spicy garlic mayonnaise, omit the mustard and stir in 2.5ml/½ tsp harissa or red chilli paste and 5ml/1 tsp sun-dried tomato purée (paste) with the garlic.
• Use roasted garlic purée or puréed smoked garlic to create a different flavour.
• Beat in about 15g/½oz mixed fresh herbs such as tarragon, parsley, chervil and chives.

CONFIT of SLOW-COOKED ONIONS

This jam of caramelized onions will keep for several days in a sealed jar in the refrigerator.
You can use red, white or yellow onions, but yellow onions will give the sweetest result.

SERVES SIX TO EIGHT

30ml/2 tbsp olive oil
15g/½oz/1 tbsp butter or
    non-hydrogenated margarine
500g/1¼lb onions, sliced
3–5 fresh thyme sprigs
1 fresh bay leaf
30ml/2 tbsp unrefined light muscovado
    (brown) sugar or rapadura,
    plus a little extra
50g/2oz/¼ cup prunes, chopped
30ml/2 tbsp balsamic vinegar,
    plus a little extra
120ml/4fl oz/½ cup red wine
sea salt and ground black pepper

1 Reserve 5ml/1 tsp of the oil, then
heat the rest with the butter in a
small, heavy pan. Add the onions,
cover and cook gently for 15 minutes,
stirring occasionally.

2 Season with salt and plenty of pepper,
then add the thyme, bay leaf and sugar.
Cook slowly, uncovered, for another
15–20 minutes, or until the onions are
very soft and dark.

3 Add the prunes, vinegar and wine
with 60ml/4 tbsp water and cook over
a low heat, stirring frequently, for a
further 20 minutes, or until most of the
liquid has evaporated. Add a little water
and reduce the heat if the mixture dries
too quickly.

4 Adjust the seasoning, adding more
sugar and/or vinegar to taste. Leave the
confit to cool, then stir in the remaining
5ml/1 tsp oil. The confit is best stored
for 24 hours before eating. Serve either
cold or warm.

VARIATION
Baby onions with tomato and orange
Gently fry 500g/1¼lb peeled pickling
(pearl) onions or small *cipollini* in 60ml/
4 tbsp olive oil until lightly browned, then
sprinkle in 45ml/3 tbsp of unrefined soft
light brown sugar or rapadura. Let the
onions caramelize a little, then add 7.5ml/
1½ tsp crushed coriander seeds, 250ml/
8fl oz/1 cup red wine, 2 bay leaves, a few
thyme sprigs, 3 strips orange zest and
45ml/3 tbsp tomato purée (paste) and the
juice of 1 orange. Cook very gently,
uncovered, for 1 hour, stirring
occasionally until the sauce is thick and
reduced. Uncover for the last 20 minutes
of cooking time. Sharpen with 15–30ml/
1–2 tbsp sherry vinegar and serve cold,
sprinkled with chopped fresh parsley.

APPLE and TOMATO CHUTNEY

This mellow, golden, spicy chutney makes the most of fresh autumn produce.
Any type of organic tomatoes can be used successfully in this recipe.

MAKES ABOUT 1.8KG/4LB

1.3kg/3lb cooking apples
1.3kg/3lb tomatoes
2 large onions
2 garlic cloves
250g/9oz/1¼ cups pitted dates
2 red (bell) peppers
3 dried red chillies
15ml/1 tbsp black peppercorns
4 cardamom pods
15ml/1 tbsp coriander seeds
10ml/2 tsp cumin seeds
10ml/2 tsp ground turmeric
5ml/1 tsp sea salt
600ml/1 pint/2½ cups distilled malt vinegar
1kg/2¼lb/5¼ cups unrefined granulated
    sugar or rapadura

3 Pour in the vinegar and sugar and then leave to simmer for 30 minutes, stirring occasionally. Add the red pepper and cook for a further 30 minutes, stirring more frequently as the chutney becomes thick and pulpy.

4 Spoon the chutney into warm, dry, sterilized jars. Seal each jar with a waxed circle and cover with a tightly fitting cellophane top. Leave to cool, then label and store in a cool, dry place.

1 Peel and chop the apples. Peel and chop the tomatoes, onions and garlic. Quarter the dates. Core and seed the peppers, then cut into chunky pieces. Put all the prepared ingredients, except the red peppers, into a preserving pan.

2 Slit the chillies. Put the peppercorns and remaining spices into a mortar and roughly crush with a pestle. Add the chillies, spices and salt to the pan.

FOCACCIA

This is a flattish bread, originating from Genoa in Italy, made with flour, olive oil and salt.
There are many variations from many regions but this is the traditional type.

MAKES 1 ROUND 25CM/10IN LOAF

25g/1oz fresh yeast
400g/14oz/3½ cups unbleached strong
    white bread flour
10ml/2 tsp sea salt
75ml/5 tbsp olive oil
10ml/2 tsp coarse sea salt

1 Dissolve the yeast in 120ml/4fl oz/
½ cup warm water. Allow to stand for
10 minutes. Sift the strong white bread
flour into a large bowl, make a well in
the centre, and add the yeast, salt and
30ml/2 tbsp oil. Mix in the flour and add
more water to make a dough.

2 Turn out on to a floured work surface
and knead the dough until smooth and
elastic. Return to the bowl, cover with a
cloth, and leave to rise in a warm place
for 2–2½ hours until doubled in bulk.

3 Knock back the dough and knead
again for a few minutes. Press into an
oiled 25cm/10in tart tin, and cover with
a damp cloth. Leave the dough to rise
again for 30 minutes.

4 Preheat the oven to 200°C/400°F/
Gas 6. Poke the dough all over with your
fingers, to make little dimples in the
surface. Pour the remaining oil over the
dough, using a pastry brush to take it to
the edges. Sprinkle with the salt.

5 Bake for 20–25 minutes, until the
bread is a pale gold. Carefully remove
from the tin and leave to cool on a rack.
The bread is best eaten on the same
day, but it also freezes very well.

OLIVE BREAD

Variations of this strongly flavoured bread are popular all over the Mediterranean.
For this Greek recipe use rich, oily olives or those marinated with herbs.

MAKES TWO 675G/1½LB LOAVES

2 red onions, thinly sliced
30ml/2 tbsp olive oil
225g/8oz/2 cups pitted black
 or green olives
50g/2oz fresh yeast
800g/1¾lb/7 cups strong white bread flour
7.5ml/1½ tsp salt
45ml/3 tbsp each roughly chopped parsley,
 coriander (cilantro) or mint

1 Fry the onions in the oil until soft.
Roughly chop the olives.

2 Dissolve the yeast in 250ml/8fl oz/
1 cup warm water. Allow to stand for
10 minutes. Put the flour, salt and herbs
in a large bowl with the olives and fried
onions and add the yeast mixture.

3 Mix with a round-bladed knife, adding
as much warm water as is necessary to
make a soft dough.

4 Turn out on to a lightly floured surface
and knead for about 10 minutes. Put in a
clean bowl, cover with clear film (plastic
wrap) and leave in a warm place until
doubled in bulk.

5 Preheat the oven to 220°C/425°F/
Gas 7. Lightly grease two baking sheets.
Turn the dough on to a floured surface
and cut in half. Shape into two rounds and
place on the baking sheets. Cover the
dough loosely with lightly oiled clear film
and leave until doubled in size.

VARIATION
Shape the dough into 16 small rolls. Slash
the tops as in step 6 and reduce the
cooking time to 25 minutes.

6 Slash the tops of the loaves two or
three times with a knife, then bake for
about 40 minutes, or until the loaves
sound hollow when tapped on the
bottom. Transfer to a wire rack to cool.

CHAPATIS

More and more types of organic bread are available, but chapatis simply have to be made by hand. These chewy, unleavened breads are eaten throughout Northern India. They are usually served as an accompaniment to spicy dishes.

MAKES SIX CHAPATIS

175g/6oz/1½ cups *atta* or wholemeal
    (whole-wheat) flour
2.5ml/½ tsp sea salt
120ml/4fl oz/about ½ cup water
5ml/1 tsp sunflower oil
melted ghee, butter or non-hydrogenated
    margarine, for brushing (optional)

COOK'S TIP

Atta or *ata* is a very fine wholemeal flour, which is only found in Indian stores and supermarkets. It is sometimes simply labelled chapati flour. *Atta* can also be used for making rotis and other Indian flat breads.

1 Sift the flour and salt into a large mixing bowl. Add the water and mix to a soft dough using your hand or a round-bladed knife. Knead in the oil, then turn the dough out on to a lightly floured surface.

2 Knead for 5–6 minutes until smooth. Place in a lightly oiled bowl, cover with a damp dishtowel and leave to rest for 30 minutes. Turn out on to a floured surface. Divide the dough into six equal pieces. Shape each piece into a ball.

3 Press the dough into a larger round with the palm of your hand, then roll into a 13cm/5in round. Stack, layered between clear film (plastic wrap), to keep moist.

4 Heat a griddle or heavy frying pan over a medium heat for a few minutes until hot. Take one chapati, brush off any excess flour, and place on the griddle. Cook for 30–60 seconds, or until the top begins to bubble and white specks appear on the underside.

5 Turn the chapati over using a metal spatula and cook for a further 30 seconds. Remove from the pan and keep warm, layered between a folded dishtowel, while cooking the remaining chapatis. If you like, the chapatis can be brushed lightly with melted ghee or butter immediately after cooking. Serve warm.

PITTA BREAD

There are many different types of pitta bread, ranging from very flat ones, to those with pockets, to a thicker cushiony one, as here. They are fun to make, and look all the better for a little wobbliness around the edges.

MAKES TWELVE

25g/1oz fresh yeast
500g/1¼lb/5 cups unbleached strong white
    bread flour, or half white and
    half wholemeal (whole-wheat)
15ml/1 tbsp sea salt
15ml/1 tbsp olive oil
250ml/8fl oz/1 cup water

1 Dissolve the yeast in 120ml/4 fl oz/ ½ cup warm water. Allow to stand for 10 minutes. Put the bread flour and salt in a large bowl and stir in the yeast mixture. Mix together the oil and water, and stir enough liquid into the flour mixture to make a stiff dough.

2 Place the dough in a clean bowl, cover with a clean dishtowel and leave in a warm place for at least 30 minutes and up to 2 hours.

3 Knead the dough for 10 minutes, or until smooth. Lightly oil the bowl, place the dough in it, cover again and leave to rise in a warm place for about 1 hour, or until doubled in size.

4 Divide the dough into 12 equal-size pieces. With lightly floured hands, flatten each piece, then roll out into a round measuring about 20cm/8in and about 5mm–1cm/¼–½in thick. Keep the rolled breads covered with a clean dishtowel.

5 Heat a large, heavy frying pan over a medium-high heat. When smoking hot, gently lay one piece of flattened dough in the pan and cook for 15–20 seconds. Carefully turn it over and cook the second side for about 1 minute.

6 When large bubbles start to form on the bread, turn it over again. It should puff up. Using a folded clean dishtowel, gently press on the bread where the bubbles have formed. Cook for a total of 3 minutes, then remove the pitta from the pan. Repeat with the remaining dough until all the pittas have been cooked.

7 Wrap the pitta breads in a clean dishtowel, stacking them as each one is cooked. Serve the pittas hot while they are soft and moist.

VARIATION
To cook the breads in the oven, preheat the oven to 220°C/425°F/Gas 7. Fill an unglazed or partially glazed dish with hot water and place in the bottom of the oven. Alternatively, soak a handful of unglazed tiles in hot water and arrange them in the bottom of the oven. Use either a non-stick baking sheet or a lightly oiled ordinary baking sheet and heat in the oven for a few minutes. Place two or three pieces of flattened dough on to the hot baking sheet and place in the hottest part of the oven. Bake for 2–3 minutes. They should puff up. Repeat with the remaining dough until all the pittas have been cooked.

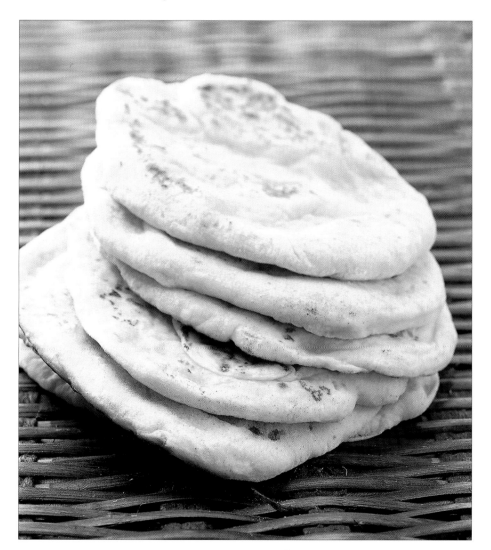

SAN FRANCISCO SOURDOUGH BREAD

There are many sourdough bread recipes, but this is a great one to start with. The bread is leavened using a flour and water paste, which is left to ferment with the aid of airborne yeast. Use unbleached organic flour and the finished loaves will have a moist crumb and crispy crust, and will keep for several days.

MAKES TWO ROUND LOAVES

For the starter
50g/2oz/½ cup wholemeal (whole-wheat) flour
pinch of ground cumin
15ml/1 tbsp milk or soya milk
15–30ml/1–2 tbsp water
1st refreshment
60ml/4 tbsp water
115g/4oz/1 cup strong white bread flour
2nd refreshment
60ml/4 tbsp water
115g/4oz/1 cup strong white bread flour

For the bread: 1st refreshment
75ml/5 tbsp very warm water
75g/3oz/⅔ cup unbleached plain
    (all-purpose) flour
2nd refreshment
175ml/6fl oz/¾ cup lukewarm water
200–225g/7–8oz/1¾–2 cups unbleached
    plain (all-purpose) flour

For the sourdough
280ml/9fl oz/scant 1¼ cups warm water
500g/1¼lb/5 cups unbleached white bread flour
15ml/1 tbsp sea salt
flour, for dusting
ice cubes, for baking

1 Sift the flour and cumin for the starter into a bowl. Add the milk and sufficient water to make a firm but moist dough. Knead for 6–8 minutes. Return the dough to the bowl, cover with a damp dishtowel and leave in a warm place, 24–26°C/75–80°F, for about 2 days. When it is ready the starter will appear moist and wrinkled and will have developed a crust.

2 Pull off the hardened crust and discard. Scoop out the moist centre (about the size of a hazelnut), which will be aerated and sweet smelling, and place in a clean bowl. Mix in the water for the 1st refreshment. Gradually add the flour and mix to a dough.

3 Cover with clear film (plastic wrap) and return to a warm place for 1–2 days. Discard the crust and gradually mix in the water for the 2nd refreshment to the starter, which by now will have a slightly sharper smell. Gradually mix in the white flour, cover and leave in a warm place for 8–10 hours.

4 For the bread, mix the sourdough starter with the water for the 1st refreshment. Gradually mix in the flour to form a firm dough. Knead for 6–8 minutes until firm. Cover with a damp dishtowel and leave in a warm place for 8–12 hours, or until doubled in bulk.

5 Gradually mix in the water for the 2nd refreshment, then gradually mix in enough flour to form a soft, smooth elastic dough. Re-cover and leave in a warm place for 8–12 hours. Gradually stir in the water for the sourdough, then gradually work in the flour and salt. This will take 10–15 minutes. Turn out on to a lightly floured surface and knead until smooth and very elastic. Place in a large lightly oiled bowl, cover with lightly oiled clear film and leave to rise, in a warm place, for 8–12 hours.

6 Divide the dough in half and shape into 2 round loaves by folding the sides over to the centre and sealing.

7 Place seam side up in flour-dusted *couronnes* bowls or baskets lined with flour-dusted dishtowels. Re-cover and leave to rise in a warm place for 4 hours.

8 Preheat the oven to 220°C/425°F/Gas 7. Place an empty roasting pan in the bottom of the oven. Dust two baking sheets with flour. Turn out the loaves seam side down on the prepared baking sheets. Using a sharp knife, cut a criss-cross pattern by slashing the top of the loaves 4–5 times in each direction.

9 Place the baking sheets in the oven and immediately drop the ice cubes into the hot roasting pan to create steam. Bake the bread for 25 minutes, then reduce the oven temperature to 200°C/400°F/Gas 6 and bake for a further 15–20 minutes, or until it sounds hollow when tapped on the base. Transfer to wire racks to cool.

COOK'S TIP
If you'd like to make sourdough bread regularly, keep a small amount of the starter covered in the refrigerator. It will keep for several days. Use the starter for the 2nd refreshment, then continue as directed.

PUMPKIN and WALNUT BREAD

Walnuts, nutmeg and pumpkin combine to yield a moist, tangy and slightly sweet bread with an indescribably good flavour. Serve partnered with meats or cheese.

MAKES ONE LOAF

500g/1¼lb pumpkin, peeled, seeded and
   cut into chunks
75g/3oz/6 tbsp caster (superfine) sugar
5ml/1 tsp grated nutmeg
50g/2oz/¼ cup butter, melted
3 eggs, lightly beaten
350g/12oz/3 cups unbleached strong white
   bread flour
10ml/2 tsp baking powder
2.5ml/½ tsp sea salt
75g/3oz/¾ cup walnuts, chopped

1 Grease and neatly base-line a loaf tin (pan) measuring 21 × 12cm/8½ × 4½in. Preheat the oven to 180°C/350°F/ Gas 4.

2 Place the pumpkin in a pan, add water to cover by about 5cm/2in, then bring to the boil. Cover, lower the heat and simmer for about 20 minutes, or until the pumpkin is very tender. Drain well, then purée in a food processor or blender. Leave to cool.

3 Place 275g/10oz/1¼ cups of the purée in a large bowl. Add the sugar, nutmeg, melted butter and eggs and mix. Sift the flour, baking powder and salt into a large bowl and make a well in the centre.

4 Add the pumpkin mixture to the centre of the flour and stir until smooth. Mix in the walnuts.

5 Transfer to the prepared tin and bake for 1 hour, or until golden and starting to shrink from the sides of the tin. Turn out on to a wire rack to cool.

COOK'S TIP
If you have more pumpkin purée than you need, use the remainder in soup.

WHOLEMEAL SUNFLOWER BREAD

Organic sunflower seeds give a nutty crunchiness to this hearty wholemeal loaf.
Serve with a chunk of cheese and a rich tomato chutney.

3 Cover the bowl with a damp dishtowel and leave the dough to rise in a warm place for 45–50 minutes, or until doubled in size.

4 Preheat the oven to 200°C/400°F/ Gas 6. Turn out the dough on to a lightly floured work surface and knead for about 10 minutes until elastic – the dough will still be quite sticky, but resist the temptation to add more flour.

MAKES ONE LOAF

25g/1oz fresh yeast
450g/1lb/4 cups strong wholemeal (whole-wheat) flour
2.5ml/½ tsp sea salt
50g/2oz/scant ½ cup sunflower seeds, plus extra for sprinkling

1 Dissolve the yeast in 120ml/4fl oz/ ½ cup warm water. Allow to stand for 10 minutes. Grease and lightly flour a 450g/1lb loaf tin (pan).

2 Put the flour, salt and sunflower seeds in a large mixing bowl and stir to combine the ingredients. Make a well in the centre and gradually stir in the yeast mixture. Mix vigorously with a wooden spoon, adding sufficient extra warm water to form a soft, sticky dough.

5 Form the dough into a rectangle and place in the loaf tin. Sprinkle the top with sunflower seeds. Cover with a damp dishtowel and leave to rise again for a further 15 minutes.

6 Bake for 40–45 minutes until golden. When ready, the loaf should sound hollow when tapped underneath. Leave for 5 minutes, turn out of the tin and cool on a wire rack.

VARIATION
Other seeds would be good in this bread – try sesame seeds, pumpkin seeds or a mixture of sesame, pumpkin, hemp and sunflower seeds.

CHEESE and ONION CORNBREAD

Full of flavour, this tasty organic cornbread is delicious served freshly baked, warm or cold in slices, either on its own or spread with a little butter. It makes an ideal accompaniment to soups, stews and chillies.

MAKES ONE 900G/2LB LOAF

15ml/1 tbsp sunflower oil
1 onion, thinly sliced
175g/6oz/1½ cups corn meal
75g/3oz/⅔ cup rice flour
25g/1oz/¼ cup soya flour
15ml/1 tbsp baking powder
5ml/1 tsp unrefined caster (superfine)
    sugar or rapadura
5ml/1 tsp sea salt
115g/4oz/1 cup coarsely grated mature
    Cheddar cheese
200ml/7fl oz/scant 1 cup tepid milk or
    soya milk
2 eggs
40g/1½oz/3 tbsp non-hydrogenated
    margarine, melted

1 Preheat the oven to 190°C/375°F/ Gas 5. Lightly grease a 900g/2lb loaf tin (pan). Heat the oil in a frying pan, add the onion and cook gently for 10–15 minutes until softened, stirring occasionally. Remove the pan from the heat and set aside to cool.

2 Place the corn meal, rice flour, soya flour, baking powder, sugar and salt in a large mixing bowl and combine thoroughly. Stir in the grated cheese, mixing well.

3 In a jug (pitcher), beat together the milk, eggs and melted margarine. Add to the flour mixture and mix well using a wooden spoon.

4 Stir the cooled, cooked onions into the corn meal mixture and stir well until the onions are evenly incorporated.

5 Spoon the onion mixture into the prepared tin, level the surface and bake for about 30 minutes until the bread has risen and is golden brown.

6 Run a knife around the edge to loosen the loaf. Turn out on to a wire rack to cool slightly and serve warm. Alternatively, leave it on the rack until completely cold, then cut into slices. To store the loaf, wrap it in foil or seal in a plastic bag.

VARIATIONS
• A wide selection of organic flours is available. In addition to a range of wheat flours, you can choose from buckwheat, rice, rye or maize.
• Reserve a little of the grated cheese and cooked onion and scatter it over the top of the bread before baking.

COOK'S TIP
A loaf tin that has drop-down sides is useful when making corn bread. Because it has a much softer texture than conventional yeast breads, you need to take care when turning out the cooked bread onto the wire rack.

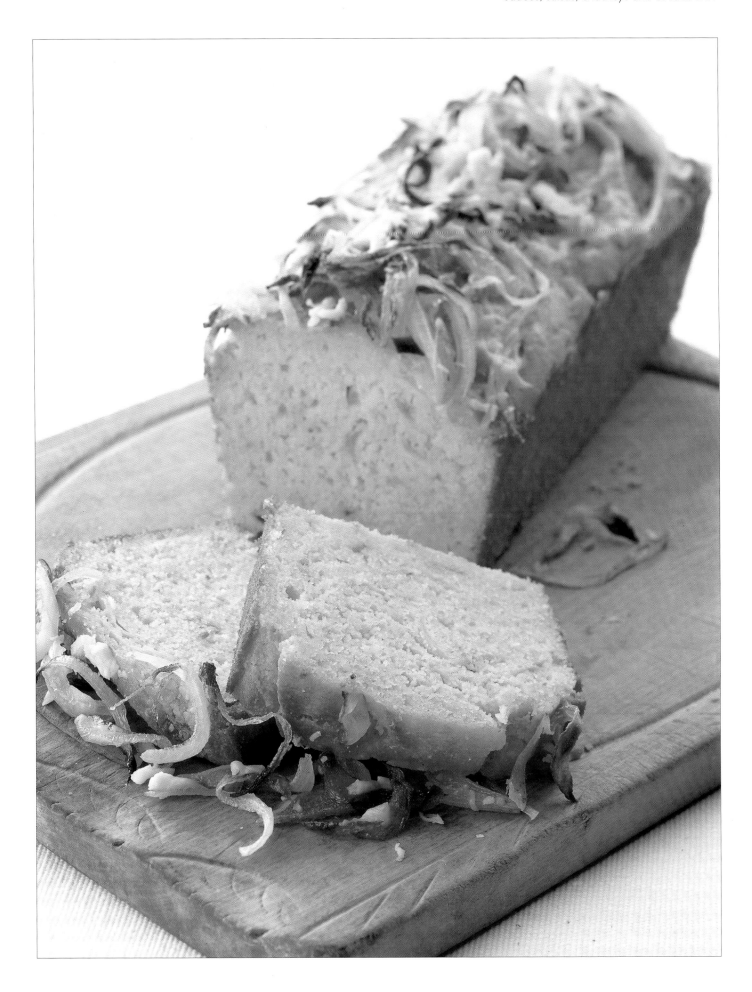

GLOSSARY

As in every specialist area, organics has its own language. The following is a guide to some of the specialist terms in common usage.

Agriculture The cultivation of crops and raising of livestock for the production of food and other products.

Agrochemical A chemical or chemical compound used in farming. Also an adjective to describe produce derived from farms that extensively use these chemicals, or the method of agriculture that utilizes agrochemicals.

Aquaculture The farming of fish and other creatures that live in fresh or sea water e.g. salmon and prawns.

Artificial additives Chemicals and chemical compounds added to foods in order to manipulate their taste, colour, texture or shelf life. These include powerful toxins such as tartrazine, a neurotoxin that is used in cordials and soft drinks (sodas) to dye them orange. Only seven of the seven thousand additives used in non-organic food may be used in organic food.

Biodiversity The wide diversity of plants and creatures that occurs in nature.

Also the ideal of organic systems of farming, biodiversity is a term to describe farms rich in different species of plants and animals, whether intentionally cultivated and bred, or those which occur naturally.

Biodynamics Based on the work of the early twentieth century theosophist Rudolph Steiner, biodynamic farming relies on companion planting, homeopathic preparations and a seven-year cycle of crop rotation to remain entirely chemical-free. Biodynamic farms are completely self-contained, integrating different crops and livestock to create a mini-ecosystem. The lunar calendar is used as a guide to planting and harvesting crops, with different star constellations signalling the most fruitful times for these activities. Biodynamics is part of the family of organic farming styles.

Certification Each organic certification board has a different code of standards. However, the basic organic standards are legally defined in international law, so every certification board throughout the world must at least comply with these standards. Check details with each certifier if you want to know if they enforce standard organic standards or stricter ones.

Companion planting A method of growing plants in combinations that optimize their beneficial effects while minimizing their negative effects on each other. For example, growing potatoes near tomatoes weakens their resistance to potato blight, so this should be avoided. Growing chamomile and peppermint in proximity is beneficial, as both plants produce more active essential oils in combination. Companion planting is a practical way of conserving and utilizing biodiversity.

Compost Vegetable and animal matter that has been purposefully decomposed (aerobically fermented) to create a natural source of nutrients for growing crops. Encourages good soil quality and beneficial enzyme production. Organic farmers must follow strict procedures to produce composts and

manures. They compost for lengthy periods to ensure that e-coli and other bugs are killed off. Also extensively manufactured and utilised by organic home gardeners.

Crop rotation A traditional method of effectively managing soil fertility on a farm by systematically rotating crops between different fields. This method often includes leaving fields to lie fallow, meaning that they are rested from production to regain their naturally fertile soil.

Fair trade The concept that a fair price will be paid for goods produced by farmers and workers in the developing world. Many poorer farmers are forced to sell their products for much less than is just if there is no other outlet for them. Fair trade means that a buyer from the developed world will not exploit this opportunity to pay less money than a commodity is worth. Effectively, honourable behaviour rather than exploitation. The official Fairtrade Mark prohibits child and forced labour, and

guarantees that workers receive a decent standard of housing, health and safety protection and employment rights. It also promotes programmes for environmental sustainability.

Fertilizers Generally refers to synthetic chemicals and chemical compounds based on synthetic nitrates used by farmers to give plants extra nutrients for growth. An excess of nitrates is known to cause cancer in humans and animals. Organic farming uses natural fertilizers instead, such as manure, seaweed, clays and rockdust.

Free range A term to describe farm animals and birds that have been able to gain some access to open pastures and skies. When applied to chickens and their eggs, it may simply mean that the chicken house has "popholes" but does not guarantee that the birds will have used these exits, especially if they have been bred in confinement. In the UK the Soil Association has the highest standards for free range poultry and eggs – prohibiting debeaking and overcrowding, and ensuring that all birds range properly in daylight. If in doubt, check with your local certification board for details of their guidelines.

Fungicides Chemicals and chemical compounds used to prevent moulds growing on crops or food products by killing fungal spores. Organic farming prohibits their use. However, where the whole crop might otherwise be lost to something like potato blight or mildew, small amounts of traditional chemicals, such as copper and sulphur compounds may be used by organic farmers. This practice is restricted to extreme cases, and permission must be granted from an organic certifier.

Gardening The practice of organic gardening is an extremely valuable activity. The United Nations' Food and Agriculture Organisation has calculated that small biodiverse gardens can produce thousands of times more food per acre than large intensive monocultures. Home gardening in Indonesia provides around 40 per cent of all food, and in Eastern Nigeria, the 2 per cent of land cultivated as domestic gardens provides 50 per cent of the food. Gardening provides people in industrialised nations with a connection to the food they eat, whether it is growing herbs in a window box or fruit and vegetables in a garden.

Genetic modification The manipulation of genetic material between different unrelated species of living entities. In agriculture, the creation of crops known as Genetically Modified Organisms (GMOs) or Transgenic Organisms by extracting genes from one species and inserting them in another. GM farming is part of the family of farming styles that makes up agrochemical farming.

GMOs Genetically Modified Organisms (see previous entry).

Herbicides Chemicals and chemical compounds used to kill weeds. Organic farming prohibits their use.

Hydroponics A modern method of agrochemical farming that grows plants in a purely synthetic environment. The plants are suspended in a liquid mixture of

nutrient compounds in a medium of sand or gravel. Bright lights are often used to stimulate plant growth. Many non-organic potato and tomato crops are now routinely grown without soil.

Insecticides Chemicals and chemical compounds used to kill insects.

Irradiation The passing of food through a radiation field to preserve it beyond its natural shelf life. The use of ionizing irradiation to preserve food is prohibited under organic standards.

Legumes Crops related to the bean family. Planted extensively in organic agriculture to maintain beneficial levels of nitrogen in the soil. Legumes have the capacity to fix nitrogen from the air into the soil through nodules in their roots. They are often planted as part of the crop rotation system in fallow fields.

Monocultures Agrochemical farms that continually grow only one kind of crop over a vast area. Monocultures are the antithesis of biodiversity, and they are the prevalent form of agriculture in most industrialized nations at the beginning of the 21st century. Four per cent of

all farms in the USA produce half of the food grown there on huge swathes of land growing only a single species.

Organic A method of farming based on the cultivation of good soil quality and biodiversity. The use of agrochemicals is strictly regulated and kept to the absolute minimum. It prohibits GMOs (even in animal feed), and is a legally binding term defined in international law. The rearing of organic animals must be according to strict welfare standards, and they may only be treated with chemicals such as antibiotics as a last resort to cure illness. When the term is used to describe a food product or item, at least 95 per cent of its ingredients must be certified organic and it may not be irradiated.

Permaculture This is the design and maintenance of food growing systems which have the diversity, stability, and resilience of natural ecosystems. It is the harmonious integration of the landscape with people, in cities or rural areas. Permaculture can be as small as a city balcony or as large as a forest. It is a way of providing food, energy, shelter and other material and non-material needs in a sustainable way

Pesticides Chemicals and chemical compounds used by farmers and gardeners to kill pests. These products often contain organophosphates, which belong to the same family of chemicals as nerve gases. Synthetic pesticides are applied to crops and livestock as a matter of course in agrochemical agriculture for the prevention and treatment of pests. In organic farming, they may only be applied to crops if all other non-chemical actions to tackle a pest problem have failed, and then only with

permission from a certifier. Organic farming relies on biodiversity to provide natural predators to control pests, or uses natural plant-based pesticides. Standards are rigorous and organic farms unfortunate enough to be affected by pesticide drift from neighbouring agrochemical properties have on occasion had their licences revoked.

Prevention The method utilised by organic farmers to minimise the use of agrochemicals, hormones and antibiotics in farming practices. Pesticide use is minimised by careful management, from companion planting to the use of satellite technology to detect potential parasites. Chemical use for livestock is minimised by keeping numbers of animals and fish lower per pen, and encouraging more freedom of movement within the farm or fish tank.

Processed Food Food that has been ready prepared from its raw state for consumption. This can be through a great variety of processes, including boiling, slicing, and baking. Processing food by its very nature removes nutrients and vitality. 70 per cent of all food grown in the USA is processed before it reaches the shops. Only 1 per cent of food grown in India is processed before it is retailed. Indian citizens do not eat their produce raw, but simply process the ingredients themselves at home.

Selective Breeding A traditional genetic technique that produces plants or animals with a particular genetic profile. Reasons may include creating a distinctive taste, unusual colour or hardier variety. It is unrelated to modern genetic modification, as selective breeding takes part between plants of the same species through interbreeding rather than between differing species using DNA displacement technology.

SUPPLIERS and INFORMATION SOURCES

UK and Eire

Biodynamic Agricultural
Association
+44 (0)1453 759501

British Nutrition Foundation
+44 (0)20 7101 0304

Cambrian Organics
+44 (0)1559 363151
www.cambrianorganics.com

Centre for Alternative
Technology
+44 (0)1654 702400
www.cat.org.uk

Circaroma Organic Skincare
+44 (0)20 7249 9392
www.circaroma.com

Clearspring
+44 (0)20 8740 1781
rudkin@dircon.co.uk

Compassion in World Farming
+44 (0)1730 264208
www.ciwf.co.uk

Fairtrade Foundation
+44 (0)20 7405 5942
www.fairtrade.org.uk

Farmers' World Network
www.fwn.org.uk

Food and Agricultural
Organization (United Nations)
www.fao.org

Fresh and Wild
+44 (0)800 9175 175
www.freshandwild.com

Friends of the Earth
+44 (0)20 7490 1555
www.foe.co.uk

Graig Farm
+44 (0)1597 851655
www.graigfarm.co.uk

Green Endings
+44 (0)20 7424 0345
www.greenendings.co.uk

Greenfibres
+44 (0)1803 868001
www.greenfibres.com

Green People
+44 (0)1444 401444
www.greenpeople.co.uk

Hambledon Herbs
+44 (0)1823 401104
www.hambledonherbs.co.uk

Henry Doubleday Research
Association
+44 (0)120 330 3517
www.hdra.org.uk

Himalayan Green Tea
+44 (0)1895 632409
www.nvspharmacy.co.uk

Irish Organic Farmers and
Growers Association
+353 (0)506 32563
www.irishorganic.ie

Kinvara Irish Organic Smoked
Salmon
+353 (0)916 37489

Llain Farm Fresh Meats
+44 (0)1348 831210

Marine Stewardship Council
+44 (0)20 7350 4000
www.msc.org

National Association of Farmers'
Markets
+44 (0)1225 787914

Neal's Yard Bakery
+44 (0)20 7836 5199
www.nealsyardbakery.co.uk

NHR Organic Oils
0845 310 8066
www.nhr.kz

Organic Delivery Company
(London)
+44 (0) 20 7739 8181
www.organicdelivery.co.uk

www.organicfood.co.uk –
Ysanne Spevack's organic food
and lifestyle website.

Organic Wine Company
+44 (0)1494 446557
www.organicwinecompany.com

Permaculture Magazine
0845 458 4150
www.permaculture.co.uk

Pero Organic Pet Foods
+44 (0)1690 710457
pero@perofsbusiness.co.uk

Pesticide Action Network UK
+44 (0)20 7274 8895
www.pan-uk.org

Planet Organic
+44 (0)20 7221 7171
www.planetorganic.com

Race and Race Artisan Foods
+44 (0)1647 277454
raceorganic@aol.com

Ravens Oak Dairy
+44 (0)1270 524210
www.ravensoakdairy.co.uk

Rocombe Farm Organic Ice Cream
+44 (0)1482 575884
icecreamcentre@netscapeonline
.co.uk

Scottish Quality Salmon
+44 (0)1738 587000
www.scottishsalmon.co.uk

Seasoned Pioneers
+44 (0)800 0682348
www.seasonedpioneers.co.uk

Sheepdrove Organic Farm
+44 (0)1488 71659
www.sheepdrove.com

Simply Soaps
+44 (0)1603 720869
www.simplysoaps.com

Slow Food Movement (UK)
c/o The Village Bakery
+44 (0)1768 881515
www.slow-food.com

Soil Association
+44 (0)117 929 0661
www.soilassociation.org
Special Diets News –
+44 (0)20 7722 2866
www.inside-story.com

Solar Homes
+44 (0)1275 540112
www.solarsense-uk.com

Sustain +44 (0) 7837 1228
www.sustainweb.org

Swaddles Green Farm
+44 (0)1460 234387
www.swaddles.co.uk

Triodos Bank
+44 (0)117 973 9339
www.triodos.co.uk

UK Register of Organic Food
Standards (UKROFS)
+44 (0)20 7238 5915

Vintage Roots
+44 (0)800 980 4992
www.vintageroots.co.uk

Well Hung Meats
+44 (0)1752 830282
www.carswellfarm.co.uk

Wiggle Wigglers
+44 (0)1981 500391
www.wigglywigglers.co.uk

Willing Workers on Organic
Farms (WWOOF)
+44 (0)1273 476286
www.phdc.com/wwoof

Women's Environmental
Network +44 (0)20 7247 3327
www.gn.apc.org/wen

USA and Canada
Biodynamic Farming and
Gardening Association, Inc.
+1 (415) 561 7797
www.biodynamics.com

Canadian Organic Growers
www.gks.com/cog/

Diamond Organics
+1 (888) ORGANIC
Ecological
Agriculture
Projects
http://eap.
mcgill.ca/general/
home_frames.htm

Institute for Agriculture & Trade's
National Organic Program
+1 (202) 720 3252

Organic Grapes into Wine Alliance
www.isgnet.com/ogwa

Organic Style
www.organicstyle.com

Organic Trade Association
www.ota.com

Organic Trading and
Information Center
www.organicfood.com

The Permaculture Institute
PO Box 3702, Pojuaque,
New Mexico, NM 87501
Rodale Institute
+1 (610) 683 1400
www.rodale.com

Seeds of Change
+1 (888) 762 7333
www.seedsofchange.com

Transfair +1 (510) 663 5260
www.transfairusa.org

Whole Foods
+1 (512) 477 4455

Wild Oats +1 (800) 494 9453

Australia
Biodynamic Marketing Co Ltd
+61 (3) 5966 7370

Biological Farmers of Australia
Co Op Ltd
+61 (7) 4639 3299

NASSA (National Association
for Sustainable Agriculture)
Australia +61 (8) 8370 8455
www.nassa.com.au

Organic Federation of Australia
www.ofa.org.au

Organic Herb Growers of
Australia (OHGA)
+61 (2) 6622 0100
www.organicherbs.org

Organic Retailers and Growers
Association of Australia
+61 (1800) 356 299
www.orgaa.org.au

Robinvale Organic & Bio-
Dynamic Wines Australia
+61 (3) 5026 3955
www.organicwines.com.au

New Zealand
Bio-Gro New Zealand
www.biogro.co.nz

New Zealand Organics +64 (9)
376 1330 www.nzorganics.co.nz

Author's Acknowledgements

Ysanne Spevack would like to
thank the following people for
their assistance. Without people
like you, this book could never
have happened …

John Barrow at Organic Delivery
    Company
Peter Bradford at Fresh & Wild
Lynda Brown
Steve Chandra
Charles, Prince of Wales
Carol Charlton
Caroline Conran
Gilli Davies
The Dkiks
Julie Edgar at Scottish Quality
    Salmon
The Finelli-Blowers
Dido Fisher
Jenni Fleetwood
Lou Gibbs
Patrick Holden, Sue Flook and
    Sarah Jeffs at the Soil Association
Peter Kindersley at Sheepdrove Farm
Guy Lafayette and David Lee at
    Consultancy for Corporate
    Change

Margaret Malone
Mia Manners
Vini Medley
Kate Pengelly
Miriam Polunin
Sarah Ratty
Anita Roddick
Craig Sams
Howard-Yana Shapiro
Brian Spevack
Michael van Straten
Amy Williams at Marine
    Stewardship Council
Antony Worrall-Thompson
Joy Wotton

Picture Credits
The Publishers would like to
thank the following for supplying
photographs for use in this book:
Anthony Blake Photo Library: 6 top,
6 bottom, 7, 8 right, 60 bottom left;
A-Z Botanical Collection Ltd: /Bjorn
Svensson 12 right, /Sylvia Sroka 14
right; Science Photo Library: /Simon
Fraser 48 left, Fletcher & Baylis 50
right. Author's portrait on jacket by
Lou Gibbs.

Bibliography

Bissell, Frances – *The Organic
    Meat Cookbook* (Ebury Press,
    1999)
Boyd, Hilary – *Banishing the Blues*
    (Mitchell Beazley, 2000)
Brown, Edward Espe – *Tassajara
    Bread Book* (Shambhala,
    1970)
Brown, Edward Espe – *Tomato
    Blessings and Radish* (Riverhead
    Books, 1997)
Brown, Lynda – *Organic Living*
    (Dorling Kindersley, 2000)
Charlton, Carol – *Organic Café
    Cookbook* (David and Charles,
    1999)
Clayton, Dr Paul – *Health Defence*
    (Accelerated Learning Systems,
    2001)
Elliot, Rose – *Beanfeast* (White
    Eagle Publishing Trust, 1975)
Elliott, Renée and Trevillé, Eric –
    Organic Cookbook (Dorling
    Kindersley, 2000)

Heaton, Shane – *Organic Farming,
    Food Quality and Human
    Health* (Soil Association,
    2001)
Lifespan Community Collective –
    Full of Beans (L C C Ltd,
    1982)
Lucas, Dr Caroline MEP – *Stopping
    the Great Food Swap* (Earthscan,
    2000)
Miller, Mark – *Red Sage* (Ten Speed
    Press, 1999)
Shapiro, Howard-Yana and
    Harrisson, John – *Gardening for
    the Future of the Earth* (Bantam,
    2000)
Spevack, Ysanne – *Branding Healthy
    Foods* (Reuters Business Insight,
    2001)
van Straten, Michael – *Superfoods*
    (Dorling Kindersley, 1990)
van Straten, Michael – *Organic
    Superfoods* (Mitchell Beazley,
    1999)

INDEX

goose, 46
marmalade-glazed goose, 200
grains, 56–7
granita, watermelon, 130
grapefruit: three-fruit
marmalade, 226
grapes, 40
gratin, salmon and rice, 166
gravy, onion, 233
Greek fruit and nut
pastries, 224
greens, 25
grouse, 47
guacamole, 234

H
haddock: seafood lasagne, 212
smoked haddock with mustard
cabbage, 211
hake au poivre with red pepper
salsa, 129
halva, semolina and nut, 223
harissa, 128
hazelnuts: hazelnut ice cream, 170
semolina and nut halva, 223
hemp, 8–9
herbs, 34–5
drying, 35
oils, 35
tisanes, 69
see also individual herbs
hijiki, 33
honey, 60
honey baked figs with hazelnut
ice cream, 170
hormones, in meat, 13
Hungarian fruit bread, 185
hydrogenated fats, 11

I
ice cream: hazelnut ice
cream, 170
rhubarb and ginger ice
cream, 99
spicy pumpkin and orange
bombe, 214
immune system, 11

J
jam, strawberry, 141
Jerusalem artichokes, 22
Jerusalem artichokes with
garlic, 194
juices, 20, 68

K
kebabs: grilled skewered
chicken, 113
kidney beans, 54–5
chilli con carne and rice, 206
kiwi fruit, 42–3
koftas, spiced onion, 192
kombu, 33
kumquats: chocolate mousse with
glazed kumquats, 216
spiced poached kumquats, 226

L
lamb, 45–6
braised shoulder of lamb with
pearl barley and baby
vegetables, 203
herb-crusted rack of lamb with
Puy lentils, 90
lamb burgers with red onion
and tomato relish, 91
lamb shanks with beans and
herbs, 204
lamb stew, 92
Moroccan spiced lamb soup, 189
moussaka, 160
roast leg of lamb, 88
lasagne, seafood, 212
laver, 33
leeks, 21
barley risotto with roasted
squash and leeks, 197
braised leeks in tarragon
cream, 79
braised leeks with carrots, 79
chicken, leek and celery
soup, 190
leek and carrot rice, 96
leek and mussel tartlets, 76
vichyssoise, 110

lemons, 41
asparagus with lemon sauce, 78
citrus and caramel custards, 102
three-fruit marmalade, 226
Tuscan citrus sponge, 105
lentils, 54
chicken casserole with winter
vegetables, 202
grilled mackerel with spicy
dhal, 168
herb-crusted rack of lamb with
Puy lentils, 90
lentil dhal with roasted
garlic, 193
lettuces, 26
limes, 41
lobster, 51
local produce, 18–19

M
mackerel, grilled with spicy
dhal, 168
mangoes, 42
maple syrup, 61
baked maple and pecan
croissant pudding, 220
butternut squash and maple
pie, 175
marmalade: marmalade-glazed
goose, 200
orange marmalade chocolate
loaf, 222
three-fruit marmalade, 226
marrows, 24
mayonnaise: garlic
mayonnaise, 235
Provençal aioli with salt
cod, 112
tomato mayonnaise, 87
meat, 44–6
see also beef, lamb etc
melons, 40
frozen melon, 131
meringues: chocolate meringues
with mixed fruit compote, 132
rhubarb meringue
pie, 104
milk, 52
millet, 56
minerals, 10
mint sauce, 88
molasses, 60
Moroccan fish tagine with
couscous, 128
Moroccan rice pudding, 219
Moroccan spiced lamb soup, 189
moules marinière, 50
moussaka, 160
mousse, chocolate, with glazed
kumquats, 216
muffins, blueberry, 140

mushrooms, 30
boeuf bourguignonne, 207
clam, mushroom and potato
chowder, 144
garlic chive rice with
mushrooms, 152
red onion and mushroom
tartlets with goat's cheese, 148
seafood lasagne, 212
shiitake rice, 147
slow-cooked shiitake with
shoyu, 147
sole with wild mushrooms, 169
steak, mushroom and ale pie,
208
mussels, 49
leek and mussel tartlets, 76
moules marinière, 50
mutton, 45

N
nectarines, 38
noodles: chicken with noodles
and cashew nuts, 159
cold somen noodles, 111
nori, 33
toasting, 32
nuts, 62–3
nut butter, 62

O
oats, 56
oat and raisin drop scones, 184
oils, 63
herb oils, 35
olive oil, 63
olive oil roasted chicken with
summer vegetables, 124
olives: olive bread, 239
tapenade with quail's eggs and
crudités, 74
onions, 21
baby onions with tomato and
orange, 236
beetroot and red onion
salad, 81